Our Lady of

GUADALUPE

Our Lady of
GUADALUPE

MOTHER OF THE CIVILIZATION OF LOVE

Carl A. Anderson

Msgr. Eduardo Chávez

DOUBLEDAY

NEW YORK LONDON TORONTO SYDNEY AUCKLAND

232.917
AND

To Our Lady of Guadalupe, in the confidence that guided by her,
the people of the Christian Hemisphere will work together
to encounter her son, Jesus Christ.

ⅅⅅ
DOUBLEDAY

Copyright © 2009 by Carl A. Anderson

All rights reserved.
Published in the United States by Doubleday Religion, an imprint of the Crown
Publishing Group, a division of Random House, Inc., New York.
www.crownpublishing.com

The images on pages 52, 66, 67, 69, 70, 73, and 75
are courtesy of the Archdiocese of Mexico

DOUBLEDAY and the DD colophon are registered trademarks of Random House, Inc.

Library of Congress Cataloging-in-Publication Data
Anderson, Carl A.
Our Lady of Guadalupe: Mother of the civilization of love / Carl A. Anderson, Eduardo
Chávez.—1st ed.
Includes bibliographic references.
1. Guadalupe, Our Lady of. I. Chávez, Eduardo. II. Title.
BT660G8A63 2009
232.91'7097253—dc22   2009012120

ISBN 978-0-385-52772-9

Printed in the United States of America

10 9 8 7 6 5 4 3 2 1

First Edition

CONTENTS

Part III: Unified in Dignity

Acknowledgments

The authors wish to acknowledge the contributions of the many people who contributed to the completion of this book. Among them are His Eminence Cardinal Norberto Rivera Carrera, Archbishop of Mexico, who so graciously allowed Msgr. Chávez to work on this book and a variety of other Guadalupe projects in the United States; Trace Murphy and the staff at Doubleday, who so patiently and carefully guided us through the process of writing and editing this book; Joe Tessitore, who has assisted us with many details of this project; the members of the Instituto Superior de Estudios Guadalupanos; and especially Maureen Hough, Jennifer Daigle, Andrew Walther, and Luis Guevara of the Knights of Columbus, whose work on so many aspects of this project is greatly appreciated.

Introduction

Mother of the Civilization of Love

TWO NEW EVANGELISTS

The genesis of this book occurred on July 31, 2002, the day Pope John Paul II canonized Juan Diego Cuauhtlatoatzin in the Basilica of Our Lady of Guadalupe in Mexico City. We were both present that day in the basilica, but we had not yet met. One of us was participating in the liturgical event that he had worked to achieve for more than a decade as postulator of the Cause for Canonization of Juan Diego. The other had traveled to the basilica eighteen months earlier for his installation Mass as the head of the world's largest organization of Catholic laymen, the Knights of Columbus. Both of us were deeply touched by our experience that day in Mexico City, and both of us realized we had witnessed one of the most profound events in the Catholic Church during John Paul II's pontificate and indeed during our own lifetimes, an event that would give deep and lasting hope to the Catholic Church in North America.

This may strike many as an extraordinary claim; after all, John Paul II is now regarded universally as one of the greatest popes in the two-thousand-year history of the Catholic Church. As pope, he canonized and beatified hundreds of people, wrote numerous encyclicals on theological, moral, and social topics, and commissioned the *Catechism of the Catholic Church*, the first definitive work of its kind in more than four hundred years. He brought interreligious dialogue to new and unexpected levels while guiding the Church into the new millennium with the focus of hope in Christ. Beyond the Church, he changed the political map of Europe and the very course of history by helping to liberate nations trapped behind the Iron Curtain during the Cold War and aiding in their cause for self-determination within the Soviet Union. Beyond Europe's borders, his concerns for the poor, the disadvantaged, and the war-torn brought a greater commitment to human rights and democracy, especially to Latin America and Africa. But in Mexico that day, as he knelt and prayed awhile before the image of Our Lady of Guadalupe after the ceremony, it was clear that he did not want to leave; when he rose to leave, he entrusted all people to the intercession of the newest saint in the Church. He had not only canonized a man of the past but also given our continent a saint for the future.

Yet, early in John Paul's pontificate, Our Lady of Guadalupe in Mexico was an important, perhaps even indispensable, presence. In an interesting way, John Paul II's first invitation to the basilica was not intended for him; the Latin American Bishops Conference had extended the invitation to his predecessor the month before, and it was only his predecessor's death that opened this opportunity to John Paul II.[1] In a telling way, it was John Paul II's determined desire to pray at the Basilica of Our Lady of Guadalupe and to personally engage in the meetings regarding the future of the Church in America that caused him to accept the invitation his predecessor had declined. (Twenty-three years later, Mexico would see this same determination; shortly before his trip for Juan Diego's canonization, John Paul II met with his medical specialists, who advised against his making the trip. But at the end of the consultation, John Paul II thanked them for their concern and concluded the meeting by saying: "I will see you in Mexico.") Later, John Paul II would reflect on his first visit to Mexico, recalling that "to some degree, this pilgrimage inspired and shaped all of the succeeding years of my pontificate."[2]

If John Paul's pilgrimage to Mexico shaped the rest of his life as the universal pastor of the Church, his choice to visit Mexico first and his words commending Juan Diego as an evangelist expressed a new importance and new understanding of the Church in the Americas.[3] He recognized the Americas as a hemisphere with a unique, rich Catholic history, and thus as a hemisphere with a unique, rich place in the future of the Church, a hemisphere with great ability to respond to and benefit from a renewed living out of the Gospel of love seen in the witness of the saints. It was in this context that a few months later, the cause for Juan Diego's canonization was officially opened and the Church in the Americas was reexamined and given a new focus: the new evangelization.

NEW SAINT, RENEWED DEVOTION

The story of St. Juan Diego is, of course, the story of Our Lady of Guadalupe. The event of his canonization cannot be understood apart from the events of her appearance. As with any apparition claim, every detail of the Guadalupan accounts must be examined: each word spoken, each miraculous or extraordinary event that deviates from the everyday, the sequence of events, the character of the people involved, their reactions to the event, their lives afterward, and especially any lingering miraculous effect. For this, we begin with Antonio Valeriano's *Nican Mopohua*, an account of the Guadalupan apparitions in 1531, the earliest extant edition of which is currently housed in the New York Public Library.[4] The historical record suggests that Valeriano may have derived the information in the *Nican Mopohua* directly from Juan Diego himself, writing it down sometime before Juan Diego's death in 1548 and within two decades of the apparition. Besides this significant work, numerous historical records recall in varying degrees of detail the Guadalupan apparitions, the miraculous image, the church on Tepeyac hill, and Juan Diego's own life; some of the most substantial works include the *Nican Motecpana*, the *Información de 1556,* and the *Informaciones Jurídicas de 1666*. Other items composing the complex record of the Guadalupan event include written accounts, artwork, recorded oral testimonies, investigations, wills, and other works.

Because Juan Diego would be the first Mexican indigenous saint of that time and place, the canonization process demanded extensive research, requiring a grasp of both the history of colonization in New Spain and pre-Colonial culture and religion. Contemporary scholars, historians, and anthropologists specializing in the culture and history of Mexico's Indian people were consulted, and nearly four thousand documents related to Our Lady of Guadalupe were reviewed. Ultimately, the knowledge and insights from such research have revealed the profound relevance and symbolic richness of the apparitions and the miraculous image on Juan Diego's *tilma* (a cloak-like garment), showing how the Guadalupan event conveys in the language and culture of the Indians a message of hope and love.

While the facts regarding Colonial Mexico cannot be changed, the perspective advocated by historians and even the public at large has changed. Unlike many scholars of the nineteenth and early twentieth centuries, contemporary biographers and historians often highlight the Spanish conquest and occupation of Mexico as a volatile period of spiritual repression, conflict, and violence. By bringing to light the complexity of this period, contemporary research has played an enormous role in helping us to better comprehend—and even test the veracity of—the Guadalupan apparitions. But unfortunately, while the idea of "conversion by the sword" is now familiar, some people may view the Guadalupan apparition and devotions as a mere by-product of colonization: as a strategic devotion fabricated by missionaries seeking to convert or pacify the Indians with a Christian-Aztec story, or as a subversive devotion adopted by Indians who were confused or sought to preserve elements of Aztec religion with a façade of Christianity. Undoubtedly, the Guadalupan devotions were a cause of concern and confusion at some times, but for us this should not be surprising, considering how even today, in the Information Age, we often encounter mixed reports even on less extraordinary events. While in this book we wish to do more than judge and debate about the Catholicity of Guadalupan devotees, nevertheless it is perhaps necessary to address some generalizations about the devotion that often sidetrack readers from the religious significance of the apparition's expression of the Gospel.

First, to write off the rise of Guadalupan devotion to manipulation and misunderstanding is not only simplistic but also historically incongruous regarding a politically and religiously complex situation. Among the missionaries, there was no unified front encouraging the apparitions, as many missionaries doubted and even tried to suppress the Indians' new devotion to the

Guadalupan Virgin.[5] Furthermore, while the missionaries desired conversions, their distrust of the Indians' Catholicity verged on the scrupulous, even by modern standards; these same missionaries, some of whom were sophisticated *letrados* (theologians) in Spain, were known to hold off giving Indians the sacraments and to eliminate symbolic elements of sacraments that were too similar to Aztec rites solely in order to keep the distinctiveness of the Christian faith obvious.[6] That is, although oversight may have occurred, purposeful theological contamination, deception, and obfuscation were largely out of character. Additionally, there was a whole range of converts among the Indians, including many who completely forsook their indigenous religious practices—but not culture—for a Christian way of life. What is more, their life as Christians went beyond practices or rites of belonging, such as baptism, to include catechesis.

Likewise, the rise of Guadalupan devotion cannot be explained as a devotion taken up to appease Christianizing government authorities; after all, at the time of the apparition, many of the Spanish authorities in Mexico were themselves incurring excommunication, caring less for Christian life and evangelization than for their greed-ridden pursuit of political gains.[7] The fact is, while the *people* in Mexico were involved in both political and religious changes, the *Guadalupan devotion* was not used politically until the devotion arrived in Spain, when an admiral in the royal Spanish fleet took up the image of Our Lady of Guadalupe in the battle of Lepanto and attributed the subsequent victory to her intercession. Moreover, even though in later Mexican history the image and devotion were appropriated to serve various political and economic causes (notably during the 1810 War of Independence), the original meaning and message of Our Lady of Guadalupe transcends the flaws and purposes of those who have turned to her.

For some, Juan Diego may seem yet another individual

"divinized" in answer to the universal human desire for heroes to look up to. This, too, reflects another trend of demythologizing the very men once lauded as great heroes. In this light, what is striking is how Juan Diego's role in the apparition—even as passed down in testimonies—is already rather humble. While he was called to a significant and meaningful task, he was not called to a "great" task by any measure of earthly grandeur. His role in the apparition itself—his first and greatest claim to renown—was not a call to conquer lands but a simple invitation to intercede on behalf of one person by communicating a request to another. In essence, it was to vouch for and trust in another person. This simple act is the kernel of meaning and truth that is served, and not obscured, by the grandeur of the divine visitations, the healings, and the miraculous tilma. It was by answering this simple invitation that Juan Diego set himself apart; his was a gesture of humility, communication, advocacy, and trust, a gesture that we perform in less miraculous ways and situations every day of our lives. It is one of the most fundamental gestures of our humanity and the foundation of any society that wishes to live beyond selfish utilitarianism.

THE NEWNESS OF GUADALUPE

Consequently, although we believe the appearance of Our Lady of Guadalupe to be a historical fact, we do not think that it should be consigned only to the pages of history books. In fact, in a unique way, the full radicalness of Our Lady of Guadalupe's apparition can only be understood fully now, when Catholicism's most expressed model for society is a Civilization of Love and its greatest explication of human dignity is the Theology of the Body. For at the time, the violence institutionalized in Aztec religion was not the only place where harsh practices could be found: the European justice system employed in Colonial Mexico and many of the "standards" of holiness among Catholics often included severe punishments and harsh penitential practices that still make us uneasy, even if the practices were less violent and more theologically different from the Aztec human sacrifices. What is notable is that this harshness is not corroborated in the words of the Virgin. In fact, while other Marian apparitions (such as those at Fatima and Lourdes) included words of admonishment or even warnings, Our Lady of Guadalupe's only words of spiritual guidance are her gentle but persistent reminders to Juan Diego about love: a love that can be trusted, a love that gives dignity, a love that is personal. If we are to see in her words an answer to a spiritual problem, the spiritual problem it answers is a lack of love and a lack of understanding about love as relationship rather than as practice. The Guadalupan message is, in its originality, a spiritual education, an education in love.

Today, as life is often characterized by a lack of love and by misunderstandings and misgivings about love, her message is one to take to heart. For this reason, like John Paul II, we think that one of the greatest influences of Our Lady of Guadalupe upon the history of the Western Hemisphere may still be before us. In the sixteenth century, Our Lady of Guadalupe became an expression of hope and unity for millions throughout the Americas. We are convinced that Our Lady of Guadalupe's message is *today* capable of being not only an expression but a true catalyst of hope and unity for millions more throughout North America and the world.

In the Christian sense, this hope and unity are spread through evangelization—that is, through helping one another to find in Jesus Christ the "adequate dimension" of our own life.[8] A clear picture of how Christians in this hemisphere can approach this task spiritually can be seen in the triptych that Benedict XVI presented in Aparecida, Brazil, on his first apostolic journey to the Western Hemisphere, depicting St. Juan Diego "evangelizing with the Image of the Virgin Mary on his mantle and with the Bible in his hand" and inscribed below with the phrase "You shall be my witnesses."[9] To evangelize in the future is to evangelize from and through these first witnesses of Christianity.

Historically in our continent, Mexico was not the only country to be changed by this Marian evangelization. As later missionaries left Mexico for the neighboring countries in the hemisphere, including to the lands of the future United States, their evangelization was defined by their devotion to Our Lady of Guadalupe. As John Paul II wrote in his apostolic exhortation *Ecclesia in America*:

> The appearance of Mary to the native Juan Diego on the hill of Tepeyac in 1531 had a decisive effect on evangelization. Its influence greatly overflows the boundaries of Mexico, spreading to the whole continent . . . [which] has recognized in the mestiza face of the Virgin of Tepeyac, "in Blessed Mary of Guadalupe, an impressive example of a perfectly enculturated evangelization."[10]

For this reason, the pope continued, Our Lady of Guadalupe is venerated throughout the Western Hemisphere as "Queen of all America," and he encouraged that her December 12 feast day be celebrated not only in Mexico but throughout the hemisphere.[11]

Just as Mary's enculturated evangelization overflowed Mexico's borders, so it overflows the confines of the era and the culture of the apparition. For this reason, she is not only the "Patroness of all America" but the "Star of the first and new evangelization" who will "guide the Church in America . . . so that the new evangelization may yield a splendid flowering of Christian life."[12] Our Lady of Guadalupe is more than an event; she is a person. As part of her continuing witness to Christ, she continues to aid the men and women of the Western Hemisphere and lead them to a greater encounter with Christ.

While two oceans may delineate our hemisphere and define us as a single community, the solidarity of the Christian life proposed by Our Lady of Guadalupe brings us to a greater solidarity, a global solidarity, when she leads us to a greater encounter with "the uniqueness of Christ's real presence in the Eucharist."[13] Through the Eucharist, believers of all nations and cultures find themselves on a path of communion. This communion finds its ultimate source and summit in the communion within the Holy Trinity. As John Paul II wrote:

> Faced with a divided world which is in search of unity, we must proclaim with joy and firm faith that God is communion, Father, Son and Holy Spirit, unity in distinction, and that he calls all people to share in that same Trinitarian communion. We must proclaim that this communion is the magnificent plan of God the Father; that Jesus Christ, the Incarnate Lord, is the heart of this communion, and that the Holy Spirit works ceaselessly to create communion and to restore it when it is broken.[14]

At Aparecida, Benedict XVI raised this conviction with even greater eloquence and at the same time emphasized its transformative power: "Only from the Eucharist will the civilization of love spring forth which will transform Latin America and the Caribbean, making them not only the Continent of Hope, but also the Continent of Love!"[15]

To venerate Our Lady of Guadalupe as Patroness of the

Americas and Star of the first and new evangelization is to venerate her precisely as a Eucharistic woman, a woman through whom
Christ came to humanity, a woman who experienced a unique
closeness with the Holy Trinity. By leading millions more to her
Son, and especially to her Son's real presence in the Eucharist, she
will guide the people of the Western Hemisphere to a greater
unity whose source is itself Trinitarian communion. For her love
surpasses herself, and leads us to the source of love, a Source which
demands from us and enables us to love our neighbor without
reservation, without hesitation, without borders. For this reason,
Our Lady of Guadalupe should also be venerated under the title
Mother of the Civilization of Love.

According to tradition, after approving the patronage of Our
Lady of Guadalupe over New Spain in 1754, Pope Benedict XIV
quoted Psalm 147, saying, "God has not done anything like this
for any other nation." We may never understand the full uniqueness of this apparition. But through the devotion to Our Lady of
Guadalupe, we can expect to see the beauty and power of this
event in the transformation of our lives and blossoming of our
communities and ultimately our continent.

PART I

Approaching an Apparition

I.

An Apparition of Reconciliation and Hope

I am the handmaid of the Lord.

—WORDS OF MARY IN
THE GOSPEL OF LUKE[1]

JUAN DIEGO

The Basilica of Our Lady of Guadalupe has witnessed many grand and reverent ceremonies through the centuries, but few like the Mass celebrated July 31, 2002 for the canonization of St. Juan Diego. Thousands of people attended the three-hour canonization Mass, while thousands more watched on screens set up just outside the basilica and throughout Mexico City. Entire boulevards were closed down to make room for pilgrims. Among those attending the Mass was Mexico's president, Vicente Fox, whose presence marked a historic occasion: the first time a Mexican chief executive attended a papal Mass. Priests read from the Bible in Spanish and in the indigenous language Náhuatl, and while a portrait of

Juan Diego was carried to the altar, Indians in colorfully plumed headdresses danced up the main aisle of the basilica.

Twelve years earlier, Juan Diego's beatification had been the result of rigorous historical research and examination into his life and later testimonies about him. Through this research, evidence of early devotion to Juan Diego and recognition of his saintliness dating back to the sixteenth century was uncovered. With this, the approval of an immemorial cultus was granted and the requirements for beatification were met. For Juan Diego's canonization, however, something more was needed: a miracle. But as it happened, on the same day that John Paul II was celebrating Juan Diego's beatification Mass, that miracle happened.

On May 3, 1990, in Mexico City, nineteen-year-old Juan José Barragán suffered from severe depression and, wanting to commit suicide, he threw himself from the balcony of his apartment, striking his head on the concrete pavement thirty feet below, despite his mother's frantic attempts to hold onto him as she cried out to Juan Diego for help. The young man was rushed to the nearby hospital, where the doctor there noted his serious condition and suggested that the boy's mother pray to God. To this, the young man's mother replied that she already had prayed for Juan Diego's intercession. For three days, examination and intensive care continued, and physicians diagnosed a large basal fracture of the skull—a wound that normally would have killed at the moment of impact, and even now destroyed any hope of survival or repair. Given the mortal nature of the wounds, on May 6 all extraordinary medical support was ceased, and young Juan José's death was thought to be imminent. But that same day, Juan José sat up, began to eat, and within ten days was entirely recovered, with no debilitating side-effects, not even so much as a headache. In the scans, the doctors could see clear evidence of the life-threatening fracture, but to their surprise they noticed that the bone was mended, with the arteries and veins all in place. Astonished, they requested more tests by specialists for second opinions, only to have their original assessment confirmed. Impossible, unexplainable, it was declared a miracle.[2]

As enormously as it changed Juan José's life, the miracle affirmed the life of another: an Indian convert born five centuries earlier at the height of the Aztec Empire, Juan Diego Cuauhtlatoatzin. Ultimately, it was this miracle that led to Juan Diego's canonization.

Juan Diego was born around the year 1474 in Cuautitlán of the Texcoco kingdom, part of the Triple Alliance with the Aztec Empire. Known by his indigenous name Cuauhtlatoatzin, meaning "eagle that speaks," he belonged to the Chichimecas, a people that had assumed Toltec culture whose wise men had reached the conception of only one God.[3] As a *macehual*, a middle-class commoner, he owned property through inheritance.[4]

The first of many great changes in his life came around 1524, when the fifty-year-old Cuauhtlatoatzin and his wife requested baptism from one of the early Franciscan missionaries to Mexico and received their Christian names, Juan Diego and María Lucía. Together, they were one of the first Catholic married couples of the New World. Five years later, María Lucía died, leaving Juan Diego alone with his elderly uncle, Juan Bernardino, also a recent convert, in the town of Tulpetlac, near Mexico City.[5]

Juan Diego's conversion had been made possible just ten years earlier, when Hernán Cortés and his men conquered the great Aztec Empire, ultimately laying waste to the Aztec capital of Tenochtitlán and its main temple, the Templo Mayor (Great Temple). Having lived in the town of Cuautitlán in the nearby kingdom of Texcoco and then in the town of Tulpetlac, Juan Diego was no doubt familiar with the Aztecs and their campaign for empire. He also would have been familiar with their religious practices, which demanded human sacrifices to sustain the Aztec gods and maintain the harmony of the cosmos. The introduction of

Christianity to the New World came with the Spanish conquest of Mexico; missionaries were sent to teach the faith, and the Indians were discouraged from practicing their own religion. Human sacrifice was prohibited and temples were torn down. Despite these efforts, missionary activity in the New World met with only very modest success. It is this history of conquest and its aftermath, along with the cultural and religious heritage of the indigenous people, that constitutes a vital lens in interpreting the significance of the Guadalupan apparitions for the Colonial Indians. More than that, it shows how the apparitions at Guadalupe resolved some of the deep-seated problems posed by the Aztec religion—problems that were doubtless exacerbated in the Indians' encounter with Spanish colonialism.[6]

After María Lucía's death, Juan Diego continued to grow in his faith; to the missionaries, who were accustomed to meager resources and unsuccessful efforts, Juan Diego's dedication to the Christian faith must have been a welcome surprise. Although there was no established church in the area, every Saturday and Sunday Juan Diego rose at dawn to walk nine miles to the nearest *doctrina* (place of religious instruction) in Tlaltelolco, where he could attend Mass and receive instruction in the faith. At the time, Mexico City was a small island in Lake Texcoco, and so in order to attend these services in Tlaltelolco, Juan Diego would have to travel south from Tulpetlac, walk around the western side of Tepeyac hill, and then along a great causeway connecting Mexico City to the mainland.

THE FIRST APPARITION

On one of his Saturday trips for catechesis, on December 9, 1531, when he arrived at the Tepeyac area, Juan Diego heard beautiful singing that seemed to be coming from the top of Tepeyac hill.[7] The singing sounded like a chorus of birds, but more beautiful than the song of any birds Juan Diego had ever heard before. Juan Diego wondered as he looked eastward toward the top of the hill:

> By any chance am I worthy, have I deserved what I hear? Perhaps I am only dreaming it? Perhaps I am only dozing? Where am I? Where do I find myself? Is it possible that I'm in the place our ancient ancestors, our grandparents, told us about: in the land of the flowers, in the land of corn, of our flesh, of our sustenance, perhaps in the land of heaven?[8]

In these moments before Juan Diego encounters the first apparition of Our Lady of Guadalupe, signs of renewal are already present. In Christianity, the east, the direction of the rising sun, is often used to symbolize resurrection and renewal, themes especially evident in Juan Diego's initial words of wonderment. Drawing on images from his indigenous heritage, Juan Diego attempts to describe something of the indescribable mystery of heaven, referring to it as "the land of the flowers, the land of corn, of our flesh, of our sustenance." For the Indians, both flowers and corn held great religious and cultural significance. On one hand, flowers, like song, were evocative of the truth and were considered the only things that, as an Aztec sage once wrote, "will not come to an end";[9] on the other hand, corn was an essential food staple, relied upon heavily by the Aztecs and without which Aztec life would have suffered greatly.[10]

Suddenly, the singing stopped, and a woman's voice called out to him: "Juantzin, Juan Diegotzin," the Náhuatl affectionate diminutive form of his Spanish baptismal name.[11] Acknowledging the woman's affectionate greeting, Juan Diego ascended the hill and found himself before a beautiful woman adorned in clothing that "shone like the sun."[12] She stood upon stones that seemed to send forth beams of light like precious jade and other jewels; the "earth seemed to shine with the brilliance of a rainbow," and the foliage had the brightness of turquoise and quetzal feathers.[13] She asked Juan Diego where he was going, and Juan Diego replied that he was on his way to "your little house in Mexico, Tlaltelolco, to follow the things of God."[14] Notably, he said this even before the Virgin introduced herself, thus underscoring Juan Diego's early awareness of the important relationship between Mary and the Church.

Then, speaking to Juan Diego in his native language Náhuatl and using Texcocan religious phrases, the woman introduced herself in an unmistakably clear way, saying:

> I am the ever-perfect holy Mary, who has the honor to be the mother of the true God [*téotl Dios*] by whom we all live [Ipalnemohuani], the Creator of people [Teyocoyani], the Lord of the near and far [Tloque Nahuaque], the Lord of heaven and earth [Ilhuicahua Tlaltipaque].[15]

By using both the Náhuatl and Spanish words for God (*téotl Dios*), the Virgin reaffirms the supremacy, oneness, and universality of God. In her humility, she speaks very little of herself, while referring to God by many titles; importantly, when she does speak of herself, she calls herself "mother" and the "ever-perfect holy Mary." This title identifies her as the Immaculate Conception, a title not officially recognized until Pope Pius IX approved it more than three centuries later, in 1854. By introducing herself in this way, Mary significantly underscores the humanity and divinity of her Son. As Christ's mother, Mary shows the humanity of her Son, since she is herself a human being; but as immaculate, she shows the divinity of her Son, who, as God, was singularly born of a sinless woman.

After introducing herself, the Virgin revealed the reason for her appearance:

> I want very much that they build my sacred little house here, in which I will show Him, I will exalt Him upon making Him manifest, I will give Him to all people in all my personal love, Him that is my compassionate gaze, Him that is my help, Him that is my salvation. Because truly I am your compassionate Mother, yours and that of all the people that live together in this land, and also of all the other various lineages of men, those who love me, those who cry to me, those who seek me, those who trust in me.[16]

The Virgin then explained to Juan Diego how she needed him to deliver her message to Friar Juan de Zumárraga, the head of the Church in Mexico City.

Within the context of European Catholicism, the first apparition makes poignantly clear the Virgin Mary's universal role as mother and her desire to bring all people closer to God through her loving intercession. Less obvious, though no less significant, is what the Virgin's request for the construction of a church would have meant to a learned Indian. For the indigenous, the temple was more than a religious building, and the establishment of a temple was more than a ceremonial religious occasion. So central was religion to indigenous culture that the temple was seen as the foundation of society. Historically, the construction of a new temple marked the inauguration of a new civilization. In fact, the Aztecs built a temple in the years immediately following their migration to the Valley of Mexico, and a common indigenous glyph, or pictogram, for a conquered people was the depiction of a temple toppling over, sometimes in flames.[17] Thus, the Virgin's commission to Juan Diego was rich in meaning far beyond the construction of a building, and was made richer still by the fact that it had been given to an Indian.

THE SECOND APPARITION

Juan Diego could hardly face a greater test than going to the head of the Church in Mexico, bishop-elect Friar Juan de Zumárraga.[18] Friar Zumárraga, who had arrived in the New World no more than three years earlier, was an extremely prudent man who, like the other missionary friars, fought vigorously against the idolatry of the time; in fact, in a letter earlier in 1531, he declared that he had caused twenty thousand idols to be destroyed, and in 1529, his agents had been responsible for burning countless native codices, including those in the royal repository at Texcoco.[19] He was particularly suspicious of supposed visions and apparitions, believing most of them to be forms of idolatrous Indian worship. Putting the bishop-elect's concerns in context, he and the other missionaries living in Mexico were confronted with a people and religion wholly strange to them. They feared that the old religion could interfere or undermine the Indians' understanding of and conversion to Christianity. Even so, Juan Diego went immediately to the friar's house, where he waited for a long time before Friar Zumárraga would see him.

Once admitted, Juan Diego told Friar Zumárraga of the apparition, but the bishop, while attentive, was skeptical of Juan Diego's story. Why would the mother of God appear to this recently converted Indian? Why would she request that a church be built on the flatland of Tepeyac hill, when the hill's peak had once held an ancient temple dedicated to the pagan goddess Coatlicue? It was a significant request, and the miraculous nature of an apparition was not to be taken lightly. Friar Zumárraga dis-

missed Juan Diego, telling him that he would listen more patiently to his story at another time.

Dejected by the response, Juan Diego returned to Tepeyac hill
and, after recounting to the Virgin what had happened, pleaded
with her to give the mission to someone more important than
himself:

> So I beg you . . . to have one of the nobles who are held in
> esteem, one who is known, respected, honored, have him carry
> on, take your venerable breath, your venerable word, so that he
> will be believed. Because I am really just a man from the coun-
> try, I am the porter's rope, I am a back-frame, just a tail, a wing;
> I myself need to be led, carried on someone's back. . . . My Little
> Girl, my Littlest Daughter, my Lady, my Girl, please excuse me:
> I will afflict your face, your heart; I will fall into your anger, into
> your displeasure, my Lady Mistress.[20]

Throughout the apparition account, these familiar and affectionate appellations reflect the indigenous form of address in
which people might call one another by many titles; for example,
consider how a younger boy of the nobility would greet his mother: "Oh my noble person, oh personage, oh Lady, . . . we salute
your ladyship and rulership. How did you enjoy your sleep, and
now how are you enjoying the day?"[21]

The Virgin listened with tenderness but responded firmly:

> Listen, my youngest son, know for sure that I have no lack of ser-
> vants [and] messengers to whom I can give the task of carrying
> my breath, my word, so that they carry out my will. But it is
> necessary that you, personally, go and plead, that by your inter-
> cession my wish, my will, become a reality. And I beg you, my
> youngest son, and I strictly order you to go again tomorrow to

see the bishop. And in my name, make him know, make him hear my wish, my will, so that he will bring into being, build my sacred house that I ask of him. And carefully tell him again how I, personally, the ever Virgin Holy Mary, I, who am the Mother of God, sent you as my messenger.[22]

Certainly there were others more suitable for the task, in terms of both credibility and social status. And why was there a need for an intermediary at all? The Virgin herself could have appeared before the bishop. And yet the Virgin selected Juan Diego—a selection that reflects the words of the Virgin Mary in the Gospel, when she praises God who "has cast down the mighty from their thrones and lifted up the lowly."[23] The Virgin's selection of a man of humble rank likewise resonates with Friar Zumárraga's own vocation as a Franciscan, an order valuing humility and renowned for its vows of poverty; in this spirit of humility, before coming to New Spain, Zumárraga had hoped to end his days living in a quiet, stable community, but was chosen instead for a prominent and demanding position in the New World. Juan Diego, too, seems to confirm the Virgin's selection; insisting that she find someone better for the task, he reveals himself as the perfect messenger, one who humbly withdraws in order to call attention to the message itself.

THE THIRD APPARITION

When Juan Diego returned to the bishop the next day to deliver the Virgin's message, Friar Zumárraga questioned Juan Diego on many details of the apparition. This time, before sending Juan Diego away, Friar Zumárraga requested evidence that would confirm the truth of his story. Undaunted by this request,

Juan Diego left, promising to return with a sign from the Virgin.

The bishop, disarmed by Juan Diego's confidence, sent two men to follow him to make sure that Juan Diego was not up to any tricks. The two men trailed Juan Diego for a good while but lost sight of him as he crossed the ravine near the bridge to Tepeyac. After a desperate and unsuccessful search, they returned to Friar Zumárraga's home and, infuriated with Juan Diego for having wasted their time, told Zumárraga that Juan Diego was a sorcerer and a fraud who deserved punishment to prevent him from lying again.

In the meantime, Juan Diego arrived at Tepeyac hill and found the Virgin there waiting for him. Kneeling down before her, he recounted his second meeting with Friar Zumárraga and told her of the bishop's request for a sign. Again with words of kindness, the Virgin thanked Juan Diego for his faithful service to her and assured him of the success of his mission, asking him to return the next day to receive a sign for him to take to Friar Zumárraga.

THE FOURTH APPARITION

Upon Juan Diego's arrival home, however, his plans to return to the Virgin were quickly set aside. While he was away, his uncle Juan Bernardino had taken gravely ill. So the following day, instead of going to Tepeyac, Juan Diego spent his time finding and bringing a doctor to help his uncle, but to no avail; although the doctor ministered to Juan Bernardino, his efforts were too late and death became imminent.

Apart from his love for his uncle, this would have been devastating to Juan Diego because of the important role the uncle played in Indian culture.[24] As Friar Sahagún, one of the early missionaries to the New World and a scholar of Indian culture, notes: "These natives were accustomed to leaving an uncle as guardian or tutor of their children, of their property, of their wife and of their whole house . . . as if it were his own."[25] Additionally, being Juan Diego's elder, Juan Bernardino occupied another essential and well-respected role in his nephew's life and in the community at large. With the absence of writing, knowledge was primarily passed from one generation to the next by oral tradition, through the accurate, word-for-word recitation of discourses from the *huehuetlatolli*, the "speech of the elders." Describing the importance of such speech, one indigenous man explained that the words of the *huehuetlatolli* were "handed down to you . . . carefully folded away, stored up in your entrails, in your throat."[26] It was through the traditions and wisdom passed down by the community elders that the contemporary indigenous world was guided and given meaning. Thus, community elders and the *huehuetlatolli*, far more than just sources of advice and education, constituted the very fabric from which indigenous identity was formed.

Although both Juan Diego and Juan Bernardino were dedicated to their new Christian faith, there is no reason to think that the special role accorded to the elders in indigenous culture would not have retained a prominent place within Juan Diego's worldview. The death of his uncle would have signaled something more than just the passing of a close family member, difficult to bear as that would have been; it also could have been seen as the irrevocable loss of a part of Juan Diego's own identity. To a certain degree, the fear and uncertainty confronting Juan Diego were experienced by many other Indian communities and families as well, some of which were decimated by disease and uprooted from their traditional religious practices.[27] And yet, even at this moment, Juan Bernardino showed the strength of his own faith and his trust in the faith of his nephew. He begged Juan Diego to bring a priest to hear his confession and prepare him for death. So the following day, December 12, Juan Diego wrapped himself in a tilma to protect his body from the cold and hurried off toward the *doctrina* at Tlaltelolco.

As he approached Tepeyac hill, Juan Diego remembered his promised appointment with the Virgin. However, aware of his uncle's condition, he did not want to delay his journey, and so he avoided his usual path in the hope of evading the Virgin. Yet as he rounded the hill he saw the Virgin descend from the top of the hill to greet him. Concerned, she inquired: "My youngest son, what's going on? Where are you going? Where are you headed?"[28]

Juan Diego, at once surprised, confused, fearful, and embarrassed, told the Virgin of his uncle's illness and of his new errand, and expressed something of the hopelessness he was then experiencing, saying, "Because in reality for this [death] we were born, we who came to await the task of our death."[29] Still, even in his distress, he remained committed to his mission. He promised: "Afterwards I will return here again to go carry your venerable breath, your venerable word, Lady, my little girl. Forgive me, be patient with me a little longer, because I am not deceiving you with this . . . tomorrow without fail I will come in all haste."[30]

The Virgin listened to Juan Diego's plea, and when he had finished she spoke to him:

> Listen, put it into your heart, my youngest son, that what frightened you, what afflicted you, is nothing; do not let it disturb your face, your heart; do not fear this sickness nor any other sickness, nor any sharp and hurtful thing. Am I not here, I who have the honor to be your Mother? Are you not in my shadow and under my protection? Am I not the source of your joy? Are you

not in the hollow of my mantle, in the crossing of my arms? Do you need something more?[31]

In this passage, the Virgin's words not only have important associations with motherhood but also have imperial associations as well. Specifically, her words bear a special resemblance to the words addressed to the Aztec emperor upon his succession to the throne:

Perhaps at some time they [your people] may seek a mother, a father [protection]; but they will also weep before you, place their tears, their indigence, their penury . . . Also perhaps the tranquility, the joy with which they will receive from you, that will be gathered in you because you are their mother, their shelter, because you love them deeply, you help them, you are their lady.[32]

The Virgin is mother and queen, and she reveals herself to Juan Diego in both of these capacities.

Interestingly, we see in this another sign of the cultural accuracy of the *Nican Mopohua*; although it was common to address persons using many different relationship titles, "inferiors never called superiors by name and rarely even referred openly to any relationship that might exist between them, whereas superiors could do both (though sparingly)."[33] In the *Nican Mopohua*, nowhere does Juan Diego address the Virgin by the name of Mary; nor does he address her as a mother. In contrast, the Virgin's first words call him by name, and from the beginning, she calls him "my dear son" and breaks the silence about their relationship by calling herself by the title Juan Diego does not address her by: mother.

MORE THAN FLOWERS

At this moment, Our Lady of Guadalupe began to reveal herself to the world—not through Juan Diego himself but through his uncle. Following her words of consolation to Juan Diego, the Virgin assured Juan Diego of his uncle's recovery, saying, "Don't grieve your uncle's illness, because he will not die of it for now; you may be certain that he is already healed."[34] In fact, as Juan Diego would later learn, at that very moment she was also appearing to Juan Bernardino. Juan Diego trusted the Virgin completely and again implored her for a sign that he could take as proof to Friar Zumárraga.

The Virgin instructed Juan Diego to go to the top of Tepeyac hill, where he would now find a variety of flowers for him to cut, gather, and bring back to her so that she could then arrange them in his tilma. Obediently, Juan Diego climbed up the hill and was amazed to find—in the arid winter environment, and in a rocky place where usually only thistles, mesquites, cacti, and thorns grew—a garden brimming with dew-covered flowers of the sweetest scent. Juan Diego quickly gathered them up in his tilma and took them back down to where the Virgin was waiting. The Virgin, taking the flowers from Juan Diego, arranged them in his tilma and said to him:

> My youngest son, these different kinds of flowers are the proof, the sign that you will take to the bishop. You will tell him for me that in them he is to see my wish and that therefore he is to carry out my wish, my will; and you, you who are my messenger, in you I place my absolute trust.[35]

Upon hearing this, Juan Diego set out once again for the bishop's house, reassured by the sign he carried and enjoying the beautiful fragrance of the flowers in his tilma.

Perhaps it is in this moment, as the Virgin stoops to rearrange the flowers in Juan Diego's tilma, that we are given the most poetically poignant expression of what the apparitions at Guadalupe would have meant to the Indian people. In her appearances on Tepeyac, the Virgin takes what is good and true in the Indian culture and rearranges it in such a way that these same elements are brought to the fulfillment of truth. In the Indian culture, flowers and song (which, you will recall, Juan Diego heard just before the first apparition) were symbols of truth—more specifically, the truth that, though somehow intuited by reason, is never comprehensively grasped.[36] Thus the Virgin's sign of flowers, which had to undo the lie told to Friar Zumárraga by the false servants, possesses a double meaning: more than a sign for the bishop that is impossible to explain away as a mere trick by Juan Diego, it is also for the indigenous people a sign of truth.

With these flowers in his tilma, Juan Diego arrived at Friar Zumárraga's residence, but the doorman and servants refused to allow him to enter, pretending not to hear his request. Nevertheless, as Juan Diego continued to wait, the servants grew curious about what he carried in his tilma and approached him. Juan Diego, afraid he could not protect the flowers from their grasping hands, opened his tilma just enough for the servants to see some of the flowers. As the servants reached down into Juan Diego's tilma, the flowers suddenly appeared as if painted or embroidered on the tilma's surface.

Amazed, the servants took Juan Diego to see Friar Zumárraga, and Juan Diego, kneeling before the bishop, told him what the Virgin had said. Then Juan Diego unfolded his tilma, letting the

flowers fall to the floor, only to reveal upon his tilma's rough surface an image of the Virgin Mary. In amazement, those present
knelt down, overwhelmed with emotion. Friar Zumárraga likewise knelt in tears, praying for the Virgin's forgiveness for not having attended to her wish. Then Friar Zumárraga untied the tilma
from around Juan Diego's neck, took it immediately into his private chapel, and welcomed Juan Diego to spend the rest of the day
in his home.

The following day, Friar Zumárraga, guided by Juan Diego,
went to see where the Virgin wished to have her chapel built. And
in this place of craggy rocks, thorns, and spiny cacti—a place
whose barren landscape was reminiscent only of death and the
futility of life—people from the city and nearby towns immediately came and began construction of the Virgin's chapel.

In the account of the Guadalupan apparitions and miracles,
there are many significant moments of reconciliation. In the image
itself, one sees a perfect harmony of cultures and their respective
symbols that convey the same truth. But for the Indians and laymen, the impression of the Virgin's image on the tilma and the
acceptance of Juan Diego's tilma into the chapel are perhaps the
most significant moments. In the Indian culture, the tilma reflected social status. A peasant's tilma would be plain and undecorat-
ed, while a tilma with color or decoration was reserved for noble-
men and people of high social rank.[37] But it would have held powerful cultural meaning as well. The tilma also represented protection, nourishment, matrimony, and consecration—all elements
that would be important as the Guadalupan legacy unfolded. For
the Indians, the Virgin, by placing her image on Juan Diego's
tilma, gives a new and elevated dignity to the common person and
especially the Indian. Moreover, this dignity is recognized by the
bishop when, as the head of the Church in Mexico, he publicly and

personally accepts the tilma into his own private chapel and welcomes Juan Diego into his home. At this moment, all of Juan Diego's roles that had previously impeded his total participation in the Church after the conquest—as an Indian, a convert, a layman, and a man of limited social significance—are welcomed as having an important and decisive place in the Church and its mission of evangelization.

A NAME FOR THE VIRGIN

After fulfilling his duty, Juan Diego begged to be excused so that he could return to his uncle, who had been, when he saw him last, seriously ill and near to death. The bishop agreed and sent several men to accompany Juan Diego, ordering them to return with Juan Bernardino if he was in good health. When they arrived at the town of Tulpetlac, they were astonished to find Juan Bernardino completely recovered; he, on the other hand, was just as astonished to find his nephew so highly honored by the accompaniment of persons sent by Friar Zumárraga. Juan Diego then explained to his uncle where he had been, only to learn that Juan Bernardino already knew: the Virgin—exactly as Juan Diego had described her—had come to Juan Bernardino too. She had healed him, instructed him to show himself to the bishop, and told him everything that his nephew was doing for her.

What is more, the Virgin revealed to Juan Bernardino something even more important—her name. Henceforth, she was to be known as "the Perfect Virgin HOLY MARY OF GUADALUPE."[38]

It is significant that the Virgin chose to disclose her full name not to Juan Diego but instead to his elderly uncle Juan Bernardino. Now there are two witnesses to the apparitions.

While pointing to the veracity of Juan Diego's account, it also underscores the role of family relationships in learning about the faith and the value of spiritual solidarity. Even before the moment when Juan Bernardino tells his nephew of the Virgin's appearance, there is already a history of mutual trust and sharing in their relationship together as Christians.

Yet this moment especially speaks of Juan Bernardino in his combined role as community elder and Christian witness. In many of the biblical accounts of Christ's miraculous healings and those later performed by his apostles, the faith of the healer is integral, but so is the faith of those being healed. Christ would often say to those whom he healed: "Your faith has healed you."[39] As already suggested, owing to his status as a community elder—a status presumably damaged following his conversion to Christianity—Juan Bernardino represented the indigenous community, both its collective knowledge and its identity. Thus, while his illness and imminent death paralleled the condition of many, so also did his recovery foretell a spiritual recovery and renewal. Specifically, the Virgin gives Juan Bernardino her name with two complementary effects. The first is a restoration of Juan Bernardino in his role as community elder, now as a witness of hope with new wisdom to share. The second is the rooting of her name in the collective knowledge of the Indian people, thus giving them a means to seek her intercession and to be spiritually healed in the hope of her promises. This is true renewal: a renewal of the individual in society and a renewal of culture in hope.

Both the Virgin's name and Juan Diego's name are significant within this context, pointing to the need for reconciliation between peoples of different cultures and especially to the importance of inculturation in achieving this reconciliation. While several scholars have argued that the name Guadalupe is of Náhuatl origin—a mistake that began with Luis Becerra Tanco in 1675, but was subsequently shown inaccurate—the fact is that the Virgin chose a name known by the Spaniards. The true origins of the Virgin's name run deeper still, once again bringing together elements of the New World and Spain.[40] (The name "Mary," of course, is originally Hebrew, not Spanish.) In Spain, there was a river named Guadalupe that ran through Extremadura, Spain; the name itself was of Arabic origin and meant "river of black gravel."[41] As legend has it, in the thirteenth century, after a statue of the Black Madonna was found on the banks of the Guadalupe River, the Royal Monastery of Santa María de Guadalupe was built in the Virgin's honor.[42] But the historical record shows that the Spaniards did not give the Mexican Virgin the name "Guadalupe." She chose it—and in doing so she assumed a name that reflected her mission as the one that carries or brings the living water, Jesus Christ.

While it is significant that the Virgin chose a layman as her messenger, thereby underscoring the importance of lay ministry within the Church, it is especially significant that she chose Juan Diego Cuauhtlatoatzin, "eagle that speaks." In Aztec culture, the eagle played an important symbolic role, both as the herald of the Aztec civilization and as the symbol of their patron deity, the sun god. According to Aztec mythology, at some time in the fourteenth century, the Aztecs migrated south to the Valley of Mexico, where an eagle sitting atop a nopal cactus revealed the site of their future capital city, Tenochtitlan ("place of the nopal cactus rock"). But far more than recalling the beginnings of the Aztec civilization, eagles also played an important symbolic role in the contemporary Aztec world, specifically in Aztec religious sacrifice. Revering the eagle as a symbol of the sun, the Aztecs would place the hearts of sacrificial victims in a *cuauhxicalli*, or "eagle gourd vessel," sometimes shaped like the head of an eagle; it was from these eagle vessels that the Aztecs believed the sun would be nourished.[43] Now, at the Virgin's request, Juan Diego Cuauhtlatoatzin is designated as the messenger of a new civilization. This new civilization, however, is not one in which the lives of the gods are sustained by the sacrifice of human lives for food, but rather one in which all people are called to the God who in Christ is life-giving food for them.

A HOME FOR THE IMAGE

On December 26, 1531, the chapel in the Virgin's honor was completed. Intended to be as much a home for the image on Juan Diego's tilma as it was a place for prayer, the chapel was built out of adobe, whitewashed, and roofed with straw in just two weeks. To dedicate the chapel, Juan Diego, Friar Zumárraga, and villagers from Cuauhtitlán processed to the foot of Tepeyac hill and placed the tilma over the chapel's altar. Housed in this new chapel, called the Hermitage, the tilma and its image attracted attention throughout New Spain.[44] Antonio Valeriano concluded the *Nican Mopohua*'s apparition account by noting that "absolutely everyone, the entire city, without exception . . . came to acknowledge [the image] as something divine. They came to offer her their prayers [and] they marveled at the miraculous way it had appeared."[45]

Juan Diego, too, became an important figure in the Virgin's new shrine. Many who came to the shrine identified in the Virgin's messenger a beautiful expression of holiness that they wished to imitate so that, as some of the Indians put it, "we also could obtain the eternal joys of Heaven."[46] In his homily for Juan Diego's canonization Mass, John Paul II recalled this early recognition of Juan

Diego's holiness in the developing Mexican Church. Concluding his homily, he prayed:

> Blessed Juan Diego, a good, Christian Indian, whom simple people have always considered a saint! . . . We entrust to you our lay brothers and sisters so that, feeling the call to holiness, they may imbue every area of social life with the spirit of the Gospel. . . .
>
> Beloved Juan Diego, "the Eagle that speaks"! Show us the way that leads to the "Dark Virgin" of Tepeyac, that she may receive us in the depths of her heart, for she is the loving, compassionate Mother who guides us to the true God. Amen.[47]

Nearly five centuries after the apparitions, Juan Diego remains an example for us today, especially for the new evangelization. In his role in the apparition and in his life afterward, he is a model of faith, of devotion, of sacrifice, and of the role of *every* believer to transform culture—"to imbue every area of social life with the spirit of the Gospel."[48]

II.

The Image of the Mother

He who falls at the feet of Christ's mother most certainly shows honor to her Son. There is no God but one, He who is known and adored in the Trinity.

—ST. JOHN DAMASCENE,
ON HOLY IMAGES [1]

A MYSTERY FOR SCIENCE

On the morning of November 14, 1921, Luciano Perez Carpio, an employee of the private ministry of the presidency, entered the Basilica of Our Lady of Guadalupe with soldiers disguised as civilians protecting him on either side. Leaning down, he placed an arrangement of flowers at the base of the Virgin's image. Moments later, a bomb hidden inside the flowers detonated. The explosion was of such a magnitude that it ruined the basilica's altar, the candelabra, and the bronze crucifix set atop the altar, and it even shattered windows of neighboring homes within a one-kilometer radius. But just inches away, Juan Diego's tilma and its glass covering remained perfectly intact. While persecution of Catholics was prevalent in Mexico during the anticlerical regimes in the nineteenth and twentieth centuries, this attack reached a new level; yet even such an orchestrated effort as this could not undo the miracle, but rather only further underscored its supernatural origins.[2]

More than a century earlier, in 1785, the tilma had already proven resistant to ordinarily devastating occurrences when nitric acid was spilled on it during a routine cleaning of the frame. As one eyewitness of the accident testified:

> The spilling of a great deal of acid occurred while the side of the frame was being cleaned . . . , enough to destroy the whole of the surface being cleaned. . . . I have personally seen, on those occasions when the glass case has been open . . . that the [nitric acid] left a somewhat dull mark where it was spilled, though the painting is without any damage.[3]

Remarkably, Juan Diego's tilma was barely damaged, having nothing to show from the incident except a dull mark where the acid was spilled, visible on the right side when looking at the image. But as for the unfortunate silversmith, the eyewitness testimony explained, "I also know that the silversmith responsible for the accident was so upset that it was believed he would become seriously ill . . . for everyone knows that nitric acid is so strong that it will destroy iron if it comes in contact with it."[4]

The tilma's preservation throughout the centuries has become a mainstay in any consideration of its miraculous properties. Perhaps even more remarkable than these dramatic incidents of preservation is how the tilma withstood equally harmful conditions on a day-to-day basis for the first 116 years of its history.[5] During this time, the tilma was displayed without any type of covering. Additionally, the image's lack of priming underneath the coloration is evident even today since the colors permeate the fabric all the way through and are visible from the back, producing a rough mirror image on the opposite side of the tilma. Unprotected, the tilma was particularly vulnerable to deterioration caused by a naturally corrosive substance, saltpeter, carried in the air from the lake, as well as by the blackening effect of dust and incense in the Hermitage and the "hands-on" devotion of pilgrims who would often kiss and touch the image. In addition, small pieces were even cut from the tilma in order to be venerated as relics, thus further exposing the edges of the tilma to fraying and deterioration.

Toward the end of the eighteenth century, José Ignacio Bartolache, a natural scientist and medical doctor, became interested in the tilma for its miraculous preservation. Intrigued by how the image had remained in such a remarkable state for two and a half centuries, he designed an experiment to test how long a tilma such as Juan Diego's would typically last in the inhospitable climate of the Tepeyac region. He commissioned several tilmas to be made of natural fibers, and instructed the most skilled Indian copyists to replicate the original image as faithfully as possible on each of the replica tilmas. Two replicas were then placed in the same area as the original image in order to expose them to the same environmental conditions. Unlike the original tilma, the replicas could not withstand the humidity and saltpeter characteristic of the Tepeyac hill climate. Before a short period had passed, the replica tilmas were discolored and falling to pieces.[6]

Many other scientific examinations of the tilma have been commissioned and continue to be done today. Yet, even as scientific knowledge has progressed and more studies on the tilma have been performed, the tilma's mystery has only deepened. Beginning with the first-ever examination of the tilma in 1666, we have learned more ways that the tilma is miraculous than we have answers explaining the miracle. In the mid-seventeenth century, with the increasing popularity of Our Lady of Guadalupe in Mexico, many desired to celebrate the Virgin with official Mass and church services, which in turn required a formal investigation into the image and apparitions. While in 1556 a study was commissioned by Bishop Alonso Montúfar, Zumárraga's successor, this did not include a study of the tilma; in the 1666 investigation, however, recorded in the *Informaciones Jurídicas de 1666*, interviews were conducted so as to learn of the rich Guadalupan oral tradition and the tilma itself was officially examined for the first time. Though the official Mass and liturgies for Our Lady of Guadalupe were not sanctioned until 1754, this investigation is important as the first formal inquiry into the apparitions and miraculous image.

To get permission to examine the tilma, a petition was formulated and addressed to Viceroy Marqués de Mancera. With the viceroy's approval granted, on March 13, 1666, the image was lowered from above the Hermitage's altar; watching over this solemn event were some of the highest authorities in New Spain.[7] First the image was given to a team of art specialists, then to a group of respected chemists, both with the goal of establishing how the image came to be on the tilma.

The team of artists consisted of seven professional painters and art instructors, most of whom had practiced or taught painting for more than twenty years.[8] However, despite their experience in the field, they could not explain how an image so beautiful could be painted upon a surface so rough. In a joint and unanimous statement, the artists marveled at the technique employed for the realization of the image and at its remarkable state of preservation:

> [I]t is humanly impossible that any artist could paint and work something so beautiful, clean and well-formed on a fabric which is as rough as is the tilma or ayate . . . [T]here cannot be a

painter, as skillful as he may be or as good as there have been in this New Spain, who could succeed perfectly to imitate the color, nor determine if such a painting is in tempera or oil, because it appears to be both, but it is not what it appears, because only Our God knows the secret of this painting, of its durability and preservation, of the permanence of its beautiful colors and the gold of its stars.[9]

The seven art specialists concluded that the only reasonable explanation for the image—for its beauty, delicacy, and preservation—was God.

With the artists' study complete, on March 28, three chemists were also given access to the image to conduct their own study.[10] After analyzing the environment around the Virgin's Hermitage, the chemists, too, were astounded. Given the location of the Hermitage—an area that was humid and filled with saltpeter— they noted that the tilma should have been destroyed by these environmental elements many years earlier. After all, the saltpeter in the air ruined even the Hermitage's stone ornamentation, and would have done the same with the silver adorning the inside of the Hermitage "if it were not for the very frequent care it receive[d], . . . since it is far less resistant than stone." Nevertheless, the image remained remarkably well preserved.[11] Touching the image, the chemists were puzzled by the fact that, though the surface of the image was soft and gentle like silk, "on the backside, it is rough and hard."[12] How could such a delicate and detailed painting, with such soft and gentle features, they wondered, be done on a surface with such a coarse weave? The chemists concluded their report in the same way as did the artists, saying: "Our limited intelligence cannot account for it."[13]

Since 1666, as technology has developed, subsequent studies

of the tilma have been numerous and diverse, underscoring the mystery of the tilma in new areas. With the rise of photography, Alfonso Marcue (1929), Carlos Salinas (1951), and ophthalmologist Dr. Javier Torroella Bueno (1956) took close-up photographs of the eyes of Our Lady of Guadalupe, and reported that the image's coloration not only depicts her pupils but also depicts the types of images one would see reflected in the eyes of a living human being—in this case, the reflected images of people. A few years later Dr. Rafael Torija Lavoignet (1958) and Dr. Charles Wahlig (1962) studied the Purkinje-Sanson effect in the image on the tilma. More recently, in 1981, Dr. José Aste Tönsmann likewise studied this same effect in the Virgin's eyes, and wrote of his findings: "The presence of the images in both of the eyes of the Virgin of Guadalupe constitutes, without doubt, one of the most forceful proofs . . . of the difficulty of obtaining a natural explanation for its creation."[14]

Over the years, these studies have continued to deepen our understanding of the unnatural, inexplicable, and miraculous qualities of the tilma. Even as science has advanced and the complicated theories of earlier examiners have proved inadequate, it has become increasingly clear that there is no natural explanation for the phenomenon of the image of Our Lady of Guadalupe on Juan Diego's tilma. Moreover, with advancements made in our understanding of the history, religion, and culture of the New World Indians, it is becoming increasingly clear that the richness of the tilma is not exhausted by its physical properties, but extends to the profound symbolic relevance of its message.

Though people marvel that the tilma has survived corrosive air, an accident with acid, and even a bombing, as with any miracle, we should look beyond its miraculous elements and survival. Without God and the Virgin, the miracle of the tilma becomes unintelligible, since this miracle is not a mere event but an action—an ongoing action that we today are also gifted in bearing witness to. And like any action, this action has an agent and a purpose. By surveying the history of the tilma, we get a better idea not only of what science can tell us about the image but at the same time a better sense of its deeper spiritual message. This is not to suggest that every facet of the tilma and its history is imbued with meaning or is theologically explicable, or even that we can ever fully grasp its mystery. Rather, the implication is simpler: it is an invitation to reflect on what historical circumstances and science have revealed about the tilma in light of the ever deepening mystery and message to which they point.

CONTEMPLATING THE IMAGE

As we will hear more about in the following chapters, the Virgin's miraculous image spoke profoundly to the Indian people of the New World in a way the missionaries never could. In his account of the history of the Guadalupan apparitions, the missionary Fernando de Alva Ixtlilxóchitl recalled:

> [The Indians], submerged in profound darkness, still loved and served false little gods, clay figurines and images of our enemy the devil, in spite of having heard about the faith. But when they heard that the Holy Mother of Our Lord Jesus Christ had appeared, and since they saw and admired her most perfect Image, which has no human art, their eyes were opened as if suddenly day had dawned for them.[15]

Appearing in this way, the Virgin herself affirms and continues a tradition already well established in the Church: that of artis-

tic patronage and development of talent as a means to achieving or inculcating spiritual growth. While serving an important peda-gogical function as a way to teach basic articles of the faith, art was also seen as having a deeper, spiritual significance as a means to contemplation and conversion. Yet in the early Church it was pre-cisely this efficacy and purpose of art that was questioned. Some, popularly called iconoclasts, argued that to venerate images of Mary and the saints was idolatrous; instead of leading to God, they claimed that veneration of icons focused merely on the creature. But in A.D. 787, the historic Second Council of Nicaea upheld the value of holy images against the iconoclasts, stating: "For by so much more frequently as [the saints] are seen in artistic represen-tation, by so much more readily are men lifted up to the memory of their prototypes, and to a longing after them; and to these should be given due salutation and honorable reverence."[16] More than seven hundred years later, Our Lady of Guadalupe issued her own statement on the matter; even today, her holy image stands as a singular example of the power of holy art to bring about spiritu-al growth and conversion.

Artistically, the image of Our Lady of Guadalupe achieves a harmony of two seemingly incompatible styles. On one hand, the use of shading and color to produce depth and lifelikeness in her face, figure, and clothing is reminiscent of European techniques and styles. On the other hand, the two-dimensional gold designs over her tunic, which do not follow the folds of the tunic, are more similar to what we find in ancient Indian codices. In this chapter, we will consider the image apart from these gold designs found on the Virgin's tunic, an important feature of the image that will be discussed in the following chapter. Here, we will look at the three-dimensional features of the image—which of course include the Virgin herself—in view of the special way that these features convey important Christian concepts in an understandable and completely relevant way for the Indians of the New World.

In the image, we can easily recognize Mary as the woman described in the Book of Revelation—the woman "clothed with the sun, with the moon under her feet" (Rev. 12:1). But to understand how her Child's presence is evoked, we have to look at the dark purplish ribbon tied high above her waist. Typically, Indian women would wear this belt just at the waist, unless a woman was pregnant, in which case the belt would be worn higher up, as in the case of Our Lady of Guadalupe. (Interestingly, there is a nice parallel in the Spanish language, where the word for pregnant is *encinta*, which literally means "adorned with ribbon.") In this way, the Virgin is a lady of Advent, of hope, patiently awaiting the birth of her Son.

Her pregnancy, as a symbol of birth and renewal, takes on greater meaning in that she is pregnant with God himself. In this, the clouds surrounding her would have elicited respect, and possibly even indicated something supernatural. It was written that when the Aztec emperor Moctezuma first greeted Cortés, he said: "I have been expecting this for some days, days in which my heart was looking at those places from where you have come *from among the fog and from among the clouds*, a place unknown to all."[17] Numerous scholars have debated what these words tell us about what Moctezuma actually believed about Cortés—for instance, did he really believe Cortés to be a god, or are these words mere mockery or simple etiquette? For us, however, what is important is not what these words actually meant in that context, but rather what they tell us about how the Indians spoke of supernatural things: "from among the fog and from among the clouds"—*mixtitlan ayauhtitlan* in Náhuatl. These are also the same words reportedly spoken to the first twelve missionaries to the New World when they met both the Aztec priests and nobles.[18] Here in the Virgin's image, she is surrounded by clouds, not because she herself is a god, but because she is with God as his mother.

A related kind of renewal is evoked as well: the renewal of the Indian civilization. Beneath her feet is an angel, bald but with the countenance of a child, thus evoking both wisdom and youthful innocence. His wings are those of an eagle, decorated by a rainbow of blue-green, white, and red. It is important to recall the eagle's role both as herald of the Aztec civilization and as the symbolic conveyor of the Aztecs' sacrificial offerings to their gods. Echoing these roles, this eagle-angel transports in his hands a new sacrifice, Christ present in the Virgin's womb. Christ the Redeemer comes to free the Indians from their perceived need for ritual sacrifice.

The clothing the Virgin wears tells us more about who she is; her mantle is adorned with stars. Some who have studied the stars on the Virgin's mantle have reported a remarkable coincidence between this pattern of stars and the constellations that appeared in the sky above Mexico City on the morning of December 12, 1531, the day the Virgin revealed herself on the tilma.[19] The Virgin's mantle is of a rich blue-green color, which for the Aztecs was a color that had significant imperial associations. Traditionally, only the Aztec emperor wore a blue mantle, which typically was festooned with emeralds, thus symbolizing the heavens. Decorated in gold flowers, her earthy pink tunic evoked the earth, the land. At her feet, these two pieces of clothing, her tunic and mantle, are held by the eagle-angel, thus indicating the Virgin's reign over the whole cosmos; in her, the sky and earth are joined together. This revelation was not merely theoretical but profoundly incorporated into the Indians' understanding of their own lives. In a 1995 interview, the Indians of Zozocolco, Veracruz, while preparing to celebrate the feast of Our Lady of Guadalupe, explained:

With the harmony of the angel, who holds up the Heavens and the Earth, a new life will come forth. This is what we received from our elders, our grandparents, that our lives do not end, but rather that they have a new meaning. . . . This is what we celebrate today . . . the arrival of this sign of unity, of harmony, of new life.[20]

These words, passed down through a centuries-old oral tradition, give us insight into ancient perspectives on the image and its meaning for the Indian people, who were able to see it in the context of their own lives, thus assuaging fears and imbuing hope.

Importantly for the Aztecs, this new harmony is illustrated specifically with depictions of the sun and the moon, the first set behind the Virgin, bathing her in a peaceful light, the second at her feet. These solar bodies were objects of great importance and fear for the Aztecs, who associated the sun and moon with gods and believed these gods to be in constant conflict with one another. Fearing that the sun would somehow perish in this cosmic battle, the Aztecs sustained their god with human sacrifices intended ultimately to achieve cosmological harmony and the preservation of life on earth.[21] The Virgin's image speaks specifically to this fear, wherein the sun and moon are shown no longer as gods but as objects under her governance. While eclipses were often believed to be bad omens and a sign of the sun's defeat, in her image the Virgin eclipses the sun, but not in a menacing way; in doing so, she brings focus to her own womb, wherein is kept the true God. Interestingly, December 12, 1531, the day of the Virgin's last appearance, was the winter solstice, thus inaugurating the time of year when the sun increasingly conquers the darkness and the days become longer.[22]

The moon set beneath the Virgin's feet has a superadded significance. While indicating her governance over the moon, and thus assuaging fear of cosmic collapse, the Virgin at the same time visually roots herself in the very origins of the Mexican civilization, which derives its name from a combination of three Náhuatl words: *meztli*, "moon"; *xic* (tli), "navel"; and *co*, "in." Taken together, these three words mean "in the center of the moon."[23] In the image, the Virgin literally stands in the center of the moon. However, though rooting herself in these origins, the Virgin at the same time suggests to the Indian people a radically new spiritual conception of the universe.

While her imperial-colored clothing and cosmic surroundings indicate that the Virgin is a heavenly queen, her posture indicates that there is someone greater than she, someone to whom she humbly prays. For us, the Virgin's clasped hands immediately indicate prayer; this would have been the same for the Spaniards at the time as well. But even more, for the Indians, her entire body would have indicated the Virgin was praying. For them, prayer was expressed not only in words or song but in solemn dance. In the image, the Virgin can be seen as in motion, with her weight on one foot and the other knee bent, in the dance-step position. This for the Indians was the highest form of prayer. As one missionary at the time explained, the Indians' religious ceremonies were elaborate events, with "many roses and green and bright things, and with chants solemn in style, and with dances . . . of great feeling and importance, without disagreeing in tone or step, since this was their main prayer."[24] The Aztec emperor would also participate, uniting himself to his people in song and dance for their gods.[25]

In this we can see a deeper meaning in the bright colors and beautiful birdsong that Juan Diego observed before his first encounter with the Virgin. With song and the transformation of Tepeyac hill into a place of brightness and light—the ground like jade and the foliage like the bright feathers of the quetzal bird—the Virgin prepares the hill as a place of worship and sacred celebration. And in this we are at the same time shown the true source of the Virgin's queenship; in her prayerful dance, lowly posture, and downcast eyes, she is queen precisely as handmaid, precisely through her humble openness to God.

The tilt of her head and direction of her gaze have another important meaning. Though for us the idiomatic phrase "to look sideways at" has a negative connotation and is often associated with indifference, in Náhuatl it was the reverse. To look sideways at someone or something was actually more complementary, meaning "thinking of he who is looked upon, not forgetting who is looked upon."[26] In this case, the side of her face is turned toward the viewer. Even today, this was one of the things pointed out in the 1995 interview with the Indians of Zozocolco: "This Woman is important because She stands before the Sun, steps on the Moon and dresses herself with the Stars, but her countenance tells us that there is someone greater than She, because She is looking down, as a sign of respect."[27]

One of the aspects of Our Lady of Guadalupe given most attention is the color of her skin. Neither white like the Spaniards nor dark like the Indians, the Virgin is a mestiza—a combination of the two. Specifically, the mestizos were people of mixed blood, having both European and Indian ancestry. In this way, she identifies herself completely with the people of the New World, since the first appearance of mestizo children was in the New World. At the same time, she does not exclude the Spaniards; they are a part of her as well. In this way, the Virgin borrows from the Spaniards and the Indians, reaffirming both in their uniqueness but at the same time representing an important link between them: she is their mother.

As their mother, she leads them to her Son. If we look closely at the Virgin's image, we can see that she is wearing a brooch with a bare cross. The Indians would have seen similar crosses worn by the New World missionaries, who wore bare crosses for fear that the Indians would mistake any depiction of the Crucifixion as an affirmation of their own human sacrifices.[28] Yet the Virgin does much more than identify with the missionaries: while pointing to Christ's Crucifixion, the bare cross also points to his victory over death in the resurrection. With plagues drastically reducing the Indian population, and their sufferings compounded by the mistreatment they received at the hands of some of the Spanish officials and settlers, the Virgin's cross stands as an acknowledgment of their sufferings.

A CULTURE OF THE IMAGE

In her miraculous image, the Guadalupan Virgin bequeathed something both enduring and physically concrete. Why she chose to perform a second miracle is a message in itself. After all, the flowers in wintertime, growing atop the barren Tepeyac hill, would likely have been miraculous enough to inspire a chapel, making the second miracle not only unexpected but completely unnecessary. Still, the Virgin chose a sign that achieved much more. Like the flowers, Juan Diego's tilma is composed of an organic, highly corruptible material—agave fibers—and yet, unlike the flowers, the tilma has neither fallen into obscurity nor suffered from the processes of normal decomposition.[29] Rather, the tilma exists as a synthesis of the earthly and the heavenly whose enduring nature belies an enduring message and request, one that far exceeds the original purpose of the flowers.

The message contained in the Virgin's image, while certainly of universal import, is one whose presentation is geared specifically toward the Indian people. Drawing upon pictographs, myth, symbols, and ways of thinking already familiar to the Náhuatl mind, the Guadalupan Virgin provides us with an extraordinary model of enculturation, as Benedict XVI wrote:

> Our Lady of Guadalupe is in many respects an image of the relationship between Christianity and the religions of the world: all of these streams flow together into it, are purified and renewed, but are not destroyed. It is also an image of the relationship of the truth of Jesus Christ to the truths of those religions: the truth does not destroy; it purifies and unites.[30]

In her miraculous image, the Guadalupan Virgin borrows potentially good and fruitful elements from the Indian culture—those "seeds of the Word" that, until unearthed, lie dormant in every civilization. In this way, she reaffirms these elements, while at the same time purifying them and bestowing upon them the fullness of Christ. Thus, far from being outright rejected or condemned, the basic truths recognized in the Indian culture are confirmed and perfected in the Virgin's miraculous image, where they are pictorially united to the truth of Christ.

In any authentic Christian evangelization, the message is always truth—specifically, the truth of Christ—and enculturation speaks to how that truth is conveyed in a cultural "language" each recipient can understand. At the first Pentecost, the apostles were sent out from the upper chamber to evangelize the world. We are told that Mary was with them, praying in the cenacle. Biblically, no passage suggests that she too spoke in tongues. Still, we know that she has done so historically, through her various apparitions.

Among these, none more beautifully points to the intimate link between love and communication than the apparitions at Guadalupe. Here, in the apparition, the Virgin Mary spoke in Náhuatl. Additionally, in looking at the image, the Indians could see reflected their own language and culture, and a codex with profound meaning.

The fact that this great and lasting miracle came as both an image and a codex was one way that this evangelization truly showed itself to be enculturated according to the New World culture rather than an imposition of European culture. In many ways, European culture could be understood as a "culture of the word," heavily influenced by its dependence upon written language— from the philosophy and literature of the ancient classical world to the study of sacred scripture and the spiritual writings of the Church Fathers. That culture was greatly advanced by medieval theologians such as St. Thomas Aquinas and during the Renaissance with the invention of the printing press some decades before the apparition. Yet the missionaries in New Spain faced a people who were entirely different in this regard. Communicating and recording ancient truths through their pictographs, the Indians of the New World lived in a culture more accurately described as a "culture of the image."

Today, we have seen a significant shift in our own culture, from a culture of the word to a new and very different culture of the image, suggested and reinforced by the prevalence and popularity of new technologies. As with any cultural shift, new problems and possibilities arise. Speaking of the special problems posed today, the late Cardinal Alfonso López Trujillo wrote, "The complex theme of language has to be taken up: 'Christ himself asks us to proclaim the Good news using a language that brings the Gospel closer and closer to today's new cultural realities.'"[31] Undoubtedly, the theme of language and dialogue is one of central importance in Christianity, not only historically, as an indispensable means to sharing the faith, but more deeply as an expression of its very origin and sublime prototype: the communion of Trinitarian love. Today, this dialogue has been opened up to a variety of new forums. And yet if it is to be effective, it must remain personal, tailored to the unique values, language, and mediums of expression present in each culture. What is more, it must always manifest itself, as John Paul II once said, in the form of "an act of love which has its roots in God himself."[32]

Enculturation requires dialogue. It requires a level of trust and understanding that makes it easy for the recipient to grasp the fundamental truths being taught. Paul VI spoke of the requirements for dialogue in this way:

> Since the world cannot be saved from the outside, we must first of all identify ourselves with those to whom we would bring the Christian message—like the Word of God who Himself became a man. Next we must forego all privilege and the use of unintelligible language, and adopt the way of life of ordinary people in all that is human and honorable. Indeed, we must adopt the way of life of the most humble people, if we wish to be listened to and understood. Then, before speaking, we must take great care to listen not only to what men say, but more especially to what they have it in their hearts to say. Only then will we understand them and respect them, and even, as far as possible, agree with them.
>
> Furthermore, if we want to be men's pastors, fathers and teachers, we must also behave as their brothers. Dialogue thrives on friendship, and most especially on service. All this we must remember and strive to put into practice on the example and precept of Christ.[33]

One of the most extraordinary examples of this enculturated, personal dialogue is that of the image of Our Lady of Guadalupe. First made manifest to a people within a culture of the image, Our Lady of Guadalupe is becoming increasingly popular today, in a global community now transitioning to a new culture of the image. Thus, while she may come to us differently—in different times and circumstances—this ancient image of Our Lady remains as contemporary as when it first appeared nearly five hundred years ago. And more than any other dialogue, the conversions and hope that she inspires make clear that the gift of her image was and continues to be an act of love rooted in God.

III.

Message of Truth and Love

I am the Way, the Truth, and the Life.

—GOSPEL OF JOHN 14:6

THE TILMA: A NÁHUATL CODEX

While in Mexico for the installation Mass as the Supreme Knight of the Knights of Columbus, I purchased an oil painting depicting the Guadalupan apparition. Painted sometime between 1675 and 1700, it depicts in vibrant colors Our Lady of Guadalupe appearing to Juan Diego, accompanied by two angels, one gazing at the Virgin, the other laying a reassuring hand on Juan Diego's shoulder. The blue veil and stars, the Virgin's positioning, even the folds of her clothing and the bending of her knee are just as depicted in the image of the Virgin on Juan Diego's tilma. But upon examining the Guadalupan Virgin's image further, it became clear that something significant was very different 'in the later painting of the Virgin. The vinelike gold design over the Virgin's tunic lacked the most important, unduplicated flower—the four-petaled jasmine flower, representing God.

Rather than a unique "error" in copying, the anonymous painter of the picture was just another in a long history of artists who viewed, or at least painted, the floral design as mere "decoration"—something extraneous, undefined, and thus perfect for artistic license. Often, instead of the spacious, logical, even repetitive design, the Colonial-era artists would paint diverse, even radically ornate, baroque floral patterns. But this "error" is also understandable, since only recently has Náhuatl and Guadalupan scholarship uncovered the reason for the flowers to take the particular shape and position they have on the tilma: each flower resembles the pictographic writing, or glyphs, found in Náhuatl codices. That is, the flowers are more than flowers; they are symbols, words, and concepts. In this, the tilma becomes more than an image; it is a codex, conveying in the Náhuatl language and culture of the Indians the most fundamental elements of the Christian message: the relationship between God and man, a relationship of love and truth.[1]

As in most civilizations, the indigenous manuscripts played a significant role in communicating information on topics of communal importance, including religious ceremonies, the gods, and special dates and feast days. Yet unlike European manuscripts written using alphabetic language, Náhuatl codices were primarily pictorial, comprising images and glyphs. Often the text was written in a circle or a square on the page, unlike the parallel lines in European text. Also, unlike bound books, these codices were more like folded stacks of long pages. When taken out to be read, the codices were unfolded flat on the floor, where their pages could be viewed from all sides. Most of the codices from central and southern Mexico we have today are composed of paper made primarily from the soft interior of tree bark, and a few from the maguey plant, the same plant family from which Juan Diego's agave tilma is made.[2] Visually, the idea of the tilma and the Virgin's image being a codex is accentuated by the fact that the floral symbols or glyphs do not follow the folds of the Virgin's tunic, as it would if the pattern were merely a design on the tunic, but rather the floral glyphs overlie the tunic area, leaving the glyph lines undistorted and entirely visible.

BASIC COMPONENTS

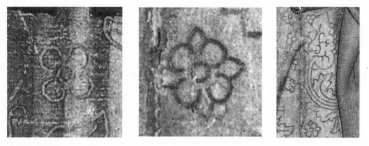

The floral design overlying the Virgin's tunic consists of three kinds of flowers: a four-petaled jasmine (appearing once), an eight-petaled flower (appearing eight times), and a flower cluster (appearing nine times). The meaning of these glyph-flowers is derived from their correspondence to ancient Náhuatl glyphs and from their relationship to the rest of the tilma image, described in the previous chapter. Additionally, because of the way these arabesque flowers are composed, they can resemble several different glyphs at the same time according to the direction they are viewed (just as the letter *p* can resemble a *d* when viewed upside down). Importantly, these multiple meanings of the glyphs are not simply common or generic glyph associations from other Náhuatl codices; rather, they are unique to the tilma, and thus imply a unique and multifaceted message and meaning.

JASMINE FLOWER

 The four-petaled jasmine flower (the flower absent in the seventeenth-century painting described at the beginning of the chapter) is the only one of its kind found on the Virgin's tunic. While basic in design, it is both central to the image of the Virgin and central to the identity of the Virgin and her Child.

For the Indians, the design of this four-petaled jasmine flower had many interrelated meanings in their religious thought. Cosmologically, it symbolized the four directions (north, south, east, and west), covering the whole universe.[3] The design represents what the indigenous called the *Nahui Ollin,* meaning "always in movement." Its fifth point, in the center, symbolizes the Fifth Sun, and is therefore the sun flower that represented in the theology of the *tlamatinime* (wise men) of the Toltecs the only living and true god, whom they called *Ometéotl.*[4] The Texcocans, of which Juan Diego was one, were heirs to Toltec thought and culture. Some of the titles attributed to this "unknown deity" were *Ipalnemohuani* ("Him for whom one lives"), *Teyocoyani* ("Creator of people"), *Tloque Nahuaque* ("Owner of the near and close") and *Ilhuicahua Tlaltipaque* ("Lord of heaven and earth"). However, in the Toltec mentality, *Ometéotl* resided in the highest part of the heavens where no human being could have access to him and where this divinity would not have to concern himself with insignificant human beings.[5]

In the apparition account, Our Lady of Guadalupe speaks of her Son using these titles (Him for whom one lives, Creator of people, Owner of the near and close, Lord of heaven and earth).[6] And yet, it is absolutely clear that she is speaking of Christ. In the image of Our Lady of Guadalupe, this takes shape as a magnificent inculturated evangelization through the positioning of the jasmine flower on the womb of the image, just below her pregnancy belt, thus identifying her Child as divine. In this, the symbol of the four-petal jasmine shows the Indians that the omnipotent God is reachable by any human being; and not only is he interested in them but he delivers himself to them: it is wondrous that this omnipotent God, the deeply rooted God, now comes to find and deliver himself to mankind through his mother.

The fathers of the Second Vatican Council spoke of the "seeds of the Word"—the glimpses of the truth about God—that can be found in various cultures.[7] This can be seen in the limited understanding the Indians had of this "unknown God," reflected in the four titles referenced above expressing certain truths about the omnipotent creator. In a special way, this harks back to St. Paul's address at the Areopagus, when he spoke to the Athenians about their worship of the "unknown God," whom they detected but could not understand. As St. Paul explained, this God is revealed fully in Christ as the one who created man and the natural order "so that people might seek God, even perhaps grope for him and find him, though indeed he is not far from any one of us. For 'in him we live and move and have our being,' as even some of your poets have said, 'for we too are his offspring.'"[8]

Of course, there are many differences between the God of Jesus Christ and Ometéotl, the god of the Toltecs. The image on the tilma addresses a number of these differences. One of the fundamental differences addressed by the jasmine's placement over the Virgin's womb is a difference of love, presence, and care. For these Indians, despite Ometéotl's authority over the whole world, the god was believed to be indifferent to the affairs of the world; though sustaining all things in existence, he was inaccessible. Here, the flower over the Virgin's womb speaks to one of the radical concepts brought by Christianity, specifically by the belief in Christ's incarnation: the omnipotent God of the earth whom these Indians sought is near to mankind, and cares for them so deeply that he comes in a vulnerable and loving relationship, through his mother.[9]

EIGHT-PETALED FLOWER

 Besides the implicit promise of birth in pregnancy, in this eight-petaled flower a different kind of beginning is expressed: the beginning of a new age, indicated by the harmony among the cosmic spheres. The eight-petaled flower, appearing eight times, symbolizes the planet Venus, also known as either the "morning star" or the "evening star," depending on whether it rises in the sky at sunrise or sunset.[10] Among the Indians, the calendar system was very complex and was entrusted to their priests educated in astronomy and the cosmological rhythms. In particular, these priests followed three calendars of varying lengths: a ritual calendar, a solar calendar, and a calendar following the movements of the planet Venus. Over several centuries, without adequate compensation for leap years, the Indians' calendar system and feast days got off, so much so that eventually the feast days were being celebrated many months away from the corresponding seasons—for example, the rituals for use during the drought season were performed long before the droughts typically occurred. On the tilma, not only are the sun and moon "subdued" and eclipsed by the Virgin and now in harmony with each other, but the two orbs governing the calendars are in harmony as well. The sun and the planet Venus are present on the tilma, but neither is dominating the other, suggesting a harmony in the calendars .[11]

Like many elements of the apparition, this peaceful timeliness reflects the birth of Christ. The Roman emperor at the time of Christ's birth, the Gospel of Luke tells us, was Caesar Augustus, who established the Pax Romana (Roman peace). During this time, an age of peace was welcomed into the empire and most of the continent. Thus, Christ was born at a time "when the whole world was at peace."[12] Likewise, coming historically ten years following the conquest, "when the arrows and shields were put aside, when there was peace in all towns," Our Lady of Guadalupe is shown to be pregnant with Christ at an interval of peace.[13]

FLOWER CLUSTER

The most intricate design on the Virgin's tunic is the cluster of flowers. Importantly, this cluster begins to address the universal and timeless questions: Who am I? How do I relate to God? How does this affect how I relate to other persons and the world? Appearing nine times, each time with slight variations, this cluster has three main parts: a triangular blossom, a curving stem with leaves, and small flowers attached to the outside of the blossom. Comparing this flower cluster with symbols found in other Aztec codices, we uncover similarities between the designs of the pictographs and the design of the parts of the flower. The blossom, with its triangular shape and bumpy slopes, resembles the glyph for "hill" (*tepec*) and the hill-like temple, while the curving stem corresponds to the glyph for "river."

In Náhuatl, it was standard to combine glyphs to create a new word or thought, especially to designate items that are unique, such as personal names or place names. In this case, the combination of glyphs for "hill" and "water" was an established combination: the *altepetl* (hill + water) was a communal concept, ranging in meaning from a village to the larger concept of nation or civilization.[14]

Historically for the Aztecs, with religion so deeply imbedded in the everyday life of the people and state, this larger concept of nation or civilization was tied to the temple. Tenochtitlan, the Aztecs' capital city, was itself believed to be the fulfillment of a promise made to the Aztecs by their patron deity, Huitzilopochtli, while they were still a subjugated people living in the land north of the Valley of Mexico. According to legend, the Aztecs were told to leave in search of a sign—an eagle set atop a nopal cactus.[15] After much wandering, the Aztecs finally found the promised sign on an island in a lake. Here, on this island, they founded their capital—Tenochtitlan, "place of the cactus on a rock"—from which they forged an empire, coming to dominate the whole Valley of Mexico. Inaugurating their new nation and civilization, the Aztecs built a temple, which later was expanded upon numerous times over its long history.[16] More than just a place of worship, the Templo Mayor transcended its sacrificial function and held greater importance in the identity of the Aztec Empire and civilization. Located in the center of the city, marked by the intersection of four converging causeways, the Templo Mayor was encircled by a wall, which separated the sacred precinct from the rest of the city. Inside the sacred precinct were palaces and numerous pyramids and other religious buildings. Though set within the enclosed space of the sacred precinct, the Templo Mayor nevertheless was connected with the rest of the city as a symbol of its sustaining and originating center, and indeed as a center of the cosmos.[17]

With this history in mind, when we look at the reason for this particular combination of glyphs—the hill and river—on the Virgin's tunic, we can understand why these geographic features carried such great significance. "Mountains and water symbolized natural forces considered necessary for the life of the community."[18] A hill represented the land's protection, a place of origin, and sustenance, while the river represented life itself. Similarly, hills were associated with temples or "sacred hills," both in writing and in reality, in part because of the obvious resemblance of a pyramid and a hill, making the spiritual sustenance and protection of the temple present as well. Only with these—spiritual sustenance, physical sustenance, and life—could a civilization exist and proceed for generations. Moreover, this combination of hill and water was also in part due to the Indians' belief that the mountains held water within them; one day, they feared, the mountains might break open, flooding the land.[19]

PROPOSING A NEW CIVILIZATION

While these are the basic glyphs composing the flower cluster, these are not the only glyphs that the flower cluster resembles. In the codices, the *altepetl* glyphs often were written to reflect the distinguishing character of the city. In this case, upon fuller examination, it becomes clearer not only that a civilization is inscribed as a message, but also what kind of civilization.

The triangular blossom is not always pointing upward, but is situated differently, for instance, the flower-duster at the Virgin's

feet or the one just above her hands. In this, the tilma-codex resembles other Náhuatl codices, which were sometimes written to be looked at from various angles. Looking at the tilma glyphs in this way, we can find another meaning in the flower-duster. When we view it upside-down, as shown in the picture, we see that the triangular blossom and the curving stem come to resemble a heart and its arteries. This depiction of a heart is similar to those found in indigenous codices, which often show the heart with the attached arteries, as found in the depictions of ritual sacrifice in the *Florentine Codex,* for example. Yet, while obviously signaling the idea of sacrifice, the heart-flower does so in an entirely new way. Unlike the Aztecs' own ritual sacrifices, this sacrificial heart is shown to be a divine heart, a heart through which divine blood flows, indicating the sacrifice and thus love of God. With the heart's artery attached to the Virgin's celestial mantle, God is shown as the true Giver of life. Rather than being sustained by the Aztecs' ritual sacrifice, he is shown as the one who sustains his creation through the gift of his own divine life-giving blood.

In an obvious way, this civilization is characterized by truth in that the glyphs representing the *altepetl* are composed in such a way that they resemble a flower—with a blossom, a stem, buds, and leaves. We have already mentioned how the Indians metaphorically associated truth with flowers and song. The image of the flower had a superadded relevance if we also recall the importance the Indians placed on tradition and the ancient word. As Miguel León-Portilla noted, the Náhuatl word for "truth," *neltiliztli*, derives "from the same radical 'root,' *tla-nél-huatl*, from which, in turn, comes *nelhuáy-otl*," meaning "base" or "foundation."[20] The flower could only survive if its roots were firmly planted in the soil; without this rootedness, the flower would die. Similarly with truth; to be true meant to be rooted or to have firm foundations. Here, the flower stem of each of the nine *altepetl* flowers is rooted visually in the Virgin's mantle, that is, rooted in the heavens. The emphasis on truth—and the health of this divinely rooted truth—is seen as well in how smaller flowers are sprouting around the top of the heart-flower.

The relationship of this civilization to truth has a personal dimension as well. Looking at the interior of the hill-flower, we can see the outlined features of a face, with two squinting eyes, a large nose, and a long, smiling mouth. For the Indians, in the same way that flowers and song were a metaphor for truth, the human heart and face taken together were a metaphor for the human individual. More than that, they were specifically related to the mature and enlightened person. Since for the Indians the whole process of education was geared toward giving a "face" (personality) to the human being, believed to be born faceless, as well as humanizing his "heart" (will),[21] the face and the heart brought together in the hill-flower refer to one both wise and mature, one with a purified heart.[22] And as if to point out how such wisdom and maturity are to be nurtured and sustained in the human person, the main artery connects the face-heart (human person) to the divine, to God. Biblically, this has an important parallel in the prophetic books of Ezekiel, found in the Old Testament, when the Lord speaks to Ezekiel, saying: "I will give them [the Israelites] a new heart and put a new spirit within them; I will remove the stony heart from their bodies, and replace it with a natural heart, . . . they shall be my people and I will be their God."[23] The opposite of a stony heart is a humanized heart, depicted literally on the tilma as a heart with a human face.

The *altepetl* civilization, while rooted in the divine, is drawn over the Virgin's earth-colored tunic. In this way, the connectedness of this heart-civilization to the earth is made clear. While it is a civilization with special ties to God, it is likewise a civilization on the earth, for the earth—for the here and now. More specifically, looking again at the triangular hill part of the flower cluster, we discover that its design is not a generic hill; rather, according to the Náhuatl writing, the execution of the "hill" glyph exhibits identifying characteristics—in this case, including its topographical uniqueness. With its noticeably pointed top, this hill symbolizes Tepeyac hill, whose name in fact meant "hill of the nose" or "pointed hill." This civilization of the heart, then, far from showing itself as an abstract or indistinct concept, is linked to a real place with real people, beginning symbolically at Tepeyac hill.

The link between this heart-civilization and God is provided by the Virgin, a link pictorially shown in the connection between the heart-flower and the Virgin's mantle. Of the nine heart-shaped flower clusters, one is placed just above the Virgin's clasped hands. In the oral tradition of the Indians of Zozocolco, the Virgin's intercessory role is seen in the heart design in this way: "Our elders offered hearts to God that there may be harmony in life. This Lady says that, without tearing them out, we should place them in her hands so that she may then present them to the true God."[24] This resonates beautifully with how the Indians' ancient oral tradition spoke of the emperor and the protection his hands were said to provide:

You make yourself just like the variety of fruit trees do; you rise with gracefulness, with gentleness. Next to you different birds suck, the hummingbird, the zaquan, the quecholli, the tzinitzan, the quetzal. In your hands they take shelter from the heat, they protect themselves from the sun.[25]

Here, the large cluster of flowers is rooted in the Virgin's mantle, indicating that the Virgin takes this heart-civilization into her own maternal care. Through her, the Indians' prayers to her are offered to God. Her compassion is more than the offering of her own heart: it is the acceptance of our hearts, ourselves, within her—it is the promise of protection and continued life.

In the preceding chapter, we considered the image of Our Lady of Guadalupe in its basic composition—in the figure and face of the Virgin, and in her clothing and positioning. And with just that, already a profound message was discerned, a new conception of the universe gleaned. Now, adding to this a consideration of the two-dimensional floral glyphs on the Virgin's tunic, the message of Our Lady of Guadalupe takes on further insistence through a new expression. Not only is it a message about God but, insofar as it was a message about God—about his closeness and personal love—it was a message for them. It was a message about God, about his love for them. And insofar as it was a message for them, it is a message for us today as well. This universal message speaks to our basic human desire for God; it is God's promise to us, made through his mother, that we are never left without help. And like any promise, it always has two sides: God promises to help us, which at the same time requires that we let him. Love—even God's love—always seeks to be returned. This is the proper relationship between God and his people.

IV.

A Multifaceted Love

The key to every hope is found in love, solely in authentic love, because
love is rooted in God.

—BENEDICT XVI, "ADDRESS TO YOUNG PEOPLE"[1]

THE EVERLASTING, EVER-LOVING GOD

Each day and in every age and culture, people speak of many different kinds of love: love for a spouse, for family, friends, neighbors. Sometimes we speak of love and do not even realize it. For
example, we often speak of charity for the poor, the stranger, the
disadvantaged, without realizing that this, too, is a unique form of
love (*charity* comes from the Latin word *caritas*, meaning "love").
Even though these loves are different, they are alike in that love is
valued most when it is unconditional and flourishing. A love less
than this is unsatisfying, and could seem expendable. But what
does unconditional mean in this context? What is truly demanded here? And is it reasonable to demand it? It was just these types

of universal, human questions about love that inspired Benedict XVI to write his first encyclical on love. And in many ways the title alone, taken from the Bible, begins to explain the Christian significance of the tilma's message and, at the same time, to identify the attractiveness of the Gospel: *Deus caritas est* (God is love).[2] From him, we can learn how our love grows to become a higher, more perfect love:

> It is part of love's growth towards higher levels and inward purification that it now seeks to become *definitive*, and it does so in a twofold sense: both in the sense of *exclusivity* (this particular person alone) and in the sense of being *"for ever."* . . . [L]ove looks to the eternal.[3] [Emphasis added]

These are the two aspects of a pure, unconditional love that we seek: it is personal, and it is lasting. In a unique way, this is expressed in matrimonial vows, when the bride and groom pledge to be faithful in love to that specific person until death. But more than that, this unconditional love is shown in God's love for us—in his eternal love for each of us personally, as individuals. Importantly, God does not merely give love; he *is* love. As such, he is the ultimate model of unconditional love. There is no condition that ends love; his love refuses to be stunted.

As mentioned earlier, the four-petaled jasmine on the Virgin's tunic spoke to a significant difficulty in the Toltec religion, namely, the Indians' belief that their supreme deity was completely inaccessible to them. Thus in the image of Our Lady of Guadalupe a love that is close and personal is evoked, but also important was the permanence of this love. The Aztecs believed that temporality was governed by the gods, and yet temporality was also a constant source of fear: Would the gods hold them in existence? After all, the four ages that had preceded theirs had ended in catastrophe, usually by a violent natural disaster. In fact, many of the Aztecs' sacrificial practices were coupled with fear. This was especially true at the end of every 104-year span, called a *huehuetilítli*. In these years, the Aztecs believed, one set of years ended and another, with the cooperation of the gods, might begin through the ritual of the New Fire ceremony, during which women and children were kept in their houses for fear that they would transform into wild animals and devour people.[4] But the success of the ceremony was never certain, and each time the Aztecs feared the possibility that the gods would abandon them and end their world. These were gods who could not persevere in care for man. In this, man was more persevering, and the burden fell on all the Indian people.

The two elements of a purified, higher love—a love both personal and eternal—were lacking. Even more, these two elements were not being preached effectively, either in word or in example, by the Spanish missionaries and colonists. But in the Guadalupan apparition, these characteristics of the highest, purest love are shown symbolically in the enduring image on the tilma and expressed really in the Virgin's declaration of her motherhood and her role in the apparitions: her affectionate names for Juan Diego; her concern for his well-being; her healing of Juan Bernardino; her understanding of Zumárraga's doubt; her encouragement of Juan Diego even when he failed; her valuing of Juan Diego even when he saw himself as lowly and unworthy; her interest in his plans; her mestiza face, which made her truly one of the people of Mexico; her persistence in meeting Juan Diego even when he avoided her; even her sacrificial role in requesting a church, a lasting place of prayer, for her Son.

This last point is most significant: the Virgin comes not for herself but for God, on an errand of love. In his third epistle in the New Testament, St. John declares the depths of God's love, writing: "God so loved the world, that he sent his only son."[5] In the apparition, coming in a way that expresses the particularity of the indigenous peoples and their cultures, the particularity of God's love comes through, so much so that we can apply it to each people and each person: God so loved the Aztecs, the Texcocans, the Tlaxcalans, the Spaniards, the New Yorkers, the Puerto Ricans, and so on, "that he sent his only son." In this way the event expresses not only the Virgin's love but God's love as well. Sending the Virgin is a personal touch.

A CIVILIZATION OF TRUTH AND LOVE

We have heard significant voices express the need to improve our society through brotherly love. But that we speak of a "civilization of love" with any amount of familiarity is largely due to the writings of Pope John Paul II and more recently Pope Benedict XVI. Few have contributed so much to our understanding of the truth about the person and the truth about love, underscoring the real possibility—and necessity—of building a civilization upon love.

John Paul II's proclamation of a civilization of love first reached our ears in 1979, the day after his first visit to the Basilica of Our Lady of Guadalupe, when he postulated a specific truth for the foundation of our communication with each other: "The truth we owe to human beings," he said, "is first and foremost a truth about themselves."[6] Cardinal Ratzinger, several years before becoming Pope Benedict XVI, likewise expressed the vital need for truth about the person particularly in regard to love: "Truth is love, and if love were to turn against truth, it would be mutilating itself."[7] On the tilma, a suggestion of this can be seen in how the flower (symbolizing truth) is at the same time a heart with a face (the combination symbolizing the individual).

Of course, there are many truths about the human person that we can speak about. Many of the most popular explanations today define man by his interactions with the created world, including economics, politics, psychology and sociology. But Christ reveals the human person in light of the human person's interactions with the Creator. "The universe in which we live has its source in God and was created by him. . . . Consequently, his creation is dear to him, for it was willed by him and 'made' by him. . . . [T]his God loves man."[8] While mankind resembles the rest of creation in being created by God, only man is called to a higher level of relationship to the Creator, a relationship of personal love with God, enabling each person to address God not only as "God the Creator" but, through Christ, as "Father."

Certainly, being a creator and a father are related: both produce something that did not exist before. But parenthood implies a correspondence, a continuity, a similarity—the similarity of being made "in the image and likeness" of another.[9] And in this continuity we find in ourselves the "dignity which . . . brings demands" and our vocation to love.[10] So important is this understanding of ourselves that soon after returning from Mexico, John Paul II devoted nearly four years to a series of weekly addresses that proclaimed this truth—what is now known as the Wednesday Catechesis on the Theology of the Body.[11]

When we make the sign of the cross, praying, "In the name of the Father, and of the Son, and of the Holy Spirit," we identify the Trinity, the supreme model of a loving communion of persons, a communion of mutual love and truth. To be made in the image of God suggests something about the human person as a reflection of the Trinity: we, too, are created for a loving communion of people. We, too, are called to imitate in our lives and everyday dealings with others the same Trinitarian love and truth we are reflections of. This is the foundation of the civilization of love: that to be made in the image of God is not simply to be *fashioned* as such, but to *function* as an image of God—that is, to be ontologically destined for and capable of a life of loving communion with others.

Our connection to God goes beyond the genetic identity of our personhood. That is, God's fatherhood creates us for loving communion with others and at the same time gives us the capacity for loving communion with others. Like the heart-flower and the heart with a face on the *tilma*, which are rooted in the divine, both the root of our personhood and the source of our love are not human but divine:

> [God] has loved us first and he continues to do so; we too, then, can respond with love. God does not demand of us a feeling which we ourselves are incapable of producing. He loves us, he makes us see and experience his love, and since he has "loved us first," love can also blossom as a response within us.[12]

God's loving relationship with us and our loving relationship with others are not separate relationships but connected. Christianity is relational: our relationship with Christ does not close in on itself, but shines forth in our lives, always demanding to be concretely revealed in our love of others. Through us, Christ's divine presence is no longer kept within the Church—as the divine water under the Templo Mayor—but is able to flow within and out from us.

In guiding our relations with others, what higher truth is there than the truth that, as made in the image and likeness of God, each person shares in a unique dignity? This is fundamental to our humanity, setting us apart from creation and demanding that we relate to one another in love. "Love contains the acknowledgment of the personal dignity of the other, and of his or her absolute uniqueness."[13] Although this dignity ultimately comes from God, this is not a hidden or purely spiritual reality. Every person can—and naturally does—recognize some dignity that all people hold in common.

This is the "good news" of the Gospel that is too good to forget: that "Jesus Christ brought us a message that has emphasized the absolute value of life and of the human person, who comes from God and is called to live in communion with God."[14] What Christ makes clear—in his incarnation, in coming to man fully as a man, and in his death—is that "each of us is the result of a thought of God; each of us is willed, each of us is loved."[15] For this reason, to live as a Christian is not simply to follow rules of "being good" but to be united to a Person. As Benedict XVI said, "Christian ethics is not born from a system of commandments, but rather is the consequence of our friendship with Christ. This friendship influences life: if it is true, it incarnates and fulfills itself in love for neighbor."[16] Our relationship with Christ is deeply positive, and rather than the source of prohibitions it is the source of love that compels us to return love with love and to treat others with compassion, generosity, and justice.[17]

Even more, there is a kind of education through Christ, by which we each grow in love and become more like Christ, more like the ultimate child of God. As Christians, we understand that this becomes part of our identity: we bear the image of God and are also the face of Christ to those around us. "The Christian has the face of Christ imprinted in his heart in an indelible fashion. He is not only *alter Christus* [another Christ], but *ipse Christus* [Christ Himself]."[18] Through love, we begin to see the face of Christ in others, and we ourselves through love are called to be the presence of Christ to others. In this education, Mary accepts a prominent part. For as the mother of Christ, she has an unprecedentedly close participation in God's Trinitarian love; even as she recognized the Messiah in her child, so she can "enlighten our vision, so that we can recognize Christ's face in the face of every human person, the heart of peace."[19]

A NEW SACRIFICE

In looking at the civilization of love in the heart-flower, we cannot overlook the idea of sacrifice simply because we associate the word with the violent and bloody sacrifices of the Aztecs. This love of God for man not only enables us to love each other but also gave us the supreme sacrificial love in Jesus Christ. By his life and death, he gave mankind his heart, in the most concrete way, on the Cross. In Christ we understand sacrifice in a new way: "This insistence on *sacrifice*—a '*making sacred*' [from the Latin *sacrum facere*]—expresses all the existential depth implied in the transformation of our human reality as taken up by Christ."[20]

This act liberating mankind from sin is more than a mere declaration of dignity and worth. Likewise, this act is more than a historical event with timeless spiritual consequences. Christ's death is our salvation; his sacrifice was the only sacrifice that could truly enable man to return to communion with God. Every sacrament we celebrate depends upon the truth of Christ's sacrifice, and enables us to participate in it to some degree. In the Gospels, Christ's sacrifice is described physically after his death, when the Roman soldier pierces Christ's side with a lance and "immediately blood and water flowed out."[21] As St. John Chrysostom reflects, "The water was a symbol of baptism and the blood [was a symbol] of the holy Eucharist."[22] The water of baptism and the Eucharist are not only symbols of Christ's sacrifice and our participation therein but also a constant source.

A civilization of love engages reality. Like the barren Tepeyac that grew flowers out of the Virgin's love for man and attentiveness to Zumárraga's desire for truth, a civilization of love is the seedbed for truth. And like the hill-flower on the tilma, with its smaller flowers growing from the large flower, truth begets truth. When Benedict XVI spoke to educators in the United States, he said: "Truth means more than knowledge: knowing the truth leads us to discover the good. Truth speaks to the individual in his or her entirety, inviting us to respond with our whole being."[23] This is the other aspect of being made in the image and likeness of God: as beings capable of love we are also beings capable of seeing the truth – another important attribute of God who is love. Our relationship with God and our development of a well-formed conscience thus purifies and elevates truth to a different level with new importance.

Seeing the truth—the truth about God, about his relationship with us, about who we are—can be overwhelming. Before the image of Our Lady of Guadalupe, Friar Zumárraga fell to his knees in penitence and awe. Juan Diego, too, when he encountered the Virgin, prostrated himself in her presence. Truth inspires awe; it inspires reverence. But the complexity of truth must never be used to obscure the good. Importantly, neither Friar Zumárraga nor Juan Diego was stunned into inaction; rather, both were inspired to act. Christianity and the Guadalupan event in particular give us a model of responding to truth and reality. Before the truth about the human person, his or her dignity and capacity to love, the only appropriate response is a gift of ourselves. This is a gift not of what we have but of who we are. In the following chapters, we will discuss how the event at Guadalupe highlights exactly this: who we are, and what this means about how we give. Precisely because it is a gift of ourselves, it is a gift that can be given wherever and whenever we are. In this, love truly becomes a universal presence. When we interact with God's creation—man and other beings alike—we interact with the fruits of love, the fruits of God's love.

Through God's love, we are invited to imitate God's own creativity; we are invited to personally participate in his own being as Lord and Creator. And just as God's creative action is one of the ultimate expressions of his love, so with us: in all we do, love is the measure, the purpose, and the motivation.

PART II

Christ, a Life-Changing Event

V.

Liberated by Love

The radical freedom of man thus lies at the deepest level: the level of openness to God by conversion of heart, for it is man's heart that the roots of every form of subjection, every violation of freedom, are found. Finally for the Christian, freedom does not come from man himself; it is manifested in obedience to the will of God and in fidelity to his love.

-JOHN PAUL II,
MESSAGE FOR THE WORLD DAY OF PEACE, 1981[1]

A NEW AND TROUBLED WORLD

Shortly before becoming pope, Karol Wojtyla celebrated Mass at his homeland's much beloved Marian shrine, Czestochowa, in Poland. In his homily he reflected on the unique paths by which we engage some of the most complex and important elements of our world, saying: "To understand man, one must delve into the depth of the mystery; to understand a nation, one must come to its shrine."[2] Few shrines express this so clearly as Mexico's Basilica of Our Lady of Guadalupe. In fact, the history of Mexico becomes incomprehensible without understanding its people's devotion to

Our Lady of Guadalupe. Without this devotion, the face of the continent would be drastically different from what it is today. For Mexico of the sixteenth century, the apparition of Our Lady of Guadalupe was a dramatic invitation "to understand man" by "delving into the depth of the mystery" at a time when the Christian understanding of man—his freedom, love, and dignity—was being obscured by the most unchristian systems.

Two years before the apparition of Our Lady of Guadalupe, Friar Zumárraga penned a secret letter to Charles V, the king of Spain, a letter forbidden by the authorities from leaving Mexico's shores. For several months, the Spanish civil authorities in Mexico had feared such a letter being delivered, and did everything in their power to prevent it from being sent: they patrolled the roads, inspected ships from deck to ballast, and forbade anyone to accept letters from any friar unless the authorities read it first.[3] So to send his letter, Zumárraga himself and another friar took the letter to the port of Veracruz at great personal risk; after all, the last friars who had tried to deliver Zumárraga's message had been robbed of not only the letter but all their possessions as well. Followed every step of the way by government agents, Zumárraga and his companion narrowly avoided having the letter confiscated, and when they reached the port, the letter was kept safe only because of the ingenuity of a Basque sailor who hid it in a cake of wax placed within a barrel, where it floated beside the ship with the other buoys. So although their pursuers arrived and searched the ship, the letter left the port undetected and a few weeks later reached the hands of Charles V.[4]

The letter now resides in the Archives of Simancas, and it gives us insight into why the civil authorities during the Spanish occupation of Mexico went to such extremes to prevent Friar Zumárraga from contacting the king. It described in great detail the inhabitants' sufferings inflicted by members of the civil governing body in Mexico, the First Audience. Natives were enslaved, children sold, property confiscated, women abducted, contracts broken, dissenters knifed, workers swindled, and clergy threatened as the First Audience under Nuño de Guzman's leadership constructed a divisive, profit-seeking regime heedless of the human cost.[5] "If God does not provide the remedy from His Hand," Zumárraga wrote despairingly to Charles V, "the land is about to be completely lost."[6]

Considering the situation, it is no wonder the early missionary efforts failed. As the missionary Friar Mendieta recalled, "When the Spaniards again arrived to their lands, [the Indians] never ceased receiving the moral principles with enormous love and benevolence, until the point where they were shocked [by the First Audience's behavior] and learned their lesson."[7] Besides the temporal damage to the people's lives, Mendieta lamented that the spiritual fallout caused by the many atrocities committed by First Audience officials had "completely prevented the salvation of an infinite number of persons."[8]

Additionally, while considered some of the most learned and holy priests of their homelands, the friars themselves were unprepared to evangelize in the new language and culture, causing Friar Sahagún to lament their ignorance of Indian culture, likening it to a doctor hoping to cure a patient without knowing the illness.[9] Facing the Aztec practices, they considered the religion diabolical for its violent sacrificial rites, and they, too, resorted to violent displays in tearing down the idols and statues.[10] Such abrasive and reactionary tactics likewise proved ineffectual.

Although we often recognize Our Lady of Guadalupe's apparition as a defining moment in the life of St. Juan Diego, it was also a critical turning point for the Indians, the Spaniards, and Zumárraga himself, whose constant conflicts had led him to despair about the future of the land. History's first quantifiable indication of a massive, radical change in lives beyond Juan Diego's own was a flood of conversions after the apparitions—inspiring

John Paul II to call Our Lady of Guadalupe the first evangelist to Mexico.[11] Writing in 1537 in his *History of the Indians of New Spain*, Friar Toribio de Benevente, whom the Indians called "Motolinia" (poor one), took great pains in calculating the number of baptisms from the figures submitted by each missionary and province. He concluded: "In my opinion and truthfully, there must have been baptized in the time I mention—a matter of fifteen years—more than nine million Indians."[12] In fact, so great was the number of Indians seeking baptism that friars began abbreviating the baptismal rites, and in 1537 a council of missionaries gathered for the first of several meetings to discuss the challenges and needs of this new land. Many historians have attributed these many conversions to the effects of the Guadalupan apparitions. What is absolutely certain is that the continent for which Zumárraga had all but given up hope in 1530 was almost universally converted to Christianity in a matter of decades, and that Guadalupe is the single highest-profile Catholic event in the Americas in the sixteenth century.

A NON-EUROPEAN CONVERSION

From the apparition account and the tilma, we can see how the event communicates the Gospel message and Christian concepts through Indians' culture and language. But to understand why such a message could inspire such conversions, and why it was communicated through the person of Mary by such an extraordinary medium as an apparition, we must look into more than cultural and linguistic analysis.

As radical as the large-scale conversion of Indians was for the Church in Mexico, it was also radical in the context of the sixteenth-century Europe, where the Church was suffering religious turmoil and failed religious reconciliation. Just months before

Columbus encountered the New World, Spain had won the Reconquista, a series of wars regaining the land of Spain from Muslim rule, and Muslims and Jews in Spanish lands were forced to choose between conversion and expulsion. Similarly, two years before Cortés encountered the polytheistic Aztecs, the Catholic Church itself faced major division when Martin Luther wrote the Ninety-five Theses, marking the beginning of the Protestant movement, which drew millions of people from Catholicism. Evangelization in Europe was volatile and problematic.

In the twentieth century, several popular commentaries on the Guadalupan event compare the religious turmoil of the two continents. These commentaries often interpret the Mexican conversions as a type of healing within the Church, observing that at the same time an estimated nine million Europeans *left* the Catholic Church for Protestantism, nine million Indians in the Americas converted *to* the Catholic Church. Of course, this has its shortcomings: the conversion of one person can never make up for another person falling away, since each person's relationship with Christ is unique and irreplaceable. But this comparison is valuable for another reason: it points to the experience of the Guadalupan event and the subsequent conversions as something remarkably different from the European experience, where the king's religious belief held great sway over his people.

The Holy Roman Empire, ruled by Charles V at the time of the apparition, had been made possible through the conversion of whole countries and peoples of Europe. And in that history, often the hallmark of a country's conversion was that it was initiated by its leaders in a kind of top-down model. For example, after reverting to paganism once the Romans departed and the Anglo-Saxons invaded, England marked its new conversion to Christianity from the baptism of King Ethelbert of Kent in 597, which "had such an effect in deciding the minds of his wavering countrymen that as many as 10,000 are said to have followed his example within a few months."[13] Likewise, France marks its conversion to Christianity from the baptism of King Clovis in 496, Poland from the baptism of King Mieszko in 966, and so on. Furthermore, expectations for this top-down model continued in Europe with the rise of Protestantism. For example, Lutheranism spread systematically through Germany according to the conversions of the county princes, and the effects of this were visible even into the twentieth century, as southern Germany was more Catholic than the Protestant north.[14] Perhaps the most explicit example of this top-down model occurred just three years after the apparition, with the birth of Anglicanism in England. Rejecting the Catholic teaching on marriage and divorce, Henry VIII codified his rejection of the Catholic Church by writing the Act of Supremacy, a law establishing a new church, the Church of England, and naming himself—and all his heirs—as its leader. Even more, it commanded that all English citizens attend these Anglican services, demanding obedience to the king not only in political matters but in religious matters as well. This caused a delicate situation, to say the least, since anyone who rejected his religious mandates effectively was accused of treason, and many who resisted were punished, even put to death.

Thus for the missionaries and conquistadors, seeking out the Indian leaders was not only a savvy political move but a religious move as well. In this context, it would have been expected that the conversion of Mexico would soon follow the death of Emperor Moctezuma in 1520, the defeat of the Aztecs in 1521, the baptism of Moctezuma's sister Papantzin in Tlaltelolco in 1524, or even the baptism of Moctezuma's son. The account of this latter baptism, as Pardo notes, barely veils the obvious symbolism of his baptism as a result of political conquest. First, the event is recounted less for his request for baptism than for his dramatic shaking during the exorcism, making it seem as if "the devil was going out of him."[15]

Additionally, a sizeable part of the account of the event is devoted to the church later built upon the site of his home; the church was dedicated to St. Hippolytus, whose feast day became a major celebration throughout the land precisely because it was on his feast day that the Aztec Empire fell.[16] In this, we can see an example of how evangelization and conversion had lost, under a cloud of political significance, their personal impetus and meaning. Consequently, though the Spanish had conquered Mexico politically and militarily, toppling the Aztec religious infrastructure, conversions were few and evangelization unsuccessful.

Resistance came as well from the Aztec worldview itself, in which the weight of religious authority rested not on the emperor per se but on tradition itself. This is partly why, after the Aztecs perceived weakness in Moctezuma's dealings with the Spaniards, who did not respect their temples and religion, Moctezuma's power was severely compromised; his dethronement, while not literal, was at least symbolically shown when he was stoned by his own people.[17] This is also why, later, when the Aztec priests were challenged by the Christian missionaries to defend the Aztec religion, the priests appealed not to any traditional metaphysical argument but to tradition itself, saying in a 1524 debate: "It is a new word, this one you tell them, and because of it we are distressed, because of it we are extremely frightened. Indeed . . . our fathers . . . did not speak in this way. . . . And now are we the ones who will [perhaps] destroy the ancient law?"[18] For the Aztecs, the wisdom of the past ages rooted the present and thereby gave meaning and direction to the contemporary world. If deprived of this rootedness, the Aztecs feared, their civilization, like a flower detached from its roots, would wither and collapse.[19] And unlike their emperor or any other religious or political persons of authority, their traditions could be neither dethroned nor converted.

The drama of Cortés's campaign of conquest was more than the collapse of Mesoamerican military, social, economic, and political structures. By prohibiting sacrifices and other religious practices, he deprived their gods of their necessary sustenance, and the Indians anticipated an apocalyptic end of the world. Instead, they saw that, though the human sacrifices to the gods had ceased, the cycle of life around them continued. The result was increasing doubt among the Indians about their worldview. But doubt is not enough for conversion, especially in the face of the violence of those who practiced the religion of their conquerors. As the Aztec priests told the Franciscans:

> *What are we to do then,*
> *We who are small men and mortals;*
> *If we die, let us die;*
> *If we perish, let us perish;*
> *The truth is that the gods also died.*[20]

The collective depression from this crisis of faith was so great that some of the natives committed suicide.[21]

Even as the Indians' way of life suffered this great religious and cultural crisis, they endured another profound assault when their very humanity and thus their rights were called into question. Was it Christian to conquer a land, appropriate other people's property, and even enslave the former property owners? Could they truly justify the subjugation of another people? Such doubts were voiced strongly by many missionaries as well as by some of the more conscientious lay Spaniards. Others, however, were eager to justify the invasion and appropriation by questioning the natives' innate capability to reason. If the natives were unable to demonstrate their humanity, they argued, then they would have no rights of ownership and their property could be seized. But if the debates were waged in Salamanca's university lecture halls and in the Spanish Court, the battleground was Mexico. Thus, the

Indians needed liberation from the many forces impeding living a free life: their religion, their human sacrifices, their depression, the cruelties dealt and received, and the animosity that quickly developed between the conquered and the conquerors.

Speaking of freedom, Benedict XVI once wrote: "Freedom presupposes that in fundamental decisions, every person and every generation is a new beginning. . . . [N]ew generations can draw upon the moral treasury of the whole of humanity. But they can also reject it, because it can never be self-evident in the same way as material inventions."[22] In a particular way, the situation of the Spanish discovery and occupation of Mexico marked a radically clear beginning when the "moral treasury of the whole of humanity" was at stake.

Although the Aztec political and religious authority were intertwined, Mexico would require a completely different method of conversion than countries in Europe. Mexico demanded a reconsideration of what evangelization is and what being a Christian means. Just as the failed attempts at governing the Indians raised new questions about what it means to be human, so the failed missionary attempts raised questions about the meaning of evangelization and being a Christian. The situation in Mexico demanded a reconsideration of conversion as a relationship with Christ, proposed though Christian witness, rather than as a transfer of religious loyalties tied to political authority. To answer these challenges, the missionaries could not simply follow the traditional European pattern.

Even as the old Christian culture was passing away, this conversion required the creation of a new Christian culture, precipitated neither by new law nor by new political leadership, but by a revelation of love. And rooted in love, this new culture would express some of the greatest concepts of Christianity in a new and renewed manner. It was a new kind of evangelization, an evangelization that was peer-to-peer rather than top-down, and as such it was marked by methods substantially different from the methods that had made Europe Catholic.

The recent precipitous decline of Christianity in Europe is significantly tied to its historical entanglement with that continent's monarchies. The Church at times became identified with the political power of the state, and as Europeans chose different forms of government, they also chose different forms of religion or none at all. It is for this reason that, discussing the legacy of the Church in light of the Roman emperor Constantine, Cardinal Ratzinger wrote in the 1980s, "In the long run, neither embrace nor ghetto can solve for Christians the problem of the modern world."[23] What is needed is not a ghetto nor an embrace, but an engagement in which Christians preach primarily through the example of their own lives, of the great freedom that is brought by saying "yes" to Jesus Christ, and in this way informing the conscience of the society in which they live.

MARY: A NEW EVANGELIST

By her apparitions, Our Lady of Guadalupe has replaced the top-down model of conversion with an evangelization rooted in a personalism independent of political and social hierarchy. Two of the titles by which she is often addressed in prayers—Morenita and Tonantzin—point toward two radical aspects of her relationship with the New World people that communicated this new evangelization based on personalizing Christ's love in a new way.

The name Morenita—a Spanish word meaning "the dark woman"—refers to the Virgin's darker skin tone, as depicted in the tilma's image.[24] At the time, and especially the longer the Spaniards spent in the New World, race, ethnicity, and origin dominated the scale of social classes; Spaniards held the positions of power both socially and politically, while the Indians, as part of the conquered people, often held an inferior position. As the Morenita, the Virgin is identifiable as a mestiza. And while mestizos would later encompass most of the country, at the time these mestizo children were despised as products of the conquest and rape, and were left, as Bishop Vasco de Quiroga explained, to search among the animal stalls for food left for pigs and dogs.[25]

Interestingly, since this was fairly soon after Cortés' conquest of Mexico, this was at a time when the number of mestizos in Mexico was still small—and the oldest mestizos in Mexico City would have been still quite young. As a mestiza, she is identified not only with the ostracized and rejected but also with the most vulnerable group, the children. Through identifying herself with them, her face becomes the face of the future.

A different facet of the universality of conversion of heart—a call to Christ not limited or prioritized by status or social position—is emphasized as well when in the apparition account the Virgin refuses Juan Diego's request that she send someone else—someone of higher social recognition—as a messenger to Zumárraga. At the Virgin's insistence, Juan Diego is instructed to seek out Zumárraga, a Spaniard known and chosen personally by the King and who, though good and humble, had an elite service in the Church and society as Mexico City's bishop. By the Virgin's request, Juan Diego is given a vital role in manifesting and promoting the solidarity that comes from a unified desire for God—a desire that transcends social hierarchy. Just as the mestiza Virgin, appearing with the face of the lowly, comes as the catalyst for conversion, so Juan Diego, a member of the conquered people, is enlisted in this significant gesture of heaven's interest in even the lowest. The mestiza Virgin, and to a certain extent humble Juan Diego, express the universality—the *catholicism*—of God's desire for persons to turn to him, a universal desire that transcends the distances created by societies even as

God's love sends missionaries to traverse oceans to make the message known.

The Indian Juan Diego and the mestiza Virgin, together occupying two lowly rungs of the New World's social hierarchy, become the catalysts for conversion, thereby introducing a new model of evangelization. Rather than the European pattern of conversion, moving from the top down in society, there is an obvious reversal. Though both the old world and new world models of evangelization had at their core the missionary activity of the Catholic Church, whose priests and bishops brought sacramental life to the previously unbaptized, the catalysts that opened each of these continets to Christianity could not have been more different. In most case in Europe, the missionary activity of the church gained ground through the good graces of a prince or king. In Mexico, the miracle the bishop had seen as necessary for the conversion of the people to the Catholic faith came not through the good graces of a prince but through the obedient actions of a simple Indian who followed the request of Our Lady, herself a mestiza woman. Instead of a conversion of a nation's people, it is a conversion of persons who together forged their mestiza nation.

The other title often attributed to Our Lady of Guadalupe, Tonantzin—a Náhuatl word meaning "our dear mother" or, colloquially, "our mama." According to Sahagún, this title was quite controversial, as some missionaries feared and believed that the Indians addressed Our Lady of Guadalupe in this way simply because they saw her as a manifestation of their Aztec goddess. Nevertheless, this title in its fundamental meaning simply means "our dear mother (*to-nan-tzin*).[27] And the continued use of this title points to something very important about how the message of the Virgin was received into the lives of Mexican Christians: it was not enough to speak of the Virgin only as someone else's mother—the mother of God or the mother of Juan Diego. Her personal motherhood for each person, her motherhood to the Indians, and to all of us, was important, and the name "Tonantzin" recognized a relationship that no one should or would want to be denied in either earthly or spiritual life.

To come as a mother—mother of God, mother of Juan Diego, mother of all people—is to come precisely in the most personal capacity. Importantly, in the apparition account, the Virgin's motherhood is a continual role that is defined not by the fact of giving birth but by a relationship of love and care evidenced in her interactions with Juan Diego and Juan Bernardino, and later in her image.

At a time when the humanity of the Indians was still contested, the Virgin's mestiza face and her declaration of motherhood were a truly great expression of the Indians' humanity. When she declared she was the mother of Juan Diego, Mary removed any doubt: the Indians were indeed children of God and entitled to respect. In her mestiza face, the Indians recognized the Virgin not as a European but as a person of the New World, sharing in their distinct cultural identity and in their unique physical traits. For the Spanish, too, there is a profound message: these children were loved to such a degree that the mother of God took on their appearance, becoming family. As "our dear Mother," and specifically as "our dear mestiza mother," the relationship between the peoples of Mexico is delineated as a relationship of family.

Although this inculturation had a liberating aspect, it was not at its heart liberation through politics. It helped free the Church from the distrust of the Indians, and the Indians from the hopelessness of their own situation. In some ways, the reconstruction of the Indians' society can be seen in the historical accounts of the conversions after the apparition. Instead of conversions being inspired from the top down, that is, from political dignitaries to the people, the Guadalupan event allowed the evangelization of the New World to spread through personal exchanges between the Indians, especially within the family, working as a powerful com-

plement to the work of the Spanish missionaries. As one missionary at the time recalled:

> In the beginning, [the Indians] started going [to receive bap-
> tism] 200 at a time, then 300 at a time, always growing and
> multiplying, until they reached thousands; some from two days
> journey, others from three, others from four, and some from far-
> ther away. This caused great admiration in those who saw it.
> Grown people brought their children to be baptized, and the
> young baptized brought their parents; the husband brought his
> wife, and the wife, her husband.[28]

Throughout Mexico's history, at various times the Church has
been protected by the government and other times persecuted by
the government. Although at a later time the Church in Mexico
would be closely identified with the state, these early conversions
appear to have occurred not as a result of Spanish civil authorities
but in spite of the actions of many of them, including members of
the First Audience. Coming thus as a mother brings a new dimension to the debates about conversion, the human person, and the
building of society. The most universal element of being human—
coming from a mother—is made the catalyst for solidarity. And
the most fundamental element of society—the family—becomes
the place where this society is created.

A NEW KNIGHTHOOD

In the New World, many of those either officially knighted or
other nobles of authority carried a devotion to Mary with them,
including Cortés, who had a devotion to the Spanish Our Lady of
Extremadura. In this, they reflected a long history of European

knighthood, in which devotion to Mary constituted a strong part of the knight's identity as a Christian called to be a defender of Christianity. Even the knight's devotion to his lady was often seen as a suggestive parallel of his devotion to Our Lady, Mary. Consequently, St. Joseph was sometimes seen as the first knight, the first entrusted by God with the task of defending Christ and Mary, making him the model for the knight. (This view of St. Joseph was ratified further in 1870 when he was named patron and defender of the entire Church.) As defender of the faith, a knight was at the same time called to be a defender of those virtues and values upheld and embodied in Christianity, especially justice; as the thirteenth-century knight Geoffroi de Charny of France tells us, a knight fought "to defend and uphold the faith or out of pity for men and women who cannot defend their own rights."[29]

In the New World, there was some degree of expectation by the Spanish Crown that this behavior, this defense of the faith and the disenfranchised, would—or should—continue. Beginning with the primary financier of Columbus's first voyage, Queen Isabel, the Spanish rulers sought to protect the rights of the natives, whom they considered "vassals" of Spain.[30] In 1499, when a shipment of Indians arrived in Spain, Queen Isabel intervened directly, issuing a public proclamation demanding that the Indians be returned to their homeland in Hispaniola (today the Dominican Republic).[31] After Isabel died, her husband, King Ferdinand, commissioned a group of scholars and theologians in the hopes of reaching some solution to the many problems facing the native people. As a result of this commission, Ferdinand promulgated the Laws of Burgos in 1512, enacting thirty-five laws intended to protect the Indians from maltreatment and to promote evangelization and missionary work among the natives, detailing many goods to be afforded to the Indians.[32] Yet, an ocean away from the authorities, it became clear that legislation alone was insufficient. In practice, the rights upheld in the laws were often obscured and their enforcement lacking; the knightly defense of justice and of the poor was abandoned throughout Mexico by the very men entrusted with it, even to the point of Charles V naming Zumárraga, rather than one of the authorities or men of power, the "Defender of the Indians." The situation had reversed; the knights, nobles, and men-at-arms no longer protected the defenseless, but instead fought for personal gain. Into this situation, Mary herself enters, choosing a *macehual*, a commoner and "a poor one," to help reestablish not only the humanity of the Indians but also the true vocation of the knight.

How could Spanish knights in the New World maintain a true devotion to the Virgin Mary and at the same time oppress those whom she now called children? For as Christians, we are called to see the face of Christ in others. And yet in this situation, while devotion to Mary was strong among the Spaniards, they failed to see or treat their Indian neighbors as Christ. After the apparition, when the Spanish and the Indians looked at the face of their beloved Mary, they saw the face of the other—their neighbors, their enemies, their parishioners. To reject each other was to reject Mary. To reject Our Lady of Guadalupe as an Indian daughter is to reject she who also appears as a Spanish daughter. In Our Lady of Guadalupe, each becomes the other, bringing a new visual manifestation of Christ's command: "Love your neighbor as yourself."[33]

LIBERATED CHURCH VS. LIBERATION THEOLOGY

The conversion of the Aztec Empire after the apparition of Our Lady of Guadalupe presents an extraordinary contrast to the other massive conversion in the history of Christianity: that following Emperor Constantine in the fourth-century Roman Empire. Speaking of Mary's role in the New World evangelization, Cardinal Ratzinger observed:

> It has always been the Mother who reached people in a mission-ary situation and made Christ accessible to them. That is especial-ly true of Latin America. Here, to some extent, Christianity arrived by way of Spanish swords, with deadly heralds. In Mexico, at first absolutely nothing could be done about missionary work—until the occurrence of that phenomenon at Guadalupe, and then the Son was suddenly near by way of his Mother.[34]

Up to the time of Constantine, the spread of Christianity was originally motivated through the personal testimony of individual Christians, but suffered under the capricious whims of some of Rome's early emperors, beginning with Emperor Nero (who reigned around the time of the martyrdoms of apostles Peter and Paul). With the conversion of Emperor Constantine, Christianity gained not only a new protector but a new level of protection in law. In A.D. 313 Emperor Constantine issued the Edict of Milan, which gave official legal recognition to the Church, granted Christians freedom of worship, and restored Church properties that previously had been confiscated. In addition, in A.D. 325 Constantine convened the Council of Nicaea, which clarified the Church's teaching on Christ as both human and divine, and from which we now have the Nicene Creed. With the freedoms secured under Constantine, Christianity flourished, and by the end of the fourth century, it was declared the official religion of the Roman Empire.

In a way, there is a direct parallel between Constantine and Juan Diego: both were catalysts for the spread of Christianity in their respective times and cultures. But unlike the evangelization under Constantine, the conversion of a hemisphere begun by the Virgin of Guadalupe through her messenger Juan Diego and with the approval and implementation of the bishop was not born of political power. It was initiated first among the common people (family members Juan Diego and Juan Bernardino) and then spread by the Church throughout Mexico.

Appearing to both Juan Diego and Juan Bernardino, Our Lady of Guadalupe gives the message, based on the expression of Christ's love, to a family—which John Paul II so often called the first "school of love"—thereby accentuating the importance of the family's role in creating a civilization of love. Furthermore, through the faith and love of Juan Diego and Juan Bernardino, the loving message of Our Lady of Guadalupe immediately incorporates them into the universal family, the Church, for whom and through whom her message gains its full fulfillment and true meaning. From the family narrowly understood, as in the case of Juan Diego and his uncle, to the larger "human family" in Mexico—Indian, mestizo, and Spanish—all were united in her loving message and in a short time united also in their faith, nourished by the sacraments of the Catholic Church.

To evangelize effectively, the Church has always adapted to the situations in which it finds itself. In late antique and early medieval Europe, this often meant creating an alliance with the indigenous power structure of missionary lands, since the political hierarchy held great sway over the beliefs of its people. This "embrace," as Pope Benedict has pointed out, was not a perfect solution. With the advent of the Protestant reformation in the 16th century, the limits of this model became abundantly clear. Finding the opposite extreme in New Spain, a Church reduced to near "ghetto status," Our Lady of Guadalupe presented a perfectly inculturated message of conversion that began the process of transcending a need for an alliance with political power and drew the Church into the mainstream of the life and society of the New World.

Thus although today some see liberation as a political solution to a variety of spiritual and ethical problems, the message of Our Lady of Guadalupe could not be more different: her solution was not political but spiritual. And her solution, although articulated clearly in the Mexican situation, is one that is relevant in all ages, as Cardinal Ratzinger noted:

> The Church cannot choose the times in which she will live. After Constantine, she was obliged to find a mode of coexistence with the world other than that necessitated by the persecutions of the preceding age. But it bespeaks a foolish romanticism to bemoan the change that occurred with Constantine while we ourselves fall at the feet of the world from which we profess our desire to liberate the Church. The struggle between *imperium* and *sacerdotium* in the Middle Ages, the dispute about the "enlightened" concept of state churches at the beginning of the modern age, were attempts to come to terms with the difficult problems created in its various epochs by a world that had become Christian.[35]

The protections and limitations of close alliances between religious and civil authority were keenly visible in Zumárraga's life. On one hand, he had been named for the bishopric by Charles V himself, and sailed to the New World as the first bishop of Mexico City alongside the first Spanish civil authority, the First Audience. The First Audience, on the other hand, would use its authority to inhibit the missionaries and restrict the work of the Church. Additionally, not only was Zumárraga officiating in religious matters, but also Charles V had appointed him the "Defender of the Indians," situating him in the middle of the debates and conflicts over the mistreatment of the Indians. This was exacerbated by the fact that although he had been granted the title, his actual authority was challenged and constrained when the First Audience threatened to kill any Indian who ventured to Zumárraga for protection.

In contrast to this conflict between Church and state, the apparition account and the oral tradition passed down from the event are strikingly clear that this was a purely religious event. Juan Diego was a *macehual* commoner uninvolved in the governing of the land; Zumárraga was invoked as the bishop. The Virgin tells Juan Bernardino of Juan Diego's visit even before the bishop approves.[36] Already, it has become simultaneously a religious and a family matter. Even the accounts of the celebratory procession for the completed chapel relate how all the people—"absolutely everyone, the entire city, without exception"—came to the chapel and marveled at the image.

In a poignant way, this change toward a freed Church and a freer people is shown in how the practice of vigils was adopted by the later viceroys in New Spain. In the Middle Ages, the tradition of knighthood included praying a vigil in a chapel the eve before one's knighting ceremony, during which one would pray all night for courage, wisdom, and holiness. Continuing this tradition, newly appointed viceroys in New Spain would spend the night at Guadalupe before entering Mexico City. And at the end of their term as viceroy, many would keep another vigil with the Virgin before returning to Spain.[37] Motivating this practice was a desire for a beneficent coexistence between the Church and the state, between the practice of faith and civil commitments and roles; the one should neither hinder nor obscure the other, but rather inform and serve.

Christian social doctrine requires continuous renewal of social structures to provide greater respect for the dignity of persons. For this reason, speaking of the role of love in a civilization, Benedict XVI noted:

Love—*caritas*—will always prove necessary, even in the most just society. There is no ordering of the State so just that it can eliminate the need for a service of love. Whoever wants to eliminate love is preparing to eliminate man as such. There will always be suffering which cries out for consolation and help. There will always be loneliness. There will always be situations of material need where help in the form of concrete love of neighbour is indispensable. The State which would provide everything, absorbing everything into itself, would ultimately become a mere bureaucracy incapable of guaranteeing the very thing which the suffering person—every person—needs: namely, loving personal concern.[38]

Peace, John Paul II constantly reminded us, requires freedom, justice, love, and truth. But it is only when each person recognizes and lives according to the dignity of each person that forgiveness seems reasonable, that justice is possible, and that peace is made real. For as Pope John Paul II recalled, "peace is not essentially about structures but about people."[39] A civilization of love is strengthened with laws, but cannot be built solely with them. Fundamentally, it is only the encounter of love that can promise to renew both social structures and individuals. This was the origin of the change in Juan Diego's life, and this was the promise millions of converts saw and experienced through Our Lady of Guadalupe when they described their new faith in Christ.

Importantly, this message of love and liberation from the trials of life was not seen as the only or most significant message. After all, "the Church desires the good of man in all his dimensions, first of all as a member of the city of God, and then as a member of the earthly city."[40] When this order is reversed, both are threatened. Unfortunately, this is sometimes a danger facing Christians today, when Christianity is reduced to a program of charity without an adequate spiritual dimension. As Cardinal Ratzinger noted:

> The danger of some theologies is that they insist on . . . the exclusively earthly standpoint of secularist liberation programs. They do not and cannot see that from a Christian point of view, "liberation" is above all and primarily liberation from the radical slavery which the "world" does not notice, which it actually denies, namely, the radical slavery of sin.[41]

Only by recognizing the profound reality of good and evil can reality and progress be not only measured but judged. When theology is harnessed only to drive earthly projects of "liberation," without acknowledging the spiritual, such liberation sacrifices what is truly fulfilling. Programs based on this kind of theology, called "liberation theology," begin with the view that "all reality is political," and thus reduce liberation itself to a strictly political concept that can only be achieved through strictly political means and action. In short, it endorses the view that "nothing lies outside political commitment. Everything has a political color."[42] In effect, theology and our relationship with God are likewise reduced to the politically tangible, and any theology that is not "practical" or essentially "political" is misconstrued as "idealist" and divorced from reality. More than that, it condemns any theology that does not embrace this radical political dimension as a "vehicle for the oppressors' maintenance of power."[43]

A decade before liberation theology entered Church circles, this type of flawed view of the Church as essentially a temporal power had led to the persecution of Catholics in Mexico during the 1920s. During this time, the Mexican government, under President Plutarco Elías Calles, decreed and enforced severe penalties on clergy and laymen alike, leading to the execution of

many. Nevertheless, Mexican Catholics held on to their faith—
and to their devotion to Our Lady of Guadalupe. Despite the
hardships during this time, one of the first dual-language edi-
tions of the *Nican Mopohua* was edited and published (1926), photographer Alfonso Marcue discovered and studied the reflections
in the Virgin's eye (1929), and an examination of Tepeyac's flora
and fauna was conducted in relation to the apparition roses
(1923).[44] It was during this time that the Basilica of Our Lady of
Guadalupe was bombed (a few months after another bomb threat
had been foiled), which caused such damage within the church
but failed to destroy the main target, the tilma;[45] the event
inspired six thousand Catholics to gather in prayer at the cathedral that night, and caused the Mexican president, Álvaro
Obregón, to visit the site himself, although his reputation for
anti-Catholicism set off a protest.[46] After these bombing fiascos,
a different approach was taken. The government attempted to
bring Guadalupe under its control in order to harness what it saw
as Catholicism's "power." In another example of an attempt at
conversion from the top down, the government founded a rival
religious organization, the nationalist "Mexican Catholic
Church."[47] In addition, the leading nationalist labor organization, the Confederación Regional Obrera Mexicana (CROM),
founded an underling group called the Knights of Guadalupe as
an alternative to independent Catholic organizations such as the
Knights of Columbus.[48] The Knights of Guadalupe even went so
far as to request that the Basilica of Our Lady of Guadalupe be
turned over to the control of this nationalist organization in the
hopes that it might become the seat or "Vatican City" for the new
nationalist church.[49] However, despite the pressures to convert to
this non-apostolic church, few joined, and even the choice of
name (Knights of *Guadalupe*) could not hide the order's allegiance
to the nationalist church. In 1925, when the Knights of

Guadalupe and the rogue "patriarch" of the newly organized nationalist church entered the Soledad Church near the basilica and removed the priest while he celebrated Mass, so great was the outrage that the parishioners protested long after President Calles closed the church.[50]

(Here, for the sake of clarity, it must be noted that there is currently another existing order, also called the Knights of Guadalupe—Caballeros de Guadalupe—but this organization is in communion with the Catholic Church and bears no past or present relationship to the nationalist order of the 1920s.)

President Calles, the nationalist church, and the Knights of Guadalupe failed to understand the fundamental nature of both Christianity and the Guadalupe message. Even the Mexican president before Calles, Álvaro Obregón, two years after the failed bombing of the basilica, showed a greater understanding of the Guadalupan event: "The Virgin of Guadalupe always has been regarded as Mexico's Queen; as such she merits our gratitude and respect."[51] But even this falls short. As described in the *Nican Motecpana*:

> She not only came to show herself as the queen of heaven, our precious mother of Guadalupe, in order to help the natives in their mundane miseries, but actually because she wanted to give them her light and her help, so that finally they would know the true and only God and through him see and know life in heaven.[52]

The significance of Our Lady of Guadalupe is reducible neither to her value as "Mexico's Queen" nor to her value as an intercessor, as one to whom the Mexican people can look for material help and support. Rather, her value lies more precisely in how she never comes alone, in how she always brings her Son.

It is true that in her actions, words, and image, Our Lady of Guadalupe speaks to the need for change, but the change she specifically requests is a new church on Tepeyac, and the purpose for this church, she tells us, is to present her Son. While the Church offers programs geared toward charitable service and the improvement of society, she is not reducible to these services and programs. The Church, like Our Lady of Guadalupe, never comes alone, but always with Christ; he is her true measure and gift to the world.

Like the message of Our Lady of Guadalupe, the message of the Church is to be preached in all times and to all people. She has stood in the center of the hemisphere, through times of close Church-state cooperation, and through times of anticlerical persecution of the Church. But her message of building a civilization of love has never changed. Like Juan Diego, we are called to spread the Gospel, to build the civilization of love his "dear mother," our *"tonantzin"* represents. And we are called to do it at all times, in all political circumstances, and in all countries on the continent of baptized Christians.

GUADALUPAN EVANGELIZATION IN THE UNITED STATES

In Mexico, it may be easy to see the pervasiveness of the Guadalupan apparition in the Catholicism and devotional spirit of its people. In the United States, we need only look in our Capitol building to find a hint of how Our Lady of Guadalupe transformed our land through the faith of Catholic evangelists.

Many years before the United States had acquired its current breadth of land from the Atlantic to the Pacific oceans, Eusebio Kino arrived on his first missionary expedition to California, bringing with him an image of Our Lady of Guadalupe. As he exited the ship, a group of Indians came forward with their hunting weapons. Not knowing what to expect, Fr. Kino laid the image on the ground before them. Upon seeing the image, however, the Indians dispersed, only to return again with pearls and other precious treasures from their homes, which they strewed upon the image. Significantly, Our Lady of Guadalupe is treated not as a miracle but as a presence, as an evangelist. The missionaries trusted in the efficacy of her presence as an evangelist; she is an evangelizing mother to whom the missionaries continued to look in order to carry on the tradition of evangelization first initiated on Tepeyac. Understandably, after his encounter with the Indians, Fr. Kino established several missionary churches along the California coast for them, calling the first settlement in La Paz after Our Lady of Guadalupe.[53]

While the codex of the tilma's image and its glyphs would not have been intelligible to the Indians to whom Fr. Kino first showed the image, the message of civilization of love and truth became truly evident in Fr. Kino's work. His care for the Indians extended beyond religious practices as he attended to their civilization itself, bringing about extensive improvements in the Indians' living conditions by better connecting them to other villages and building schools, roads, rancheros, and stockyards. In Fr. Kino's work as a priest and social pioneer, we find an exemplar of the type of evangelization inspired and enabled by Our Lady of Guadalupe. So great was Fr. Kino's presence that in 1965 the State of Arizona sent a statue of Fr. Kino—complete with crucifix, compass, and rosary—to the United States Capitol's Statuary Hall as one of two heroic persons who gave so much to the people in that state.[54]

VI.

A Call to Conversion

"What does Mary mean to you, personally?"
*"An expression of the closeness of God . . . And the older I am, the
more the Mother of God is important to me and close to me."*

—JOSEPH CARDINAL RATZINGER[1]

THE MIRACULOUS FACE OF FAITH

In the New World, the growing popularity of Our Lady of
Guadalupe drew suspicion, so much so that, even after Archbishop
Alonso Montúfar delivered a homily extolling the Guadalupan
devotion, the Franciscan Provincial of Mexico, Friar Bustamante,
fired back with his own harsh critique. He condemned the
Indians' fascination with the image of Our Lady of Guadalupe on
St. Juan Diego's tilma, suggesting that "the first person to claim
that the image was capable of miracles should have been given one
hundred lashes of the whip."[2] Following this controversy, in
September of 1556, Archbishop Montufar ordered an investigation into the Guadalupan devotion. To some degree, an important
concern in this was the extent to which the Guadalupan devotion

inculcated truly Christian beliefs and practices, and especially the extent to which it pointed beyond the Virgin to Christ. The danger to be avoided was perhaps expressed best by the great twentieth-century Mexican muralist Diego Rivera, when he said: "I don't believe in God . . . But I do believe in the Virgin of Guadalupe."[3] Already the very location of the Virgin's shrine alarmed some of the missionaries who questioned how Tepeyac hill itself might influence belief, since nearby had once been an Aztec temple to the goddess Cuatlicue. Although many Catholic churches in Europe and in Italy, in particular, were built over pagan temples, in Mexico this particular spot drew suspicion, even leading some to distance their own devotion to the Spanish Virgin of Guadalupe (Our Lady of Extramadura) from the Indians' devotion to the Mexican Virgin of Guadalupe by insisting that the Virgin's title be changed to an Indian name, Tepeaquilla or Tepeaca (after Tepeyac).[4] Nevertheless, by the end of Montúfar's investigation, the testimonies given ultimately vindicated devotion to Our Lady of Guadalupe and the popularity of her miraculous image, reaffirming it as a true expression of the Christian faith and an encouragement of the Gospel message. But how?

Listening to the Gospels read at Mass, we hear of many miracles performed by Jesus during his earthly ministry. Some are extraordinary miracles like raising the dead to life and healing the severely sick, and we can easily see them as expressions of God's grandeur and power. But they are also always linked to faith. As John Paul II explains, "Faith precedes the miracle and indeed is a condition for its accomplishment. Faith is also an effect of the miracle, because it engenders faith in the souls of those who are its recipients or witnesses."[5] But, as John Paul II also points out, first and foremost, miracles are a mark of Christ's sonship, because "all that he does, even in working miracles, is done in close union with the Father."[6]

The miracles are therefore "for man." In harmony with the redemptive finality of his mission, they are works of Jesus which reestablished the good where evil had lurked, producing disorder and confusion. . . . No other motive than love for humanity, merciful love, explains the "mighty deeds and signs" of the Son of Man.[7]

Our Lady of Guadalupe's message of love and Christian personalism spoke to reestablishing a moral order that had been corrupted. But we cannot respond to this Christian personalism by interpretation alone. We live according to this Christian personalism only if we ourselves are continuously transformed. For this reason, like Christ's miracles during his public ministry, the miraculous occurrences at Tepeyac are "closely linked to the call of faith,"[8]—not only because they are "miraculous" or because they are "religious" occurrences, but because they lead us to the source of our transformation, to her Son who redeems.[9] In this, Our Lady of Guadalupe's apparition becomes a participation in Christ's sonship and Christ's mission. Through a gesture of closeness, words of compassion, and an invitation to come to Christ in our difficulties, Our Lady of Guadalupe makes a declaration of faith.

Of course, the faith of those engaged in the miracle, like Juan Diego, differs from the faith of those who approach the miracle afterward. There is no guarantee that the miracles will be received with faith or inspire faith. Even some of Christ's apostles who had witnessed his miracles betrayed him (Judas Iscariot), denied him (Peter), and doubted him (Thomas). Christ himself noted in one parable that for some, even if a person should return from the dead and give a warning to his brothers, his brothers would not change their ways, because they had already rejected the words of Moses and the prophets.[10] This parable is interesting in that it suggests that there is a certain way of approaching God through the miraculous: "'Blessed are the pure in heart, for they shall see God.' The organ for seeing God is the purified heart."[11] The miraculous is not a force, but a presentation, a communication, which can be ignored, misconstrued, or accepted only in part. It presupposes an openness of heart—an openness to transformation and to truth. This is in part "the task of Marian piety": "to awaken the heart and purify it in faith."[12] And through it, we too become blessed to see God in each other, and to recognize his work in our lives and in each other's lives.

TO JESUS THROUGH MARY

Ingrid Betancourt, an important political and social activist in Colombia, was kidnapped by Marxist guerillas while campaigning as a presidential candidate in 2002. As a rising political figure, her capture became an international cause of concern, especially in Europe, because of her dual citizenship with France. On July 2, 2008, after six years of failed negotiations and efforts for release, she and fourteen other hostages were liberated from their captors in the jungles of Colombia in a risky but ultimately bloodless military operation. Asked afterward about her trials, she spoke about her faith and her prayers to Mary. "When I thought of the Virgin, I thought of the Virgin of Guadalupe. I always felt she was very close to me. I know she is close now and is helping us and will help all those who continue in captivity in Colombia. She will bring them out, you'll see; she will do this miracle for us."[13] For Betancourt, faith was not only a support during her trials but a foundation for life. "Without faith there is no hope, without hope there is no strength, no fortitude to continue fighting. Faith is everything; it's what gives meaning to life, especially faith in Christ."[14]

Betancourt's rescue was not literally or scientifically miraculous in the sense of being absolutely impossible, nor would bringing out the rest of the captives be. However, as Betancourt suggests, obstacles do not have to be marked by scientific impossibility in order to be serious impediments. Human nature, sin, ignorance, habit, and fear can all seriously work against the hallmarks of a civilization of love and peace: truth, freedom, and justice. What is miraculous, what is worthy of our wonder (from *mirari,* to wonder), is a change of heart.

This is one of the great beauties of conversion. Recalling the profound joy of the baptized Indians and of those preparing to receive the sacrament, one missionary wrote:

> To see the fervent desire which these new converts brought to their baptism was truly something to notice and marvel at. One does not read about greater things in the primitive Church. And one does not know what to marvel at most, seeing these new people coming or seeing how God brought them.[15]

This, too, is the true marvel about the apparition: the many changes of heart that happened in the face of the miraculous. Some of these changes are very real and practical, like Zumárraga accepting Juan Diego to stay in his house after he had previously sent Juan Diego away twice before; others are changes in the face of mystery, like Zumárraga's servants refusing Juan Diego admittance, then letting him in after the roses transform in Juan Diego's tilma. The most human changes are more subtle actions of following and trusting even when the path is not entirely understood; Juan Diego considers himself unworthy to approach Zumárraga, and yet at the Virgin's insistence he does. But why? He is still, after all, "a man from the country";[16] his tilma had not yet been imprinted with an image that would bear the signs of his dignity as a child of God. But he trusts, and this trust gives him determination and directs his determination. He goes because the Virgin has helped him to understand the honor of his sonship. He goes because he trusts the Virgin, who leads him and teaches him to follow a new relationship. This is miraculous, not in the sense that it is impossible, but in the sense that, through the Virgin of Guadalupe, Juan Diego, too, experiences a conversion of the heart.

When John Paul II placed his devotion to Mary as central to his pontificate, choosing the expression *Totus Tuus* ("Entirely Yours") as his apostolic motto, he must have had Mary's role in inspiring conversion and leading others to Christ in mind. The expression was taken from one of St. Louis de Montfort's prayers to Mary, and in a personal way it became not only an expression of John Paul II's devotion to Mary but a result of his deeper understanding of the purpose of Marian devotion.

> *Totus Tuus*. This phrase is not only an expression of piety, or simply an expression of devotion. It is more. During the Second World War, while I was employed as a factory worker, I came to be attracted to Marian devotion. At first, it had seemed to me that I should distance myself a bit from the Marian devotion of my childhood, in order to focus more on Christ. Thanks to Saint Louis of Montfort, I came to understand that true devotion to the Mother of God is actually Christocentric, indeed, it is very profoundly rooted in the Mystery of the Blessed Trinity, and the mysteries of the Incarnation and Redemption.[17]

As it did for the young John Paul II, devotion to Mary leads one more closely into the mysteries of Christ and his mission of salvation in the world. Historically, it was only through Mary that God took on human flesh and became one with us. And today, like

Juan Diego centuries before, we can be brought into closer unity with God by following Our Lady of Guadalupe's message of trust and love.

In the working document written in preparation for the Synod of Bishops for America, one of the subjects proposed for consideration was the role of Mary in the health and evangelization of the church in the Americas: The "Virgin Mary will be a model of conversion, communion and solidarity for the Church in America, so that the saving activity of her Son may reach all on the continent."[18] Looking at the Gospel accounts mentioning Mary's life, we find significant moments when Mary's life, words, and interiority give a clear, concrete model. If the communion of saints truly matters, it is not only possible to detect a Marian model but a uniquely Guadalupan Marian model of conversion, communion, and solidarity.

After all, Our Lady of Guadalupe, Our Lady of Extremadura, Our Lady of Fatima, and countless other titles Mary is given throughout history and throughout the world are ultimately the same: each is Mary. There is no—and can be no—contradiction with the Virgin Mary spoken of in the Gospel. Mary is a woman for every age, and yet how she expresses herself can be different. In every age, she continues to participate in Christ's revelation of himself through miracles, just as she did in the first miracle of Christ recorded in the Gospels—the miracle of changing water into wine at the wedding at Cana. She continues to be aware of our situation and to propose to us that, as once she did at Cana, we "do whatever he tells us."[19] What is unique among Marian apparitions is how each speaks to specific persons, in a specific time and place, who have unique problems, language, and preconceptions.

Consequently, it is possible—and for us in the Americas, we have a special invitation—to reflect on and follow the example of

Our Lady of Guadalupe in our efforts toward personal conversion, communion, and solidarity. The subjects addressed in particular during the apparition—Mary's motherhood, charity, witness, intercession, trust, and truth—form the basis of the Guadalupan model of conversion, communion, and solidarity, and become the foundation of Guadalupan spirituality.

MARIAN CLOSENESS TO GOD

In the previous chapter, we considered Mary as the first evangelist, and thus her involvement in "making converts." Although we can perhaps better understand Mary as a model evangelist, we do not ordinarily think of Mary as a model of communion, solidarity, or especially conversion. We often associate conversion only with converting from one religion to another religion, like the Indians converting from Aztec beliefs to Christianity. But conversion, as Benedict XVI said, is much broader and more continual than this:

> What does "to be converted" actually mean? It means seeking God, moving with God, docilely following the teachings of his Son, Jesus Christ; to be converted is not a work for self-fulfillment because the human being is not the architect of his own eternal destiny. We did not make ourselves. . . . Conversion consists in freely and lovingly accepting to depend in all things on God, our true creator, to depend on love. This is not dependence but freedom.[20]

Conversion is not a mere declaration of beliefs or a mark of membership. It is a wholehearted adherence to a Person, a continual "yes" to the transformative power of God's love. Its requirement is a simple gesture, a simple "yes," and in this way it is something we can all do; even more, it is something we are all called to. But importantly we are not left without a model; because conversion as a constant "yes" to God is something that Mary herself did so well, so perfectly, and in such a clear manner, it is possible for us to live our lives guided by her example. And for us today, in a new time and situation, Our Lady of Guadalupe again presents a model of seeking God, following Christ, depending on God, and depending on love.

It was precisely this universality of conversion that, on the eighth centenary of St. Francis' conversion, Benedict XVI underscored, saying: "Speaking of conversion means going to the heart of the Christian message, and at the same time to the roots of human existence."[21] Of course, there are many ways we can describe the heart of the Christian message, but this is how Benedict XVI described it to a group of Catholic youth:

> Here then we have reached the heart of the Christian message: Christ is the response to your questions and problems; in him every honest aspiration of the human being is strengthened. Christ, however, is demanding and shuns half measures. He knows he can count on your generosity and coherence; for this reason he expects a lot of you. Follow him faithfully and, in order to encounter him, love his Church, feel responsible, do not avoid being courageous protagonists, each in his own context.
>
> To be converted thus means not pursuing one's own personal success—that is something ephemeral—but giving up all human security, treading in the Lord's footsteps with simplicity and trust so that Jesus may become for each one, as Blessed Teresa of Calcutta liked to say, "my All in all".[22]

Often times, God's love is present to us in ways that we can neither anticipate nor comprehend. And yet, regardless of our intellectual limitations, preconceptions, and sometimes flawed expectations, the mystery of God's love is not, to borrow a phrase from Winston Churchill, "a riddle, wrapped in a mystery, inside an enigma."[23] It is something so immense and overwhelmingly great that we can only experience and know it one part at a time. Like Juan Diego, who could not immediately understand the significance of the Virgin's miraculous apparitions and her declaration of motherhood and so tried to avoid her in his time of greatest need, we can be overwhelmed by the mystery of divine love, not immediately able to recognize its practical and profound significance. Importantly, however, the more we open ourselves up to it, the more it will make sense in our lives.

Speaking of the spiritual life, Fr. Benedict Groeschel once noted that spiritual intimacy requires three things: openness, self-giving, and vulnerability. The first two—openness and self-giving—are easy to accept in our spiritual life, precisely because we see their importance in our relationships with family and friends.[24] Openness and self-giving are often hailed as the cornerstones of a good marriage, and most erroneous views and treatments of the marriage bond often return to some basic rejection of these two necessities. However, vulnerability is less often discussed, and for many it is the real crux of spiritual difficulties. To truly love completely is to love with complete openness and self-giving, even with the knowledge that one may be changed, one may even be hurt. It is the vulnerability Christians see in Christ, "obedient unto death, even to death on a cross."[25]

Frankly, vulnerability cannot be explained as a good in a secular society. Today, we often equate vulnerability with weakness and inability and autonomy with strength and true happiness. As the German philosopher Friedrich Nietzsche wrote, happiness is "the feeling that power *increases*—that resistance is overcome, not contentment, but more power; not peace at any price, but war; not virtue, but efficiency."[26] To the contrary, in Christ men and women are called to be people of the Beatitudes. The paradox of Christianity is that in Christ "power and service went together."[27]

If to serve is to become vulnerable through a gift of self, to serve through God's love is to become vulnerable to God's love and to experience service not as a loss but as a powerful fulfillment. It is the vulnerability seen in Mary's "yes" to God. It is the vulnerability asked of Juan Diego, to change his direction and his plans and to risk the ridicule of Zumárraga's servants, the humiliation of enduring Zumárraga's doubt, the fear and disappointment of failing, the frustration of being entrusted with a task believed to be too large for his shoulders. It is a vulnerability that leads us to the edge of what is easily desirable or possible through our efforts. It is a vulnerability that demands faith.

In Mary, we learn how closely God comes to us in this way. And in Mary, we learn how to be open, giving, and vulnerable to God. We learn to trust God. Millions of people around the world remember John Paul II for saying, wherever he visited in the world, "Do not be afraid! Open wide the doors to Christ!"[28] In Benedict XVI's first homily as pope, he explained why we should not be afraid, why we should have the courage to welcome Christ in our lives: "Do not be afraid of Christ! He takes nothing away, and he gives you everything. When we give ourselves to him, we receive a hundredfold in return. Yes, open, open wide the doors to Christ—and you will find true life."[29] This was the hopeful message of the Virgin in telling Juan Diego that his uncle had been healed. This was the courage of Juan Diego in not returning to this uncle, believing in the Virgin's word that Juan Bernardino had been healed.

HUMANITY RENEWED

It is significant that Mary appeared to Juan Diego after his formal conversion to Christianity—his baptism—rather than before. Juan Diego's conversion to Christianity marked a definitive change in his life. With the Indian culture's emphasis on tradition and the wisdom of the ages, his conversion must have been very difficult. But even more, it marked a change of heart, a change in what he desired, since even after his baptism, Juan Diego pursued the faith through not only the sacraments and prayer, but also through catechesis. That is, Mary comes to a Catholic in order to encourage him to become a better Catholic. She comes to a Catholic and administers to his—and his community's—deepest needs. She comes to a Catholic and engages him in active Catholic life.

In the hagiographical writings and verbal testimonies about Juan Diego's life, often people focused on the facts of his life (marriage, location, age, etc.) and his sanctity. Juan Diego's flaws or spiritual difficulties before or after the apparition are largely or completely overshadowed by his record of holy living after the apparition. Even so, in the apparition account we can still glimpse Juan Diego's spiritual struggles to pursue God in truth and love. For example, just as the Spanish occupiers challenged the humanity of Indians like himself through exploitation, so his language in the apparition account expresses in a more subtle way how his own evaluation of himself deteriorated toward a utilitarian view of human worth and purpose: "Because I am really just a man from the country, I'm the porter's rope, I'm a back frame, just a tail, a wing; I myself need to be led, carried on someone's back."[30]

Juan Diego's expression of humility reflects the common phrases and patterns of courteous speech for the Indians, placing him among the common people. But his mission was more. His mission was to intercede on behalf of the Virgin. Only a person can be a witness for another person. Only a person can show persistence, patience, humility, and dedication. Only a person can trust and inspire trust. Only a person with free will can choose virtue. Only a person can show desire. The Virgin's reply delineates the difference and also elevates him beyond the instrumentality of being only "one of the people," beyond identifying him by how he functions: "Listen my youngest son, know for sure that I have no lack of servants, of messengers, to whom I can give the task of carrying my breath, my word, so that they carry out my will; but it is necessary that you, personally, go and plead, that by your intercession, my wish, my will, become a reality."[31]

When we come to the end of our abilities, when we approach something that our knowledge cannot explain, when we face something that we alone cannot surmount or a problem that man cannot fix, when we face something larger than ourselves, that is when we ask ourselves who we are. This happens when we face our death or the death of a loved one, serious health issues, situations "beyond our control." In a civilization of love, many of these still cannot be "fixed," but they can be approached satisfyingly when they are answered by love. It requires a trust in God's decisions, that God does not call us to something beyond us, only to abandon us without personally seeing to our help. Sometimes he calls us to face something beyond us in order to encourage—even demand—that we search him out, just as Christ did, depending on God and depending on love. Even while suffering on the cross, Christ turned to the Father, saying, "why have you abandoned me?", which was in fact a prayer, a recitation of one of the ancient psalms.[32] And even just before his death, there still was the trust in the Father that made Christ entrust himself to the Father: "into your hands I commend my spirit."[33]

The miracle of the apparition is a reminder of in whom and in what we place our trust—in God and his infallible love. Speaking of this love, Benedict XVI once wrote:

> Let us . . . be overtaken by the reconciliation that God has given us in Christ, by God's 'crazy' love for us: No one and nothing could ever separate us from his love. With this certainty we live. And this certainty gives us the strength to live concretely the faith that works in love."[34]

It is God's "crazy" love that makes him present himself to us, to be near to us; it was by this same "crazy" love that he sent his son and over fifteen centuries later that he sent his mother to Tepeyac. It was precisely trust in this love that was the trust at stake in Zumárraga's despairing letter to King Charles. This was the certainty received through Mary's apparition. Moreover, it is our certainty in God's love and the transformative power of his love that is the basis of our trust in others. It was out of his love for us that he created us and created all that is around us.

CIVILIZATION OF TRANSFORMED PERSONS

Reflecting on the canonization of Juan Diego, John Paul II wrote:

> But to return to Guadalupe, in 2002 I was privileged to celebrate the canonization of Juan Diego in this shrine. It was a wonderful opportunity to offer thanks to God. Juan Diego, having embraced Christianity without surrendering his indigenous identity, discovered the profound truth about the new humanity, in which all are called to be children of God in Christ. "I bless you, Father, Lord of heaven and earth, for although you have hid-

den these things from the wise and the learned you have revealed them to mere children. . . ." (Matt.11:25). And in this mystery, Mary had a particular role.[35]

The call to conversion is central to what it means to live a Christian life. Yet what does it mean to say that a culture itself is called to conversion? Culture is not definitive; it cannot direct itself independent of people, but it takes on the character of those who live in a community and give it life. Conversion begins with individual people and, through the lives of these individuals, culture is transformed. Whether in the form of personal prayer, small or great acts of charitable service, the daily self-renunciations and sacrifices in our family lives, or integrity and competence in our work, we are called to be mediators between God and society. In this way culture is not only transformed, but converted.

In his book *Coworkers of the Truth*, Joseph Ratzinger speaks of this kind of transformation, both in oneself and in the world:

> Those who would be Christians must be "transformed" ever again. Our natural disposition, indeed, finds us always ready to assert ourselves to pay like with like, to put ourselves at the center. Those who want to find God need, again and again, that inner conversion, that new direction. . . . Yet the truth is that what is invisible is greater and much more valuable than anything visible. One single soul . . . is worth more than the entire visible universe. . . . *Metanoeite*: change your attitude, so that God may dwell in you and, through you, in the world.[36]

Thinking of the change in Juan Diego's life following the apparitions—in how he continued to grow in Christian practice and understanding, dedicating himself to a life of service and never neglecting the opportunity to share the Virgin's message with others—it is important to keep in mind that this change has a source. When we are led to him, Christ not only changes our lives, but he also presents the possibility of positively changing the lives of others. Through God's love for us, we are given the possibility of living out the two greatest commandments: loving God and loving our neighbor. Someone once said to Mother Teresa that not for a million dollars would he touch a leper. Much to his surprise, Mother Teresa responded: "Neither would I. If it were a case of money, I would not even do it for two million. On the other hand, I do it gladly for love of God."[37] This is true conversion of the heart. Adhering to God in such a love, all else must fall beneath that love, becoming an expression of that love.

Some would call Mother Teresa unreasonable for being willing to touch a leper for the love of God, that is, to touch a leper in faith. But reason itself demands an enormous amount of trust, the fundamental trust that what has been is an indicator of what will be, that there is some order and logic to the world. This need for faith becomes all the more obvious when considering the actions and intentions of others, since a person's love for another is one value that is not a catalogue of actions. It is possible—and even easy—to do "works of charity" lovelessly. Love cannot be seen in the way that actions can be. That is why understanding a person's love requires faith. That is why faith must also be a gift, a gift from God. Faith is the gift that enables us to see and to trust his love.

This also shows the conversion of the heart in its most concrete, everyday expression. In Christ, building up a civilization of love is not an abstract good or hypothetical possibility. It is being built already. It is concrete. It is personal. It is found in the individual witness offered by all people truly touched by God. By converting to Christ, reality can reach its full potential. Even suffering finds its beauty in Christ. If we ourselves live close to Christ, we can bring Christ closer to other people. Personal witness is indispensable, as Pope Benedict XVI has made clear: "Only through men who have been touched by God can God come near to men."[38]

Through devotion to Mary, "people can have a direct experience of Christianity as the religion of trust, of certainty."[39] The Guadalupan event made that clear. Before the miracle of Our Lady's appearances, human efforts had failed; Christianity appeared to be neither a religion of trust nor of certainty but rather the religion of the conqueror, a religion with deadly heralds. Even with the great efforts and examples of some of the early missionaries, Christianity could not be offered as a good—not with so many witnesses against it. The fallibility of human works and the limitations of the world had become too obvious, and even human reason could not tell Friar Zumárraga of the truth of what he had heard from the Virgin's messenger. And yet, through Our Lady of Guadalupe, all of this was ultimately changed; revealing herself as a mother, suddenly trust was possible, certainty within reach.

The entire story of Guadalupe is one of transformation: from a continent of bloodletting and human sacrifice, to a continent where the mother who watched her Son pierced granted a reprieve to its inhabitants. It is the story of a barren hillside surprisingly covered in flowers, of a coarse tilma, imprinted with the beautiful image not made by human hands, of a bishop's heart softened, and of the beginning of millions of conversions, each of which represented an immortal victory for the civilization of love. It falls to us, to continue this sequence of conversions and through our conversion of self to become the codex that can bring conversion to those around us by our witness.

VII.

Mary and the Church

Here, at the feet of Mary, ever anew we "learn the Church," entrusted
by Christ to the Apostles and to all of us. The mystery of Mary is
linked inseparably to the mystery of the Church.

-JOHN PAUL II,
ADDRESS AT THE MARIAN SHRINE AT CZESTOCHOWA[1]

CHURCH ON TEPEYAC

One of the most interesting details of the apparition is the
Virgin's request: to build a church on Tepeyac. With other
churches in the general area, including the *doctrina* that Juan
Diego was accustomed to visit for instruction, building another
church on Tepeyac may seem superfluous from a pragmatic stand-
point. Would this chapel, uniquely requested, have a unique purpose? After all, although the tilma is now housed in the Basilica
of Our Lady of Guadalupe, in the apparition account the tilma's
image is unknown and unexpected at the time of Mary's first
request for a church. Furthermore, why would *Mary* request a
church at all?

One of the main indications about Mary's personal role regarding the church's purpose is her declaration that it be a place of intercession: "There truly will I hear their cry, their sadness, to remedy, to cure all their various troubles, their miseries, their pains."[2]

In August 1736, a painful and deadly plague of typhus broke out throughout the population of New Spain. Thousands died in the streets and in the hospitals of Mexico City. Within months, the city's nine hospitals were filled, along with nine abandoned buildings converted into makeshift infirmaries. Victims gathered in the city's plaza and in any large buildings that could be found. Soon existing cemeteries were filled, and outlying parts of the city were transformed into cemeteries that were also filled. The archbishop of Mexico paid to open pharmacies throughout the city to distribute free medicine. Despite these efforts, the plague raged on into the next year with its original intensity. During this time, Our Lady of Guadalupe remained a center of devotion. During nine days of a solemn novena to the Guadalupan Virgin, an unbroken line of pilgrims stretched from Mexico City to the Virgin's shrine at Tepeyac. A council of civic leaders was organized and vowed to have Our Lady of Guadalupe declared Patroness of the City of Mexico. At ten o'clock on the morning of April 27, 1737, the city swore its solemn allegiance to Our Lady of Guadalupe. On the eve of this consecration, only three burials took place in the city's cemetery of San Lázaro, where previously forty to fifty burials had been taking place each day.[3]

This show of devotion to the Guadalupan Virgin, while astounding, is not unique to this occasion. Historically, whenever disasters struck, the people of Mexico City turned to her; nearly three hundred years later, in the swine flu epidemic in Mexico City in 2009, Cardinal Norberto Rivera Carrera led the citizens of that city in prayers seeking the protection of Our Lady of Guadalupe. Even in personal trials, illnesses, or injuries of family members, Our Lady of Guadalupe was almost always invoked, at least in prayer, if not in pilgrimage. And today, millions of people visit the Basilica of Our Lady of Guadalupe in Mexico each year, praying for intentions and attending Mass. That people come to her, even with simple personal troubles, as once she encouraged the grieving Juan Diego to do, points to the individuality in Mary's relationship to each of us, the individuality expressible only as a relationship between mother and child.

CHRIST PRESENT

One of the greatest of Christ's promises recorded in the Gospels is this: "I am with you always, until the end of the age."[4] From the human perspective, it is also one of the most enigmatic. Speaking these words after his resurrection, he had already proven in a tangible way that his love for his apostles was so strong—despite their faults, doubts, and denials—that he returned to them in his resurrected life. But Christ promises his presence not only until his ascension but until the end of the age. He promises enduring and personal affection not only to the apostles meeting him on the mountaintop in Galilee but to all subsequent generations, causing us to ask: how is he still with us today?

The answer to this question is made clearer in the context of what was said. Meeting with the apostles as he had requested, Jesus spoke of a time beyond his resurrected life on earth:

All power in heaven and on earth has been given to me. Go, therefore, and make disciples of all nations, baptizing them in the name of the Father, and of the Son, and of the Holy Spirit, teaching them to observe all that I have commanded you. And behold, I am with you always, until the end of the age.[5]

That is, Christ is made present by his power over heaven and earth, by our evangelization, by our baptism, and by our observance of his commandments. Aside from his power over heaven and earth, the rest are actions between persons and within the Church.

At its heart, the Guadalupan event points to Christ's presence precisely in this way. In the previous chapter, we looked at the apparition's Christocentric element, with Mary as a model of conversion to Christ and as a mother through whom Christians are led to a greater union with Christ. Much of this focused on her acceptance of God's will at the Annunciation, in the moment when she said "yes" to God, conceiving Christ, and thus becoming Christ's mother. However, Mary's motherhood also opens us up to a new dimension of encountering Christ, encountering Christ in the Church. The stated purpose for the Tepeyac chapel clearly speaks to this continuing presence of Christ.

I want very much that they build my sacred little house here, in which I will show Him, I will exalt Him on making Him manifest, I will give Him to all people in all my personal love, Him that is my compassionate gaze, Him that is my help, Him that is my salvation.[6]

Only here is the full purpose for the church—and our full place in this church—made clear: it is a place where Christ is made present, a meeting place for God and man.

In the original Náhuatl, the personhood of what is given at

the church is made more apparent in these last lines. Often, it is translated simply as "my compassionate gaze, my help, my salvation," but in the Náhuatl there is the affix *te*, indicating a person. In this way, this compassionate gaze, help, and salvation are personified, or, more specifically, are a person. Christ is made present in a way that is personal, just as each person is loved particularly in a way that is lasting. This makes both the request for a church and the entire apparition Christocentric, centered on Christ.[7]

For us today, just as for Juan Diego and the people of the New World, the church is not a place of remembrance, like a memorial, but a place where Christ is constantly present as a person. That continuing presence is the true and lasting miracle, enabled through Christ's power as God and made known to us through the witness of others in the life of Christ's body, the Church. By requesting this chapel, the Virgin encourages Juan Diego in a sharing of the faith. She relates to us as individuals seeking Christ but also as members of the Body of Christ, the Church.

Mary's motherhood is not the only motherhood given to us. Rather, both Mary and the Church are mothers in a spiritual sense, and the motherhood of each complements the other's. As John Paul II explained: "The two mothers, the Church and Mary, are both essential to Christian life. It could be said that the one is a more objective motherhood and the other more interior."[8] While the motherhood of the Church is inextricably linked to the preaching of God's word and the sacraments, "Mary's motherhood," John Paul II continued, "is expressed in all the areas where grace is distributed, particularly within the framework of personal relations. They are two inseparable forms of motherhood: indeed both enable us to recognize the same divine love which seeks to share itself with mankind."[9]

UNDER MARY'S ROOF

This personal presentation of Christ is indicated in the second way the Virgin is identified with the church in the apparition account: It is her church and—what is more—her *home*. And Mary is identified not only with the church on Tepeyac but even with the doctrina in Mexico City: "I am going as far as your little house in Mexico, Tlaltelolco, to follow the things of God that are given to us, that are taught to us by those who are the images of the Lord, Our Lord, our priests."[10]

The first conversation between Juan Diego and the Virgin, in which the Virgin asks Juan Diego where he is going, establishes more than where Juan Diego is headed. It is an opportunity for Juan Diego to express the continuity of the Church and of its teaching. Our Lady already appears in the context of Christ and the Church. She already is associated with the clergy, the "images of God," who teach. She already participates in the education of her children. In this context, the entire apparition, the entire mission entrusted to Juan Diego, brings Juan Diego to fuller participation in the Church's "yes" to God.

Giving birth to Christ began with an extraordinary "yes" to God's will. More extraordinary is the "yes" to Christ's life throughout his childhood and mission. Speaking of Christ's life, Benedict XVI highlights Christ's time in Mary's home as a formative period in Christ's life. Christ spent most of his life in Mary's home, and Mary was present at the wedding at Cana, the beginning of Christ's public ministry. Christ constantly calls himself the Son— and as Son he has both a father (God the Father) and a mother (Mary).[11] Benedict XVI concludes that something in Christ's childhood and upbringing enabled him to uphold childhood as a model of our relationship with God:

"Truly I say to you, unless you turn and become like children, you will never enter the kingdom of heaven" (Mt 18:3). This means that Jesus does not regard "being a child" as a transient phase of human life that is a consequence of man's biological fate and thus is completely laid aside. Rather, it is in "being a child" that the very essence of what it is to be a man is realized, so much so that one who has lost the essence of childhood is himself lost. . . . If being a child remained so precious in Jesus' eyes and he saw this as the purest mode of human existence, then he must have had very happy memories of his own childhood days.[12]

So close is this association between spiritual childhood and the favor of God that Benedict XVI sees the New Covenant established by Christ beginning "not in the Temple or on the holy mountain, but in the simple dwelling of the Virgin, in the house of the worker, in one of the forgotten places in 'Galilee of the Gentiles,' a town from which no one expected anything good to come."[13]

Consequently, the Church continually returns to the home of Mary to discover, as Christ discovered, the calling to unite to God through the free and loving acceptance of his will and love.

What does Jesus learn from his mother? He learns to say Yes, *fiat*. Not just any Yes, but a Yes that goes ever farther, without getting weary. Everything that you desire, my God . . . This is the Catholic prayer that Jesus learned from his human mother, from the *Catholica Mater* who was in the world before him and who was inspired by God to be the first to speak this word of the new and eternal covenant.[14]

It is this prayer and outlook that each Christian learns from Mary; this too is how the Church follows the model of Mary.

Mary's home is closely tied to the future of the Church. "The universal Church can grow and flourish only if she is aware that her hidden roots are kept safe in the atmosphere of Nazareth."[15]

MARY'S MOTHERHOOD AND WOMANHOOD

Just as Mary's motherhood of Christ went beyond birth, so with Juan Diego—and us. Her motherhood is not mere spiritual "fact," like a name on a birth certificate. Rather, she comes to Juan Diego making present her continued role as mother.

In the apparition account, one of the most striking moments is when Mary calls herself God's mother and Juan Diego's mother: *inantzin* (dear mother) and *nohuacanantzin* (compassionate mother). Both words have the same ending (*-tzin,* dear). This ending was also used when she called to Juan Diego in the beginning: "Juantzin, Juan Diegotzin." This word ending was used to express affection, reverence, and intimacy. It is often loosely translated as "dear." However, it was significant whether this affectionate form was given to someone else or whether one called oneself by this endearing form. While calling another by this respectful form could indicate one's own feelings toward or relationship with the other person, to call oneself by this form indicates a degree of acceptance of this familiarity as a joy, an honor. In this case, the Virgin calling herself God's dear mother and Juan Diego's dear mother revealed a relationship that was both preexisting and honorable.[16]

Of course, Mary was Christ's mother in a way different from her motherhood for us. She was Christ's biological mother: he was conceived within her, she carried him in her womb, and she gave birth to him. It is a relationship none of us has with her. But spiritually, she is the mother of all of us, the brothers and sisters of Christ. And this motherhood, too, was given by God, in Christ's words from the Cross when he entrusted Mary and the apostle John to each other:

> When Jesus saw his mother and the disciple there whom he loved, he said to his mother, "Woman, behold, your son." Then he said to the disciple, "Behold, your mother." And from that hour the disciple took her into his home.[17]

Christ did not ask for anything specific; he does not tell John, "Let her stay with you." He gives a relationship. He gives his mother a son. He gives this son a mother.

Even more, he entrusts his mother not only to John but to "the disciple there whom he loved." Through Christ's love for each of us, and through our discipleship to Christ, we too are both entrusted to Mary and entrusted with Mary: "Mary's motherhood, which becomes man's inheritance, is a gift: a gift which Christ himself makes *personally* to every individual."[18] This is seen, too, in the Guadalupan apparitions; not only is the Virgin's spiritual motherhood expressed to another "John" ("Juan" Diego), but the Virgin's words express how this is a relationship that already exists. She is already his mother. She already holds Juan Diego in her arms. Mary's motherhood affects each of us individually, as she intercedes and cares for us. Just as John, out of care for this relationship, accepted his new mother into his home, just as Our Lady of Guadalupe entered the home of Juan Bernardino and requested of Juan Diego a home, so each of us is called to invite her into our homes and our hearts.

Together and inseperably, Mary and the Church aid the person in continual conversion to Christ, helping us to show our faith in action, work for love and persevere through hope in Christ.[19] In this task, Mary's womanhood bears special significance:

> Mary is the believing other whom God calls. As such, she represents the creation, which is called to respond to God, and the freedom of the creature, which does not lose its integrity in love but attains completion therein. Mary thus represents saved and liberated man, but she does so precisely as a woman.[20]

For Catholics, Mary provides the example of the perfect woman. Not only was she sinless, but also she displayed an incredible sense of interiority, a capacity to listen, and above all a trust in God that allowed her to say yes to his will, even when what was asked required heroic trust.

We can imagine that the Virgin Mary, as the wife of a carpenter, had to work very hard to help sustain her family and to raise Jesus. Yet even as a woman of great activity, Mary was also a woman of advent, of prayerful waiting for the Word. Mary's womanhood is significant since she is in a very real way Christ's mother, but it is also important in terms of the unique moral and spiritual values embodied therein.[21] Mary exemplifies values integral to the affective, personal, and interpersonal life of the human person. Values such as attention, openness, receptivity, waiting, and patience—often called "ethic of care" values—are all deeply characteristic of Mary in her relation to God and to others. Through these values, Mary showed above all a trust in God that allowed her to say "yes" to his will, welcoming God into her womb and into her life. Precisely through her womanhood, she made her whole life "a response of God's love."[22]

Of course, we must remember that in the New World, the face of mature Christians was not only European, but also male. In the apparition of the Virgin, the Church in the Americas is given anew the protoevangelist, Mary, who precisely as Virgin and mother represented saved and liberated humankind in a loving way. As in the life and person of Mary, action and prayer are shown to be integrally united in the single gift of self to God, as an action stemming from prayerful union with him. It is Mary's continued response to God's love, from Nazareth to Tepeyac, which inspires Juan Diego to the seek the same sensitivity to the will of God when he accepts God's plan for him—a plan he had not envisioned personally, but was able to recognize when proposed to him lovingly as a "response of God's love."

THE CHURCH: BRIDE AND MOTHER

Within the Church, Mary's motherhood takes on a concrete character of care. Importantly, however, as a woman espoused to God, Mary does more than point toward the Church. She is in fact a model for the Church, the Church that is the Bride of Christ, and she is a model for us precisely in our participation in the Church. While a model for each individual believer, Mary's motherhood is also a model for the Church. In fact, as John Paul II wrote in his apostolic letter on the dignity of women, "Unless one looks to the Mother of God, it is impossible to understand the mystery of the Church, her reality, her essential vitality."[23] In a fundamental way, the Church finds a model in Mary, who in her "yes" to God became that place where God and humanity met. The Church is called to an analogous vocation, bringing Christ in the sacraments to all people and, at the same time, giving birth through her preaching and the sacraments to a new community of believers.

Speaking of the Church, there are two terms most often used. One is *populus Dei*, meaning the "people of God"; the other is *ecclesia*, meaning "church." Together they describe two different aspects of the Church's relationship to Christ. As Cardinal Ratzinger explains:

> In contrast to the masculine, activistic-sociological *populus Dei* (people of God) approach, Church—*ecclesia*—is feminine. . . . Church is more than "people," more than structure and action: the Church contains the living mystery of maternity and of the bridal love that makes maternity possible. There can be ecclesial piety, love for the Church, only if this mystery exists. When the Church is no longer seen in any but a masculine, structural, purely theoretical way, what is most authentically ecclesial about *ecclesia* has been ignored.[24]

The Church as *ecclesia* points to the way the Church relates to Christ in a feminine manner. Several times in the Gospels, Christ spoke in parables of himself as the bridegroom with his bride. This bride is the Church. The Church incorporates into her own self-understanding the mystery of Mary, "the listening handmaid who—liberated in grace—speaks her *Fiat* and, in so doing, becomes bride and thus body."[25] Without the values of femininity and an ethic of care, as embodied in the person of Mary, the proper relationship between God and the Church is threatened. To lose sight of the Church as the patient bride of Christ risks reducing the relationship between human and divine to an exclusively human dialogue. Coming to the Indians and missionaries as a woman, Our Lady of Guadalupe awakens them to the femininity of the Church. Just as Mary's receptivity to God enables her to bring us to Christ, so the Church's continual receptivity to Christ enables the Church to bring Christ to all peoples. The image and codex of Our Lady of Guadalupe, which carried the symbol of divinity in the four-petaled flower at its center, brought to the Indians in a feminine form the message and truth of Christ. In the same way, our *ecclesia*, our Church with its feminine aspects, brings Christ to our life both through its teaching and through its sacraments.

This understanding of the Church as *ecclesia*, as feminine, does not preclude action, does not preclude the masculine. On the contrary, it is the very presupposition upon which the Church's charitable action is based. The choice is not between God and works of charity but rather between God and charity on one hand and mere action on the other. In the same way that the human person finds fulfillment only through a duality of both the so-called masculine and feminine, so too with the Church, who in her charitable work with others actively offers God to the world. This activity is not sought in and of itself, as a mere social service or program; neither is it proselytism. It is, rather, one of the many forms in which we open ourselves up to God's free gift of love to us, in our own free gift of love to others.

MARY, THE CHURCH, AND THE SACRAMENTS

To speak of the motherhood of the Church in terms of her preaching and the sacraments may sound abstract and removed from the familiar reality confronting us in our individual church communities; it is not. At baptism, we are each individually born into the Body of Christ. Each person receives his or her name, is anointed individually, and is welcomed personally—by family, by godparents, and by the priest—into a living human and spiritual family.

The reality of the Church manifesting Christ's presence to us in the sacraments would have been particularly clear for those converting after the apparition. As the Náhuatl scholar Fr. Mario Rojas Sánchez points out, the Náhuatl word for "sacrament" itself suggested this reality of meeting Christ through the sacraments.

While in English, as in Latin, the word *sacrament* derives from the word for "holy" or "sacred," the Náhuatl word created for "sacrament" speaks more of the person. It is composed of three words: *celilia* (to receive) + *tla* (thing, object) + *te* (someone, a person). Thus, the Náhuatl word for "sacrament" was *tetlaceliliztli*, meaning to "receive something which is also a Someone."[26]

For the missionaries of Mexico after the apparition, maintaining this personal element in baptism was one of their great concerns. In one of the accounts of the many baptisms, this personal element was stressed, noting that the missionaries placed chrism on each person being baptized. And despite the added work, as one priest explained, he "felt in his heart something more joyful in baptizing them than others."[27]

This desire for Christ leads to a desire to live a Christian life, because only a life that has truth and love as its basis can bring closeness with Christ. The persistence of this desire was exemplified by the many Indians who had to travel great distances to be baptized, crossing over gorges and traveling through rough, mountainous terrain. Yet getting to a church or monastery where they could be baptized was not their only difficulty. Because there were so many Indians who wanted to receive the sacrament of baptism, often they would have to wait months before being baptized. In the convents of Guacachula and Tlaxcala, close to two thousand Indians were counted waiting in the courtyards, begging any missionary they saw to baptize them. This became such a problem that the friars of New Spain wrote to the pope in order to request permission to perform an abbreviated form of the baptismal ceremony.[28] The Franciscan missionary Friar Toribio recorded that in a short space of time close to nine million Indians received the sacrament of baptism.[29] Friar Juan de Torquemada, in his book *Monarquía Indiana*, informs us that "many thousands were baptized in one day."[30] In receiving baptism, the inhabitants of Mexico not only received Mary as their mother but also underwent through the process of the sacrament a spiritual rebirth. Their rebirth through Christ gave them a distinctive mother, both in Our Lady of Guadalupe and in the institution itself.

In addition to learning catechism and accepting the sacrament of baptism, the Indians often sought the sacrament of confession. As Friar Mendieta recalled:

> It happened that on the roads, hills and wilderness, one thousand, two thousand Indian men and women would follow the [friars] just to confess, leaving their homes and lands [completely unattended]. Many of them were pregnant women, some giving birth on the way, and almost all of them carrying their children on their backs. Others were old men and women who could hardly stand with their canes and [some were] even blind. . . . Many would take their wife and children and their small amount of food as if they were moving to another place. They might stay one or two months waiting for a confessor, or a place to confess.[31]

In this testimony, it is easy to see the hardships and persistence. But in comparison to the forms of confession practiced by the Aztecs, one may also see the way in which Christianity transformed the Indians' understanding of repentance—and forgiveness—as part of a continual conversion to Christ.

For the Aztecs, the goddess who tempted them to sin was the same goddess who could forgive them. Such forgiveness could only be granted at certain times, and the Aztec priest had to consult sources to be sure it was a proper time. Only once could a given sin be confessed and excused. Repeat offenses of the same sin were believed unpardonable, which led many to wait until very late in life before they would confess serious offenses. As Sahagún explained, only old men would confess great sins such as adultery, "from which fact we may deduce that they probably had greatly sinned in their youth but did not confess until they were old, but that they would continue sinning while young."[32] Yet once they converted to Christianity, the sacrament of confession became a significant and much desired element in the Aztecs' life in the Church.

Many aspects of Indian religous ritual had direct—if obviously different—analogs to Catholicism. Thus Our Lady of Guadalupe proposed a new way of life on Tepeyac. She offered to the Indians the fulfillment of their own culture, replacing violence with love as the solution to the problems of everyday life. Ever the loving mother, Our Lady requested the Tepeyac church be built at the bottom of the hill—the humble root, a place easily accessible to the passerby. As Fr. Peter John Cameron observes, "Our Lady of Guadalupe comes to us even in the midst of our idolatries,"[33] and there her presence as mother provides guidance, protection, and a home in which we are invited to enter into a new life, with Christ our Redeemer as our brother.

PART III

Unified in Dignity

VIII.

The Gift of Vocation

In the Church there is a diversity of ministry,
but a oneness of mission.

—PAUL VI, APOSTOLICAM ACTUOSITATEM[1]

THE VOCATION OF JUAN DIEGO

One of the striking facts about the first church built on Tepeyac is that it is almost impossible to separate the church's history from the life of Juan Diego himself. Shortly after the people of the town built the chapel in December 1531, Juan Diego requested permission from Zumárraga to live there, and a small room was attached to the chapel's east side. There, he soon found himself in the hub of Christian life. When he was not at Mass, deep in prayer, or sharing the apparition story with pilgrims, Juan Diego cared for the Virgin's chapel. One task he took upon himself was sweeping the floors, a great honor in Indian religious ritual, as the sixteenth-century missionary-historian Friar Mendieta wrote: "They have great reverence to all the temples and to all the things consecrated to God; even the principal elders take pride in sweeping the churches, maintaining the custom of their ancestors when they were pagans that, by sweeping the temples, they showed their devotion, even the important persons."[2] In this way, Juan Diego made of his life what had been an honor for his ancestors.

With Juan Diego's close connections to the Church and his reputation for eagerly speaking of God and Mary, it is understandable that some of the early paintings of Juan Diego depict him wearing the garb of the first missionaries to Mexico, the Franciscan brown habit, instead of Indian clothing.[3] For anyone familiar with the true situation of Indians regarding holy orders, this becomes rather extraordinary. Around the time of the apparition, Indians were barred from entering the priesthood; in fact, just four years before the apparition, three Indians had expressed a desire to become priests, but later word came back forbidding it.[4] Not until 1539 did the bishops accept literate Inidans and mestizos into minor orders.[5] Thus to depict Juan Diego in the Franciscan habit was in some ways an extraordinary expression of his extraordinary life. It placed his dedication to Christian life and evangelization, lived out within walking distance of his old home, on the level of the missionary friars who had given up everything and left their home continent in order to preach the Gospel and be a concrete witness of Christian life.

In a striking way, this points to the "oneness of mission" shared by all those in the Church: the call by God to holiness and to evangelization.[6] It is our "universal vocation."[7] However, although it may be poignant to depict Juan Diego in the Franciscan habit, not only is it historically inaccurate but it also overlooks the distinctiveness of Juan Diego's life and the "diversity of ministry" that is so vital to the Church—and to our world. The universal call to holiness and evangelization is lived out differently in each of our lives in what it is helpful to think of as complementary vocations—a vocation to the lay life, to the priesthood, to religious or consecrated life. In each of these, the person works toward holiness and the sharing of the Gospel in a distinct way defined by the unique opportunities of his or her way of life. Juan Diego sought Christ's love, and radiated Christ's love, precisely as a layman and a mediator between the old world and new.

This "oneness of mission" extends beyond the church walls, but sometimes it can be difficult to see how this is true. Consequently, lay men and women often view their lay vocation as the "default" vocation, and thus as less important. After all, it does not require seminary training or ordination, and except at marriage, there is rarely a definitive moment when the lay life is chosen or actively accepted. Living in the world, lay persons often engage in work and social interactions that have little or no overt connection to religious devotional practices. While the lay vocation is not a "religious" vocation in the clerical or monastic sense, religion still plays a vital part in it.

While in Rome attending the second session of the Second Vatican Council, Bishop Karol Wojtyla—who later became John Paul II—described the lay vocation in this way:

> If someone were to ask me what the role of the laity in the Church is, I [would] answer that it consists in completing the work of Christ, the Son of God, in the world and with the world's help. It consists in regaining the world, in all of its facets and manifestations, for the Eternal Father. On the road to this, however, lies an even higher aim: to regain man himself, in his humanity, for the Eternal Father.[8]

In their work, marriages, families, social life, and social interactions, lay men and women make their greatest transformations of society.

This role of lay witness is apparent in the tilma, an item that has some of the most beautiful uses in the indigenous culture—and also some of the most mundane ones. The tilma was an article of clothing bearing the indication of one's social status. It was also indispensable as a tool used to transport food and other goods, connecting it to the very life, work, and sustenance of the indigenous people. Used in the marriage ceremony, when the man's tilma was tied to the dress (*huipil*) of the woman, it symbolized the person in the bond of marriage. In Juan Diego's tilma, these various facets of everyday life are affirmed in their proper dignity as forums for witnessing to and connecting with God. In a special way, Juan Diego recognized the possibility of living a spiritually fulfilling life in the world, in whatever situation one is placed, when he encouraged Juan Bernardino to remain at his home in Tulpetlac so that his uncle could continue the type of life they had lived together. This is what Benedict XVI called "the truly great thing in Christianity, which does not dispense one from small, daily things but must not be concealed by them either," namely, "this ability to come into contact with God."[9] Witnessing to God even in the world, lay Christians offer God to the world. Transforming the world, lay Christians offer the world to God.

EUCHARISTIC PARISH

Speaking of the codex of the image, we can see how an *altepetl*-like flower represents a civilization. Joining this with the call to build a church, we see how this could have been understood as a new beginning, the establishment of a new civilization. The building of the church is not only symbolic in the indigenous historical and cultural context, where temples played a central role. In a very real way, the building of a church—specifically, the local church and its parish community—truly is the foundation and source for the building of a civilization of love.

In the codex, what is remarkable about this interpretation is that each of the flower clusters has unique elements that distinguish it from the others, and yet they all follow a certain model, continuing to maintain the *altepetl* shape. Some of the flowers have more little flowers on the top of the hill, others more leaves or more buds on the stems; some are positioned on the garment, while others are positioned on the Virgin's sleeves. That is, they bear the same resemblance not only to *a* civilization but to the *same* civilization with the same divine source, without losing their uniqueness and independence.

The elements symbolized by the tilma's codex come into a concrete synthesis in the parish. In the parish church, individuals (hearts with a face) are educated in Christ; coming to know Christ, they learn to recognize the face of Christ in themselves and in one another. In the parish, Christ's sacrifice is made truly present in the Eucharist; through receiving the Eucharist, the parish is transformed from being a collection of persons to a unity of persons, "a family of families"—relatives through the blood of Christ. Finally, through the Eucharist, the parish family receives the grace to look beyond its borders.

In the codex, all of these civilization glyphs are located around the central glyph, the four-petal flower indicative of divinity. Likewise, in the Church at large, people of all civilizations center on Christ. Today, this "catholic" (in the sense of universal) reality of the Church is made particularly apparent in the diversity within our parishes.

In his message for the eighty-fifth World Migration Day, John Paul II addressed the difficulties individuals and families face when they leave their homeland to settle elsewhere. He spoke of many needs migrants have, but in particular he spoke of the church: "The parish is the place where all the members of the community come together and interact. It makes visible . . . God's plan to call all people to the covenant established in Christ, without any exception or exclusion."[10] Called to become, individually, a spiritual center of worship for everyone, the parish is the place where the Church reaches out to the world. In the tangible witness offered by its parishioners—in their prayerful intercession, listening ears, open hearts, and willing gift of support and help—the parish manifests in concrete terms the universality and unifying power of God's love.

The church Our Lady asked to be built on Tepeyac was not simply to be another indigenous building. It was to be a place where she, like a magnet, could draw people to the presence of her Son in the Eucharist. The mission of building a church physically on Tepeyac hill, and to a greater extent the evangelization of his people, was Juan Diego's lasting contribution. The man sometimes painted in Franciscan robes was the New World corollary to St. Francis himself, who was instructed by Christ to "rebuild My church." While St. Francis rebuilt a small chapel in Assisi and had as a greater mission the role of messenger in the reevangelization of Christians in the Old World, Juan Diego was the messenger of first-time evangelization to those unfamiliar with Christ in the New World.

While the task of establishing the church was completed when Juan Diego successfully gained Zumárraga's approval, the mission of making the chapel a vibrant center of Catholic life filled Juan Diego's lifetime. Living at the hermitage with the image, Juan Diego found himself with many pilgrims coming to see the image and to hear of Mary's apparition. But many of these, we are told, came with their problems. Just as Mary asked Juan Diego to intercede for her, to bring her desire to the spiritual father within the Church on earth, Friar Zumárraga, so many pilgrims came to Juan

Diego to intercede for them to our spiritual mother in heaven. And for hundreds of years those who have come to ask the favor of Our Lady of Guadalupe have received at the foot of her image her greatest gift, her Son in the Eucharist.

As at the Hermitage or the Basilica of Our Lady of Guadalupe, the parish too is ultimately a spiritual community founded upon Christ's unifying love offered in the Eucharist. As Pope Benedict XVI writes in his first encyclical, "'Worship' itself, Eucharistic communion, includes the reality both of being loved and of loving others in turn. A Eucharist which does not pass over into the concrete practice of love is intrinsically fragmented."[11] Coming to the Eucharist, each Catholic receives Christ—and the grace to live more fully the life of Christ.

If the Church is to be the center and source of a civilization, it depends on the parish, the "family of families," that extends beyond itself to touch the lives of others. For this reason, too, shortly before becoming pope, Karol Wojtyla declared the need for families to perform service together, especially within the parish. "It is not sufficient merely to visit the sick, this should be made into a 'family' custom—but within the scope of the larger family of families which is the parish."[12] Works of charity, unity, and truth are purified and find their true expression in the parish. In its people, the civilization of love is rooted in faith, and in their concrete community, the parish.

UNIVERSAL VOCATION

In 1666, another great investigation into the Guadalupan events was conducted, in which numerous Indian elders recounted what they knew of Juan Diego and the apparition. Many of those testifying were very old, putting them within a generation of the apparition, and the details they recounted about his life, practices, and demeanor were passed down to them largely by word of mouth, making what was remembered and told a gauge of what truly struck the early Indian witnesses in the first place: the distinctiveness of his Christian life. In the many texts describing Juan Diego's life and holiness, the accounts of his practices and attitude toward others express the vitally important fact that his relationship with Christ dramatically changed the way he lived. One particularly moving testimony was given by Marcos Pacheco, who gave an account of the event as told to him by his aunt. He recalled how she was so impressed with Juan Diego's holiness that she would say to her nephew, "May God make you like Juan Diego and his uncle."[13] Greeting the Mexican people during his 2002 trip to Mexico for the canonization of Juan Diego, John Paul II echoed these words, saying: "May God make us like Juan Diego!"[14] But why look to Juan Diego's life at all?

Quite frankly, to ignore the saints is to ignore the work of God's love and to deny a vital part of our relationship to Christ as our Brother. To be a child of God means that not only do we have a fraternal relationship with Christ, but we have a fraternal relationship with all other children of God, both those living now and those who "have gone before us marked with the sign of faith."[15] To accept the reality of the communion of saints—that there is a special bond between the saints in heaven and us on earth, enabled by God's love and our love of God—is to accept the power of God's love to extend beyond an individual human person.

Our Lady of Guadalupe's presence makes manifest in a dramatic way how death does not end our vocation to witness to the saving work of Christ. Learning about the saints, we open our eyes to the manifold ways God makes his love apparent in our lives, as well as to the manifold ways we respond to God's love. That is, looking at the lives of the saints, we are inspired and informed of the true nature of holiness and the various forms that it can take. Pope Benedict XVI writes of the saints:

> Their human and spiritual experience shows that holiness is not a luxury, it is not a privilege for the few, an impossible goal for an ordinary person; it is actually the common destiny of all men called to be children of God, the universal vocation of all the baptized.[16]

The fact is, the Church does not canonize a person simply because the Virgin Mary appears to him or her. The Church has recognized Juan Diego as a saint because of his holiness after the apparition. His relationship with Christ continued to be the foremost desire in his life. How Juan Diego responded to this call to holiness not only affected him spiritually but also changed his life, and it changed the lives of those around him as well. This type of witness—this following of Christ's call to holiness—can change the face of our civilization.

THE NEW EVANGELIZATION

As an indigenous layman, Juan Diego was a new kind of witness for the evangelization in the New World. In a way, the full importance of Juan Diego's unique life after the apparition can be understood in a new dimension, in terms of his vocation as a layman, a sort of lay pioneer in a place where the majority of his people were not Catholic and none of the Indians was a priest or missionary.[17] With the Church in Mexico so young and in such a precarious position, those lay converts needed then, as we do now, reminders of the importance of the laity in serving Christ in union with the Church hierarchy. Juan Diego's lived witness after the apparition was an inspiration to generations, as is made clear by the 1666 investigation. In the same way, each of us is called to live a life of heroic witness, whatever our circumstances, evangelizing those with whom we come in contact. Our role in the new evangelization is to make present and relevant the message of the Gospel—the message of faith, hope, and charity—in a culture that has often become deaf to its message. This requires our consistent living of the Gospel message in our parishes, in our homes, and in our public lives.

On the feast of Our Lady of Guadalupe in the Jubilee Year 2000, Cardinal Ratzinger gave an address to catechists entitled "The New Evangelization: Building the Civilization of Love" in which he said:

> God cannot be made known with words alone. One does not really know a person if one knows about this person secondhandedly. To proclaim God is to introduce to the relation with God: to teach how to pray. Prayer is faith in action. And only by experiencing life with God does the evidence of his existence appear.[18]

It is impossible to introduce others to someone one does not know, and it is impossible to know Christ without at the same time loving him. Juan Diego was an effective messenger because his prayerfulness enabled him to call others to God and to show them how to recognize God's presence in their lives. His closeness to Our Lady and her Son provided such a strong witness that his intercession was frequently sought, and is still sought today.

Closeness to Christ is not always easy. The parish is not just a collection of individuals and individual families, but a living body. Of course, the reality of this community is not always clear or apparent in our parish, since "parish life is especially related to the strengths and weaknesses and needs of the families that make it up."[19] Like a family, one parish or another may become fragmented. Lack of concern, cooperation, or involvement—any ailment that can plague a family—can also affect a parish. Often, when individuals or families are affected by these, the parish is also affected, and this may lead to further discouragement in participation and interest in parish life. We may not care for every aspect of a particular parish experience: we may not like the music or the church architecture, or perhaps the homilies leave us untouched; maybe we even feel isolated or out of place. But we must remember two things. First, the Eucharist is the central and unifying element that supersedes any cosmetic issues we may see. Second, we should remember that we have an integral role to play in the parish. Its vitality depends in no small measure on the vitality breathed into it by each parishioner.

Wherever we find them, human faults and imperfections are nothing compared to God's gift of himself to us. It is this gift— the Eucharist—that truly binds us together and infuses all other parish activities with meaning.

Speaking of the future of the Church, Cardinal Ratzinger once said that "we don't have such urgent need" for reformers. What the Church really needs, he added, are "people who are inwardly seized by Christianity, who experience it as joy and hope, who have thus become lovers. And these we call saints."[20]

To be "inwardly seized by Christianity," however, requires that we live with a well-formed conscience and an awareness of our vocation as Christians, which in turn require that we be authentic in our treatment of others—that we treat them with the charity and dignity due every human person. And the truth of their own dignity needs to be spoken often. This dignity should be universally defended in every culture, however diverse and however seemingly distant from God.

At the Basilica of Our Lady of Guadalupe, John Paul II suggested that the future of our country and our continent depends on this:

> We must rouse the consciences of men and women with the Gospel, in order to highlight their sublime vocation as children of God. This will inspire them to build a better America. As a matter of urgency, we must stir up a new springtime of holiness on the Continent so that action and contemplation will go hand in hand.[21]

In the new evangelization, no pope has laid such dramatic expectations of evangelization for a continent at the feet of just a few individuals, such as the first Franciscan missionary friars; but at the feet of the laity as a whole, they have. In words addressed to bishops from the United States, John Paul II made this imperative clear, declaring that "now is above all the hour of the lay faithful," and that the success of this new evangelization depends in large part upon the laity "being true leaven in every corner of life."[22] The newness of the "new evangelization" is how it is "new in its ardor, methods and expression."[23]

This is the importance of the Virgin's chosen description of God, expressed in the words of the Indians and in the image's codex. This was in part the distinctiveness of Juan Diego: he lived a distinctively Christian life in a new way, literally living near the ruins of his people's previous religious aspirations. Not only is Juan Diego a reminder of the transformative power of witness in the evangelization of people who had never met Christ, but he is a model for us today in the new evangelization of those who have met Christ but don't know him as they should.

IX.

The Face of the Hidden Christ

May the Continent of Hope also be the Continent of Life! This is our cry:
life with dignity for all! . . . Dear brothers and sisters, the time has come to
banish once and for all from the Continent every attack against life.

—JOHN PAUL II, HOMILY AT THE BASILICA
OF OUR LADY OF GUADALUPE[1]

NEW LIFE

For us today, a pilgrimage of children to the Guadalupan basilica
may seem cute or quaint. For the children walking to the Virgin's
Hermitage in 1544, however, it was perhaps the most concrete
expression of how Christianity had changed their civilization. In
that year, Mexico suffered one of its greatest plagues and one of the
longest droughts in its history.[2] Historically for the Aztecs, a
drought not only devastated crops but also could be devastating to
families. While adults were sacrificed to the god of war, children
were sacrificed to the god of rain, Tlaloc. For example, an excava-
tion of the Templo Mayor revealed a fifteenth-century burial site

dating from a drought with the remains of at least forty-two young children who were sacrificed. Additionally, because it was considered good if the victims cried at the sacrifice, great care was taken over choosing the victims, and the bodies of the chosen children show a range of disabilities and prior painful sicknesses ranging from toothaches to bone diseases.[3] But in 1544, we find a serious and dramatic manifestation of change from a culture of death to a culture of life, when instead of a sacrifice of children, a pilgrimage of children ages six and seven processed to the adobe Guadalupe Hermitage to pray for relief—a great and early testament of trust in the Virgin of Guadalupe as the Mother of Hope and the Mother of Life.[4]

THE EXPECTANT VIRGIN

All Marian apparitions are extraordinary and unique, and the Guadalupan apparition is no exception. There is the extraordinary relevance of the Virgin's image and codex to the Mesoamericans. There is the enduring image on the tilma that is a kind of continuous apparition. But one of the most significant aspects of the Guadalupan image is its depiction of the Blessed Virgin as a pregnant woman and Christ as neither a young boy nor a grown man but a helpless child hidden and alive within the womb.

In this, the image of Our Lady of Guadalupe may be understood as an image of the Visitation, introducing the people of the New World to Christ in a way similar to his introduction to the people of ancient Israel. Reading the Gospel of Luke, we find the first revelations of Christ's identity months before his birth in Bethlehem, while he was still a child in his mother's womb. When Mary (pregnant with Christ) visits her cousin Elizabeth (pregnant with St. John the Baptist), Elizabeth recognizes the specialness of

Mary's pregnancy, saying, "Blessed are you among women, and blessed is the fruit of your womb."[5] Elizabeth goes further, identifying what makes Mary and Christ uniquely blessed: "Who am I that the mother of my Lord should visit me?"[6] Just as Mary is addressed as a mother before the birth of her Son, Christ is recognized as Lord before his birth. And just as Mary is identified by her relationship to Christ, so Elizabeth identifies Christ by his relationship to herself and to all of us.

Importantly, both Christ and Mary are acknowledged in these vital roles at a time when Christ is most helpless and vulnerable. And the next time Christ is most vulnerable, at his crucifixion, Mary is named our mother. In these moments of extreme vulnerability as a child and as a suffering man near death, Christ experiences and reveals a profound part of what it means to be human. Hans Urs von Balthasar writes:

> The developing human being . . . is intrinsically ordered to "being *with*" other persons, so much so that he awakens to self-consciousness only through other human beings, normally through his mother. In the mother's smile, it dawns on him that there is a world into which he is accepted and in which he is welcome, and it is in this primordial experience that he becomes aware of himself for the first time.[7]

What is obvious physically about the human person is that the body is made for life: lungs are created to inhale the air that is so necessary for life, while the heart pumps the blood that is so necessary for life. What is profound is how our awareness of our ultimate purpose in life depends on other people. "Being with" others leads us to understand ourselves in relation to each other, and through other people we can come to understand the truths about ourselves as individuals and as a society. We are made aware that each of us was created out of love, for love. If we are cut off from love, or if we cut ourselves off from love, our life becomes unintelligible. God's calling us to love—our vocation to love—is made apparent by the love and presence of other persons.

Our dependence on others and their dependence on us may effectively reveal love. Using pregnancy as an example, Benedict XVI describes how our "being with" others also necessitates a "being for" others: "This *being-with* compels the being of the other—that is, the mother—to become a *being-for*."[8] And after birth, children become aware of their mother's care, her "being for" them. From the earliest stages of infancy, every mother and father watches their child naturally begin to discern for himself or herself what is around, but especially what exists "for" him or her, what persons or objects communicate some element of care or happiness. As the child grows, the child learns to discern the difference between a relationship with an object (a relationship of utility) and a relationship with a person—a relationship between two freedoms. Uncoincidentally, as children learn the limits of their physical freedom, they also learn the moral limits to their freedom: "I must live my freedom not out of competition but in a spirit of mutual support."[9]

It is easy to see how a child must exist as "being with" another person in order to survive, and thus how a child depends on the "being with" and "being for" of the parents. This observation becomes especially clear looking at an unborn child. Yet important to keep in mind is the fact that "the child in the mother's womb is simply a very graphic depiction of the essence of human existence in general."[10] The human person's need for others applies as much to the physically mature as it does to a child. Although a person can be isolated socially and distanced geographically from other people, no person can survive for long without entrusting himself or herself to others. Absolute autonomy cannot exist.

Thus, in a world where absolute autonomy is construed as freedom, and freedom as happiness, it is no surprise that people often see their attempts at happiness thwarted. The problem is not in equating happiness and freedom, but in equating happiness and freedom with autonomy. Absolute autonomy is more than just impossible; it contradicts the very nature of what it means to be human. Rather, as Thomas Merton once explained, true happiness is achieved through freedom, while freedom reaches its highest expression in a profound sharing of ourselves with others:

> A happiness that is sought for ourselves alone can never be found: for a happiness that is diminished by being shared is not big enough to make us happy. . . . True happiness is found in unselfish love, a love which increases in proportion as it is shared. There is no end to the sharing of love, and, therefore, the potential happiness of such love is without limit. Infinite sharing is the law of God's inner life. He has made the sharing of ourselves the law of our own being, so that it is in loving others that we best love ourselves.[11]

"Being for" others betters not only their circumstances and person but also our own. It helps us to better become what we are. While true love is always selfless love, it is not thankless love: with it, we work to realize our own dignity as made in the image of the Trinity, the dignity of being placed first and foremost within a communion of persons, a communion of love, the dignity of being something God called "very good" from the beginning of creation.[12] Even more, as John Paul II notes, "while each day of creation concludes with the observation: 'God saw that it was good,' after the creation of man on the sixth day, it is said that 'God saw everything that he had made and behold, it was very good.'"[13] Humanity's goodness extends beyond itself.

HOPE IN ACTION

Granted, it can be difficult to see this dignity. A culture of life is more than a privilege for prosperous times. Even in the face of dramatic, decimating death, such as Mexico experienced at various times after the apparition, people are still able to build a culture of life. A culture of life respects life for what it is, not for what hardship and suffering frame it to be. A culture of life does not deny the reality of death. A culture of life deals with death as a serious but not ultimate principle. In fact, one of the most strikingly human elements conveyed in the apparition account is Juan Diego's grasp of the reality of death. As a man in his fifties, he certainly knew many people who had died, including his own wife, María Lucía. He had likewise lived during the smallpox epidemic that killed millions of Indians. And then, in a windfall of life-changing events, his uncle Juan Bernardino became ill with a swift and even visually grotesque plague. In his words to the Virgin, we glimpse how powerfully this impending death colored Juan Diego's view of life: "because in reality for this [death] we were born, we who came to await the task of our death."[14] This statement, perhaps more than any other in Juan Diego's dialogue with the Virgin, resonates with contemporary views of the person; and the Virgin's response—"Am I not here, I who have the honor to be your mother"—tests our understanding of the person and points us toward hope.[15]

The truth is that "God is not satisfied with finding his creation good; he wants it also to find itself good."[16] Each of us makes the dignity of God's creation known. While the dignity of the other inspires love, through love we open ourselves up to the innumerable riches of that dignity; through love we show this dignity to others. By loving others, we lead others to recognize their dignity and to live according to it. In his homily at the beginning of his papacy, Benedict XVI spoke of this active role in helping others to see this truth about themselves:

> The purpose of our lives is to reveal God to men. And only where God is seen does life truly begin. Only when we meet the living God in Christ do we know what life is. We are not some casual and meaningless product of evolution. Each of us is the result of a thought of God. Each of us is willed, each of us is loved, each of us is necessary.[17]

The fact that Benedict XVI's first two encyclicals have dealt with love and hope reflects how these words continue to be the measure and guide of his life as pope. These words, too, can be a measure and guide for us in our lives if we ask ourselves each day, "Am I living in a way that makes Christ's presence apparent? Am I 'being with' and 'being for' people in such a way that they are encouraged to recognize and live up to the beautiful dignity that is theirs?"

This revelation of the dignity of the human person was one of the great gifts of the Guadalupan event for both the Indians and the Spaniards. On one hand, the Indians suffered from a profound depreciation of their dignity through their own culture. Having no knowledge of the Gospel, the culture of the natives of Mexico had taken even valid concepts to terryfiying conclusions.[18] Men, women, and children had their hearts torn out above a sacrificial altar, and wars were waged to acquire more victims so that, as one Aztec chief explained, "each time and whenever . . . our god wishes to eat and feast, we may go . . . as one who goes to the market to buy something to eat."[19] Although pregnancy and birth were largely honored, an Aztec "lecture" given to a newborn child shows clearly how violence was perceived as the means to most ends—no matter how noble.

My very beloved child, very tender . . . this house where you have been born is just a nest, a shelter . . . your own land is another, it is promised elsewhere, which is the field where wars are made, where battles are engaged: you are sent for it. Your role and job is war, your role is to give the sun the blood of your enemy to drink and to give the earth . . . the bodies of your enemies to eat. Your own land, your inheritance, and your father are the house of the Sun. . . . Hopefully you will deserve and be worthy of dying in this place and receiving in it a flowered death.[20]

While the Indians had an understanding of the importance of sacrifice—and of its redemptive power—the manner in which they expressed this—through human sacrifice—was, of course, not one which was in keeping with human dignity. And after the conquest of Mexico, the Indians' dignity as persons was denied outright in the maltreatment they received from many of the Europeans. While affecting the Indians, these injustices at the same time impoverished the Spaniards, who reduced themselves to mere "things," moved not by truth or goodness but by the whims of greed and corrupt passion.

In the context of such abuse, the Virgin's response to Juan Diego's morbidness—her declaration of her motherhood—can seem a surprising counterargument to make. On the contrary, however, by speaking of her protection, her care, her nourishment, her constant being with and for us, the Virgin awakens Juan Diego to his own humanity. Through love, the Virgin puts death in perspective, thereby revealing the Marian dimension of the distinctiveness of Christian hope. Spiritually and metaphorically, there is a sense that this life is all a pregnancy. We are all waiting to be born out of this life, this life of transformation, of maturation, of becoming what we are meant to become, of becoming more aware of and sensitive to God's love. The more we become aware of and sensitive to God's love, the more we become aware of and sensitive to God's love for others, and thus our love for others grows as well. As Benedict XVI writes:

> Hope in a Christian sense is always hope for others as well. It is an active hope, in which we struggle to prevent things moving towards the "perverse end." It is an active hope also in the sense that we keep the world open to God. Only in this way does it continue to be a truly human hope.[21]

In the same way that our love of God reaches out to others, the Virgin's love of God and of each individual person reaches out to everyone. This movement of love to embrace the whole and to never exhaust itself provides another consolation and reason to trust in the Virgin's motherhood. Juan Diego can trust Our Lady of Guadalupe specifically because her motherhood is not closed in on itself but is open to all; she is a mother who rejects no one.

For this reason, too, the church on Tepeyac was requested not as a private place of prayer for Juan Diego but as a place of prayer for all, a "little home" open to all so that every person has a place to encounter Christ, not only for the Virgin's love of Christ, but specifically for her love for us: "Because truly I am honored to be your compassionate Mother . . . [T]here truly will I hear their cry, their sadness, in order to remedy, to cure all their various troubles, their miseries, their pains."[22] In a very real sense, "prayer is hope in action,"[23] and the Church a place where through the Eucharist and through prayer we encounter Christ, the ultimate transformative hope that saves.

HOPE FOR OTHERS

What is more, the Church is a place where through prayer "we undergo those purifications by which we become open to God and are prepared for the service of our fellow human beings . . . and thus we become ministers of hope for others."[24] That is, prayer leads us to charity, to the pursuit of "all serious and upright human conduct [which] is hope in action."[25]

This "hope in action" is ultimately shown in our response to one another. As Paul VI wrote, "charity must be as it were an active hope for what others can become with the help of our fraternal support. The mark of its genuineness is found in a joyful simplicity, whereby all strive to understand what each one has at heart."[26] Responding in this way can be effective only if our response is guided by the truth: the truth about who the person is and the reality of the situation. In hope, we perceive God as the beneficent giver that he is, and so in hope we at the same time perceive others as the recipients of God's graces and gifts; reflecting his merciful and generous giving to each person, we mercifully and generously give ourselves. Addressing members at a conference on the aftermath of abortion and divorce, Benedict XVI explained this, saying, "The Gospel of love and life is also always the *Gospel of mercy,* which is addressed to the actual person and sinner that we are, to help us up after any fall and to [help us] recover from any injury."[27] We truly see another person only if we appreciate that person in all his or her uniqueness and dignity; it is to understand not only what a person has done—for we have all sinned—but what a person is and by whom that person is loved.

In the Guadalupan event, this ethic of active hope and care for the person is shown especially in how the Virgin acted toward Juan Diego when he was faced with his uncle's death. Rather than expressing anger or frustration that Juan Diego disregarded her instructions, the Virgin met him where he was and showed compassionate concern for his situation. She was interested in him personally, asking: "My youngest son, what's going on? Where are you going? Where are you headed?"[28] There are moments when difficulty obscures the truth and thus obscures the right course of action. There are moments when as a culture we realize that subtle motives and fears have made inhuman practices common and even forced custom itself down a path that few had envisioned or desired. These are moments when we must ask ourselves and each other, "Where are you headed?" These are questions that must be asked because the answers may surprise us.

Although God and Our Lady meet us where we are, our society and peers often do not—even to the point of creating a great silence about the facts of abortion and its aftermath. Often it even appears that too much time is wasted condemning the person, with so little time spent caring. With this, we are reminded of how our ways are unfortunately not always God's ways:

> Christ is not a healer in the manner of the world. In order to heal us, he does not remain outside the suffering that is experienced; he eases it by coming to dwell within the one stricken by illness, to bear it and live it with him. Christ's presence comes to break the isolation which pain induces. Man no longer bears his burden alone: as a suffering member of Christ, he is conformed to Christ in his self-offering to the Father, and he participates, in him, in the coming to birth of the new creation.[29]

We too must meet people as God does: where they are, rather than where we would like them to be. By reaffirming all persons, we must be the voice and helping hand of truth and love. Financially, love costs us nothing, but gives a part of ourselves. If we truly recognize the face of Christ in the poor and disadvantaged, in the unborn, in the worried faces of mothers and fathers who, like Christ in Gethsemane, feel abandoned and betrayed, we realize that we have more to offer than advice. Finding ourselves already a part of a community—our neighborhood, workplace, school, or parish—we realize that we already have a relationship with this parent or this peer or this child. We have to reach out when difficulties in life—whether circumstantial hardship or degradation—obscure the truth about the human person, about our brothers and sisters entrusted to our care.

CARRYING CHRIST

When all we see around us are the weaknesses of human love, it is easy to lose hope and to believe that perhaps our desires for love and happiness exceed what is possible for us. To think like this, however, would be one of the greatest self-deceptions, for it would be to betray our deepest aspirations and to live as if God did not exist. While this is a very human temptation, it is especially a temptation for our time. Looking over the course of human history, we have seen some of the worst in ourselves. But at the same time, we find profound revelations of faith, hope, and love. We find that whenever people open themselves up to the reality of God, our greatest failures are less decisive: they are no longer the only reality, nor the most important part of reality. Human love in light of divine love can reach its true potential and goal: the perfection of love, hence the perfection of man.

Giving ourselves to others in "active hope" shares a part of ourselves with them, and at the same time it is an opportunity for them to share with us. We share our talents, our joys, our time, and our attention, but we also share our sufferings. We share in the sufferings of others. When Our Lady of Guadalupe first introduced herself to Juan Diego, she told him how she was the mother of God, using the Náhuatl word *inantzin*, but when she referred specifically to her role as mother to him and to us, she called herself *nohuacantzin*; here, there is one important addition, *nohuac*, meaning "compassionate." Etymologically, the English word *compassion* derives from the Latin *compassio*, meaning "to suffer together" (*com* meaning "together" and *passio* from the verb "to suffer"). This compassion, this "suffering with" others, is possible through love and supremely modeled in Christ. Christ suffered and Christ liberated. His liberation was wrought precisely through his suffering with us. Like Christ himself, who welcomed our sufferings into his very body, the Virgin suffers with us as well. It is a fundamental way that we express our nearness to Christ in our attentiveness to the concerns, sufferings, and pain of others. It is how we carry the triumphant Christ to others, and at the same time how we receive the suffering Christ from them.

To see the reality of divine love requires something from God and from us: it requires his love, which is always given, and our reception of that love. It requires that we first trust in his love, that we give ourselves over to this love, so that in time our words and thoughts and hearts may be made one with the words and thoughts and heart of the Psalmist:

> *O Lord, hear my voice when I call;*
> *Have mercy and answer.*
> *Of you my heart has spoken: "Seek his face."*
> *It is your face, O Lord, that I seek;*
> *Hide not your face.*
>
> . . .
>
> *Do not abandon or forsake me,*
> *O God my help!*

Though father and mother forsake me,
The Lord will receive me.

. . .

Hope in him, hold firm and take heart.
Hope in the Lord!"[30]

Hope in God's love calls us out of ourselves in order to seek the face of God; it opens us to care about the day-to-day realities of our lives. We hope in God, in the fact that his love is something real for us today. More than that, hope in God gives us renewed energy and hope in others; it lets us see them, failures and all, but still love them, still believe in the dignity they have and the perfection to which they are called. It helps us carry Christ to them, to see Christ in them, and to receive Christ from them.

X.

The Christian Hemisphere

Not only in Central and South America, but in North America as well, the Virgin of Guadalupe is venerated as Queen of all America.

—JOHN PAUL II, ECCLESIA IN AMERICA[1]

THE CHURCH IN AMERICA

When the Knights of Columbus sponsored a tour of a relic of Juan Diego's tilma in 2003, Our Lady of Guadalupe's role as mother of all in the Americas became very clear. In city after city, crowds of tens of thousands of people came to venerate Our Lady of Guadalupe. What was most striking was not the number of people but the number of nationalities and ethnicities represented in each gathering. From Denver to Dallas and from La Crosse to Los Angeles, people of Mexican origin and people with no connection to Mexico whatsoever prayed side by side to the Virgin of Guadalupe.

During this tour, as the outpouring of devotion to Our Lady from the laity showed, nowhere is the laity's mission more eagerly embraced than in the American hemisphere. Here, the faith was transmitted—recently—from person to person and from family member to family member. Here, a layman, Juan Diego, became the single most important evangelist of the New World, and perhaps in the history of Christianity. But here and now there is one last question that must be answered: What does faith in this God give us?

This question, posed by Benedict XVI to the bishops at Aparecida in his first apostolic visit to the Western Hemisphere, is the perennial question about the distinctiveness of Christian life. For the Indians of Colonial Mexico, the answer seemed unintelligible, as the preached goodness of Christian life was obscured by encounters with sinful Christians. For the Indians and the Spaniards, and for us in the Western Hemisphere, we can find the answer clearly in Our Lady of Guadalupe, as she exemplifies the transformative power of God's love—a love that made her his mother, that fueled her sinless life, that brought her, transformed again, to make his love present at Tepeyac, transforming Juan Diego into a messenger, a man of church and charity, and eventually into a saint. To the bishops of the Americas gathered in Aparecida, Benedict XVI expressed this gift of Christian transformation in this way:

> Faith in this God . . . gives us a family, the universal family of God in the Catholic Church. Faith releases us from the isolation of the "I," because it leads us to communion: the encounter with God is, in itself and as such, an encounter with our brothers and sisters, an act of convocation, of unification, of responsibility towards the other and towards others. In this sense, the preferential option for

the poor is implicit in the Christological faith in the God who became poor for us, so as to enrich us with his poverty.[2]

Today, we must keep this question constantly foremost, for only if our faith informs our actions, only if we live a distinctively Christian life, can our actions clearly speak the answer to others in a universal language and give the world the infallible hope it needs, a hope that cannot be found either in an individual alone or in humanity as a whole.

For this reason, a decade ago the bishops of the hemisphere met at the Synod of Bishops for America and invited all of us living in the hemisphere to rethink who we are as *Americans*:

> We believe that we are one community; and, although America comprises many nations, cultures and languages, there is so much that links us together and so many ways in which each of us affects the lives of our neighbors.[3]

That meeting itself was an excellent model of cooperation among the bishops of the Americas. But the challenge to the Church of the Americas was a challenge to all the baptized. As Pope John Paul II wrote in *Ecclesia in America,* "The renewal of the Church in America will not be possible without the active presence of the laity. Therefore, they are largely responsible for the future of the Church."[4] The question is what Catholics—lay and clergy alike—can do to advance the promise of *Ecclesia in America*. For this promise is made increasingly urgent with each passing day.

The fact is, this promise for renewal of the Church in America, articulated in *Ecclesia in America,* is based upon the reality that our unity in the sacramental life of the Church transcends every national border and joins us in a way that must have both profound and practical consequences. Speaking of the Church, Cardinal Ratzinger noted that our unity and thus our vitality come through the uniqueness of our unity and vitality as a Church:

> The Church is not an apparatus; she is not simply an institution; neither is she only one of the usual sociological entities. She is a person. She is a Woman. She is a Mother. She is alive. The Marian understanding of the Church is the strongest and most decisive contrast with the concept of a purely organizational and bureaucratic Church. We cannot make the Church; we must *be* the Church. It is only in the measure in which faith, above and beyond doing, forms our being, that we *are* Church and the Church is in us. And it is only in being Marian that we become Church. Also at the beginning, the Church was not made, but born. She was born when the *fiat* emerged from the soul of Mary. This is the most profound desire of the Council: that the Church is reawakened in our souls. Mary shows us the way.[5]

Precisely because Mary is the archetypal believer, she is also the archetype of the Church. In the Americas, we have the particular example in the figure of Our Lady of Guadalupe, providing a model for us as both believers and as the Church in America.

Although during these centuries she has come to symbolize many things, today in light of *Ecclesia in America* hers is a message of unity—she is the spiritual mother we all share, perfectly encul- turated, a symbol of the "catholic" aspect of a Church where all are full members and all are welcome as equal heirs to the kingdom of God. As John Paul II wrote in *Ecclesia in America*:

> The appearance of Mary to the native Juan Diego on the hill of Tepeyac in 1531 had a decisive effect on evangelization. Its

influence greatly overflows the boundaries of Mexico, spreading to the whole Continent. America, which historically has been, and still is, a melting-pot of peoples, has recognized in the *mestiza* face of the Virgin of Tepeyac, "in Blessed Mary of Guadalupe, an impressive example of a perfectly enculturated evangelization." Consequently, not only in Central and South America, but in North America as well, the Virgin of Guadalupe is venerated as Queen of all America.[6]

The unity of the Christians of this hemisphere—with Guadalupe at its center—continued throughout the twentieth century as well. It was at the Basilica of Our Lady of Guadalupe that the flags of twenty nations were sent in tribute in 1941, and where forty-five members of the American Hierarchy, led by Archbishop Cantwell of Los Angeles, pledged "devotion and fealty" to the "Virgin of the Americas."[7] In 1961, the basilica was also the site of a congress held during the international Marian year, and where in 1962 President John F. Kennedy insisted on attending Mass during his visit to Mexico. Just as Our Lady of Guadalupe has been the center and motivation for such historic hemispheric unity, so she should remain as we discuss issues that affect the Americas today. Her patronage of churches and families throughout the hemisphere goes back hundreds of years, and yet today she affords us a new starting point to reconsider our cultures, our methods of evangelization, our life as a country, a continent, and a Church.

Our collective American continent is one on which we can find devotion to Our Lady of Guadalupe everywhere. In the northernmost American country, Canada, she has a prominent place in the Shrine of St. Anne du Beaupré in Quebec. In the southernmost American country, Argentina, she has a basilica in her honor near the town of Santa Fe. It is not too much to say that in every country of the Americas, Our Lady of Guadalupe is mother not only in her title, Empress of the Americas, but by adoption as well. She is the spiritual glue that holds together a continent that, though diverse in language and culture, shares in common—in every country—the experience of baptism.

In this, Our Lady of Guadalupe—a woman of enculturation— can play a vital role in shaping our new culture. Our Lady of Guadalupe presented to the Spanish and Indians alike a model of enculturation and cultural dialogue. Neither exclusively Spanish nor exclusively Indian, she appeared as a mestiza—a woman of both cultures, who transcended any cultural divide and called the Europeans and Native Americans alike to her Son. She came to two cultures that had recently been at war, and called them to overcome their differences and join a common cause: the evangelization of the Americas and, in this way, the building of a new civilization.

Our future as the "continent of baptized Christians" requires that we—whatever our ethnic or national backgrounds—likewise respond to this message and overcome our differences in order to build a hemisphere that can truly be called a civilization of love.[8] As Pope Benedict XVI said in his first encyclical, *Deus caritas est*: "To say that we love God becomes a lie if we are closed to our neighbor or hate him altogether."[9] This is the message of the mestiza Virgin of Guadalupe as well, but at a more profound level. We are more than neighbors; we are all children of God, regardless of ethnic or national heritage.

When Our Lady of Guadalupe appeared to Juan Diego, there was no shortage of distrust between the Native Americans and the Spaniards. Similarly today, there is no shortage of distrust based on different cultures or nationalities. Perhaps one of the biggest hurdles to overcome is the fear by many in the United States of Hispanic immigration. Of all people, Catholics should have no trouble remembering that the same fears were harbored against the Irish and Italian immigrants of the nineteenth and early twentieth centuries. Few today would contest the contributions made by those immigrants to the United States, who not only assimilated but breathed dynamic life into the Catholic Church and helped to make it the largest single religious denomination in the United States.

For if our continental history is a shared one, so too is our future. David Rieff pointed out in the *New York Times Magazine* in December 2006 just how interwoven our collective future as "American" Catholics is, noting: "Nationally, [in the United States] Hispanics account for 39 percent of the Catholic population . . . since 1960 they have accounted for 71 percent of new Catholics in the United States."[10] At a time when Church attendance is faltering across Europe, it is stronger in this hemisphere and strongest in Latin American countries and in those places in the United States that Hispanic immigrants call home.

For Catholics in the United States, immigration from Latin America brings a unique benefit. Hispanic immigration brings with it the promise of a revitalization of our parishes through a rich tradition of spiritual devotion. It is up to the Catholics already in the United States to provide a rich spiritual environment that will feed the needs of these new arrivals. As these immigrants breathe new life into parish communities, it is our job to help them assimilate into our parishes and communities, as our parents and grandparents did, and to help them to live their faith with support from all Catholics.

ACROSS THE BORDERS

A crucial part of this future is the cooperation between Catholics in the United States and Mexico and, by extension, the rest of the continent. From the halls of government to the parish pews, the willingness and ability of Catholics to respond to the "perfectly enculturated" call of the archetypal American Christian, Our Lady of Guadalupe, and to build bridges between those in the United States and those in Mexico and throughout the hemisphere will shape our future. This is a special responsibility of Catholics in the United States—especially leaders in business and finance. As John Paul II wrote to Christian workers, "The culture of workers . . . must remain a culture of solidarity"[11]—a solidarity of equality, a solidarity that restores to each person the dignity of their work by recognizing the dignity of the human person. Likewise, the movement toward greater transparency in Mexican government and politics gives Catholics in the United States as well as those in Mexico an unprecedented opportunity for cooperation in economic and social reform.

This would not be the first time that Catholics of the United States have taken a leadership role to help their neighbors to the south. During the 1920s Mexican persecution, as thousands of Mexicans died with the words *Viva Cristo Rey, viva la Virgen de Guadalupe* on their lips, those north of the border did not ignore their plight, and voices such as the Knights of Columbus helped Catholics in the United States successfully influence their government to take an active interest in the persecution. Moreover, when up to a million Mexican refugees fled north, American Catholics opened their arms to those displaced by the violence. Seminaries were built so that young Mexicans could study for the priesthood in the safety of the United States, and Mexican exiles, from archbishops to humble rancheros, received aid, here and in Mexico, from their fellow Catholics north of the border. And when the Cristero struggle ended in 1929, it was the active involvement and cooperation of Catholics on both sides of the border that had made that peace—and rebuilding of the Church—possible.

That unity between Catholics of the hemisphere had been prepared for hundreds of years. This unity is evident from the earliest colonial periods in the bringing of the Guadalupan devotion to the northern reaches of New Spain by the missionaries of what is now the southwestern United States—men such as Fr. Eusebio Kino and Blessed Junipero Serra in the seventeenth and eighteenth centuries. Meanwhile, men such as Friar Margil de Jesús brought the devotion to Central America, and others such as Count Luis Enríquez de Gúzman carried the image farther south, to Peru and beyond.

Our hemisphere is indeed a microcosm of the globalization process occurring worldwide. What happens in America will have a profound effect on the Church and the world, and what happens between the United States and Mexico will shape the future of our hemisphere. Catholics in both countries have every reason to work for a day when such close neighbors are even closer friends.

UNITY WITHIN THE CHURCH

One model for the type of cooperation that can occur between the Catholics of the United States and Mexico is that seen in and fostered by the Knights of Columbus. Founded in 1882 in New Haven, Connecticut, the order rapidly expanded throughout the hemisphere. Canadian councils were founded in 1897, and Mexican councils in 1905. Since then, Knights from both sides of the border have accumulated more than a century of cooperation in many different forms. More recently, it has meant the support of seminarians from the United States to study in Mexico and learn Mexican culture, the support of Mexican seminarians to minister to the needs of Mexican immigrants in the United States, and the support of the Catholic Legal Immigration Network. Today, local Knights of Columbus councils along the border actively work together in Mexico and the United States on social, spiritual, and charitable projects. Increasing such cooperation is a high priority of the Knights of Columbus and it should be as well for other Catholic organizations in the United States. But all of this collaborative action is inspired by a belief that our unity as persons is stronger than any differences a border can raise, and our mission as Catholics is stronger than nationalism.

Beyond our common human family as men and women, we recognize a deeper bond of kinship as children of God and brothers and sisters of Christ, a bond that specifically orients us to the service of others. As Christians, and specifically as Catholics, we have a right to encourage in each other and expect in our dealings with each other a common measure of faith, hope, and love. In most of the countries of our hemisphere between 70 and 95 percent of the population is Catholic. In the United States, Catholics today represent one in every four people. If we, as Catholics, view one another as brothers and sisters in faith, as we have done before, and if we share that vision with the rest of our country, we truly have the opportunity to shape not just the future of the Church but the future of our own country, our continent, and our hemisphere.

It is precisely in this ecclesial childhood that we find in Our Lady of Guadalupe a true guide. Shortly before becoming pope, John Paul II spoke of the power of a mother's example of love: "This fundamental love, love for a human being who is conceived, who is carried beneath the heart of a mother, who is to be born: this is a fundamental love! The entire existence of the nation depends on it."[12] How much more perfect is the example of Our Lady of Guadalupe to us! For regardless of our own upbringing or current family situation, Our Lady of Guadalupe comes reaffirming the goodness of our childhood before God and leading us by her example of compassion, by her affection and interest, by her persistence to guide and make easier Juan Diego's decision to follow the will of God, by her own trust in us to join her in her own missions and intercessions for God. Hans Urs Von Balthasar made this point as well when he wrote:

> [Mary] is not only the maternal figure of the Church that gives birth to all the other members of the Body after it has borne the Head (Rev 12:17), and remains their Mother; she is also the archetypical member of the Church . . . , who [i.e., the Church] in all her members participates, through Christ and by virtue of word and sacrament, in the grace of being a child in the bosom of the Father. . . . [A]ll forms of the following of Christ within the Marian Church by carrying Christ's Cross with him, all priestly functions of the hierarchy and of the laity, are in the end ordered to this highest grace of childhood.[13]

Thus if all forms of Christian living find a model in Mary, and if we speak of Mary as the archetypical believer and the archetype of the Church, it is possible to speak of her as the archetype of Christian culture, the Christian culture enacted by believers but not exclusively for believers, a culture that is the intersection of the Church and community.

Perhaps more than any other region in the Western Hemisphere, and even the world, North America is known for our diverse people, for being on the forefront of trends and creators of state-of-the-art technologies. Without a doubt, our versatile and often shifting culture requires new methods of evangelization, methods often proposed by these very changes. But also it requires us to ask ourselves what the face of Christian culture in the future should look like. For this, we can choose no better guide than Our

Lady of Guadalupe when we search for those "seeds of the Word" in our culture and purify them into something supportive of all that is best in man and supportive of man's search for God.

In this, we do well to remember the words of Paul VI: "The civilization of a people is measured by its sensitivity in the face of suffering and its capacity to relieve it!"[14] We do well to remember also the words of Benedict XVI to young people: "It is up to you and to your hearts to ensure that progress is transformed into a greater good for all. And the way of good—as you know—has a name: it is called love." As we consider our civilization and our place in our communities and families, we should remember that the generosity and the "way of love" in our culture and civilization cannot be summed up by the "generosity" of impersonal systems of aid, however efficient. If for this fact alone, the personal presence of Our Lady of Guadalupe presents a strong model of the importance of maintaining the personal element in charity. It is only through this personal element that aid takes on a magnitude beyond the problem itself, and becomes the face and foundation of love.

This is especially true for us as Christians. "It is therefore natural that those who truly want to be a companion of Jesus really share in his love for the poor. For us, the option for the poor is not ideological but is born from the Gospel."[15] Just as we cannot ignore the poor on our spiritual journey to Christ, so we cannot ignore our faith as we labor for the poor. Catholics on both sides of the border should take the initiative to promote a Catholic solution to the problems of poverty and to promote economic and educational opportunities for the poor of the region. In Our Lady of Guadalupe, we have a model of "the preferential option for the poor" in a woman who came to conquered and conqueror alike in order to show to all—even the poorest and those without hope—the way to true resurrection. In her, we hear a voice expressing the true means to overcoming difficulties.

And if Our Lady of Guadalupe's message is one that has universal meaning for those in the Americas, then Juan Diego's example is also very important. On the continent where Juan Diego— a layman—was a key element in the evangelization of all those who inhabit it, we should carefully consider and follow his example. He found himself between two worlds. He was an Indian bringing this perfectly enculturated message both to his own people and to the Spanish. And he brought Our Lady of Guadalupe, and her message, to both groups consistently.

We too often find ourselves between worlds: between home and work, between our private and public lives. And yet, like Juan Diego, we are called to be witnesses of the truth—even when faced with disbelief. We must be undeterred as we bring the message of the mother of our continent and her Son to all those we encounter. We must witness by our lives, so that our example will be like a living tilma, and will provide a map to all we encounter of a civilization where love triumphs and motivates all action.

Our continent is one drawn together by shared history. On a historical level, all of its countries—to some degree—are nations of immigrants and of Native Americans. On a spiritual level, all of these countries share a common heritage of Christianity and baptism. And on a personal level, every person on this continent shares a mother: Our Lady of Guadalupe. From Canada to Argentina, all of us who live in the Americas are called, like Juan Diego, to bridge the divides of cultures, religion, and factions of any kind, by presenting to all the message of Our Lady of Guadalupe, the message of the mother of the civilization of love. What unites us as a Christian family, as children of a mother who has watched over us for nearly five hundred years, is far greater than anything that divides us.

But in this, no unity can be as great as the unity of a life with Christ, our Source. In Our Lady of Guadalupe, we find new signs of this great unity in the call for the chapel that would become the center of the parish and sacramental life for the people of not just Mexico, but of the Americas and indeed the whole world. As we prepare for the future, we do well to remember Benedict's words at Aparecida: "It is only from the Eucharist that the Civilization of Love will come forth."[16] Thus Our Lady of Guadalupe offers us the promise that the Continent of Hope may one day blossom into a Civilization of Love.

APPENDIX A

The Nican Mopohua

The Nican Mopohua *was probably written down sometime before Juan Diego's death in 1548 by the mestizo Antonio Valeriano (1520–1605), a student of the renowned missionary-scholar Friar Bernardino de Sahagún. The oldest copy of the* Nican Mopohua, *dating from the mid-sixteenth century and containing about one-third of the apparition account, resides in the New York Public Library. The account reflects the popular style of speaking used by the Indians at the time of the apparitions. The paper on which the account is written contains watermarks, an indication of the paper's European origin, and it is written using Spanish lettering in vogue at the time.[1]*

Textually, the account contains a mixture of both Spanish and Náhuatl idioms and expressions characteristic of the time.[2] Notably, the indigenous elements appear in how the narrative and dialogue between Juan Diego and the Virgin reflect the high forms of indigenous speech, the huehuetlahtolli, *the speech of the elders. As the Náhuatl scholar Miguel León-Portilla notes, this suggests that the author was familiar with ancient Indian rhetoric and songs. Náhuatl rhetoric in the account includes the frequent use of poetic phrases (such as "your face, your heart" to mean "your person"), the unique expressions of honor through both titles of rank and diminutive titles of affection (such as "My Mistress, my Lady, my Queen, my littlest Daughter, my little Girl"), and multiple phrases to compound an idea, creating a cascade of images (such as when Juan Diego approaches the beautified Tepeyac*

hill, saying, "By any chance am I worthy, have I deserved what I hear? Perhaps
I am only dreaming it? Perhaps I'm only dozing? Where am I? Where do I find
myself?").[3] Although this form of speech may seem archaic to our ears, it has been
retained in translation to give the reader the chance to experience naturally the
rhetorical ebb and flow.[4]

This translation was greatly informed by the translation done by members of
the Instituto Superior de Estudios Guadalupanos under the supervision of Msgr.
Eduardo Chávez.

Here is told and set down in order how a short time ago the Perfect
Virgin Holy Mary Mother of God, our Queen, miraculously appeared on
the Tepeyac, "nose of the hill," widely known as Guadalupe. First she
caused herself to be seen by an Indian named Juan Diego, poor but worthy of respect; and then her precious and beloved image appeared before
the recently named bishop, Don Fray Juan de Zumárraga.

[1]Ten years after the conquest of the water, mountain and city of Mexico,
when the arrows and shields were put aside, when there was peace in all the
towns, their waters and their mountains. [2]Just as it budded, faith now grows
green, now opens its corolla, the knowledge of the Giver of life, the true God.

[3]Then, in the year 1531, a few days into the month of December, it
happened that there was an Indian, a *macehual*, a poor man of the people;
[4]his name was Juan Diego, and he lived in Cuauhtitlán, as they call it,
[5]and in all the things of God he belonged to Tlatelolco.

[6]It was Saturday, not yet dawn, when he was coming in pursuit of God
and His commandments. [7]And as he drew near the little hill called
Tepeyac, it was beginning to dawn. [8]There he heard singing on the little
hill, like the song of many precious birds. When their voices would stop,
it was as if the hill were answering them. Extremely soft and delightful,
their songs exceeded those of the *coyoltototl* and the *tzinitzcan* and other
precious songbirds.

[9]Juan Diego stopped to look. He said to himself, "By any chance am
I worthy, have I deserved what I hear? Perhaps I am only dreaming it?
Perhaps I'm only dozing? [10]Where am I? Where do I find myself? Is it
possible that I am in the place our ancient ancestors, our grandparents,
told us about: in the land of the flowers, in the land of corn, of our flesh,
of our sustenance, perhaps in the land of heaven?"

[11]He was looking up toward the top of the hill, toward the direction

from which the sun rises, toward where the precious heavenly song was coming from.

[12]And then when the singing suddenly stopped, when it could no longer be heard, he heard someone calling him from the top of the hill, someone was saying to him: "Dear Juan, dearest Juan Diego."

[13]Then he dared to go to where the voice was coming from, his heart was not disturbed and he felt extremely happy and contented, he started to climb to the top of the little hill to go see where they were calling him from. [14]When he reached the top of the hill, he beheld a Maiden standing there. [15]She called to him to come close to her.

[16]And when he reached where she was, he was filled with admiration for the way her perfect grandeur exceeded all imagination: [17]her clothing was shining like the sun, as if it were sending out waves of light. [18]And the stones, the crag on which she stood, seemed to be giving out rays [19]like precious jades, like jewels they [the stones] gleamed. [20]The earth seemed to shine with the brilliance of a rainbow in the mist. [21]And the mesquites, prickly pear, and the other little plants that are generally up there seemed like quetzal feathers. Their foliage looked like turquoise. And their trunks, their thorns, their prickles, were shining like gold.

[22]He prostrated himself in her presence and listened to her venerable breath, her venerable words, which were extremely affable, extremely noble, as if from someone who was drawing him toward her and loved him. [23]She said to him: "Listen my son, my youngest son, Juanito, where are you going?" [24]And he answered her: "My Lady, my Queen, my Little Girl, I am going as far as your little house in Mexico Tlatelolco, to follow the things of God that are to us given, that are taught to us by our priests, those who are the images of the Lord, Our Lord."

[25]Then she spoke with him, she revealed her precious will; [26]she said to him: "Know, know for sure my dearest and youngest son, that I am truly the ever perfect Holy Virgin Mary, who has the honor to be the Mother of the one true God for whom we all live, the Creator of people, the Lord of all around us and of what is close to us, the Lord of Heaven, the Lord of Earth.

"I want very much that they build my sacred little house here, [27]in which I will show Him, I will exalt Him upon making Him manifest, [28]I will give Him to all people in all my personal love, Him that is my compassionate gaze, Him that is my help, Him that is my salvation.

29"Because truly I am honored to be your compassionate mother, 30yours and that of all the people that live together in this land, 31and also of all the other various lineages of men; those who love me, those who cry to me, those who seek me, those who trust in me. 32Because there [at my sacred house] truly will I hear their cry, their sadness, in order to remedy, to cure all their various troubles, their miseries, their pains.

33"And to bring about what my compassionate and merciful gaze would achieve, go to the palace of the Bishop of Mexico, and tell him how I have sent you, so that you may reveal to him how I very much want him to build me a house here, to erect my temple on the plain; tell him every-thing, all you have seen and marveled at, and what you have heard. 34And know for sure that I will appreciate it very much and reward it, 35that because of it I will enrich you, I will glorify you; 36and because of it you will deserve very much how I will reward your fatigue, your service in going to petition the matter for which I am sending you. 37Now, my dearest son, you have heard my breath, my word; go, do what you are responsible for doing."

38And immediately he prostrated himself in her presence, and he said to her: "My Lady, My Little Girl, now I will go to make your venerable breath, your venerable word, a reality; for now, I leave you, I, your humble servant."

39Then he came down the hill to put her errand into action; he returned to the path and went straight to Mexico City. 40When he reached the center of the city, he went directly to the palace of the Bishop, the Governing Priest, who had just recently arrived; his name was Don Fray Juan de Zumárraga, a Franciscan Priest.

41And as soon as he got there, he tried to see him [the Bishop], he begged his [the Bishop's] servants, his helpers, to go and tell him that he needed to see him. 42After a long time, when finally the Reverend Bishop ordered that he [Juan Diego] enter, they [the Bishop's servants] came to call him. 43And as soon as he [Juan Diego] entered, first he knelt before him [the Bishop], he prostrated himself, then he revealed to him, he told him of the precious breath, the precious word of the Queen of Heaven, her message, and he also told him everything that made him marvel, what he saw, what he heard .

44But the Bishop, having heard his whole story, his message, as if he didn't particularly believe it to be true, 45answered him, he said to him:

"My son, you will come again. At that time I will still hear you calmly, I will look at it carefully from the very beginning, I will consider the reason why you have come, what is your will, what is your wish."

[46]He [Juan Diego] left; he left sad because the errand entrusted to him was not immediately accepted. [47]Then he returned, at the end of the day, he went straight from there to the top of the little hill, [48] and he arrived before Her, the Queen of Heaven: there, exactly where she had appeared to him the first time, she was waiting for him.

[49]As soon as he saw her, he prostrated himself before her, he threw himself to the ground, and he said to her: [50]"My Mistress, my Lady, my Queen, my littlest Daughter, my little Girl, I went to where you sent me to carry out your venerable breath, your venerable word. Although I entered with difficulty to the place where the Governing Priest is, I saw him, and before him I placed your venerable breath, your venerable word, as you ordered me to do. [51]He received me kindly and listened with attention, but, from the way he answered me, it's as if his heart didn't recognize it, he doesn't think it's true. [52]He said to me: 'You will come again, and at that time I will still hear you calmly, I will look at it carefully from the very beginning, I will consider the reason why you have come, what is your will, what is your wish. [53]We shall see,' the way he answered me; it's as though your venerable divine house that you want them to build here, that maybe I just made it up, or maybe that it doesn't come from your venerable lips.

[54]"So I beg you, my Lady, my Queen, my little Girl, to have one of the nobles who are held in esteem, one who is known, respected, honored, have him carry on, take your venerable breath, your venerable word, so that he will be believed. [55]Because I am really just a man from the country, I'm the porter's rope, I'm a back frame, just a tail, a wing; I myself need to be led, carried on someone's back; there, where you sent me, it is not my place to go or to stay, my little Girl, my littlest Daughter, my Lady, my Girl. [56]Please, excuse me, I will afflict your face, your heart; I will fall into your anger, your displeasure, my Lady Mistress."

[57]The Perfect Virgin, worthy of honor and veneration, answered him: [58]"Listen my youngest son, know for sure that I have no lack of servants, of messengers, to whom I can give the task of carrying my breath, my word, so that they carry out my will; [59]but it is necessary that you, personally, go and plead, that by your intercession, my wish, my will, become

a reality. [60]And I beg you, my youngest son, and I strictly order you, to go again tomorrow to see the Bishop. [61]And in my name, make him know, make him hear my wish, my will, so that he will bring into being, he will build, my sacred house that I ask of him. [62]And carefully tell him again how I, personally, the ever Virgin Holy Mary, I, who am the Mother of God, sent you as my messenger."

[63]For his part, Juan Diego responded and said to her: "My Lady, my Queen, my Little Girl, let me not anguish you or grieve your face, your heart; truly with gladness I will go to carry out your venerable breath, your venerable word; I absolutely will not fail to do it, nor does the road trouble me. [64]I will go now, to carry out your will, but maybe I won't be heard and, if heard, maybe I won't be believed. [65]But truly, tomorrow afternoon, when the sun goes down, I will come to return to your venerable breath, to your venerable word, what the Governing Priest answers to me. [66]Now I respectfully say goodbye to you, my youngest Daughter, my young Girl, Lady, my Little Girl, rest a little more." [67]And then he went to his house to rest.

[68]On the following day, Sunday, while it was still nighttime, everything was still dark, he went to Tlatelolco directly from his house, he came to learn about divine things and to be counted in roll call; then he went to see the Governing Priest.

[69]And around ten he was ready, he had been to Mass and was counted in the roll, and everyone had left. [70]But he, Juan Diego, then went to the palace, the Reverend Bishop's house. [71]And as soon as he arrived, he went through the whole struggle to see him and, after much effort, he saw him again. [72]He knelt at his feet, he wept, he became sad as he spoke to him, as he revealed to him the venerable breath, the venerable word, of the Queen of Heaven. [73]He hoped the errand would be believed, the will of the Perfect Virgin, to make for Her, to build for Her, Her sacred little house, where She had said, where She wanted it.

[74]And the Governing Bishop asked him many, many things, he interrogated him, in order to be certain about where he had seen Her, what She was like. He told absolutely everything to the Reverend Bishop. [75]And although he told him absolutely everything that he had seen, that he had marveled at, that it appeared perfectly clear that She was the Perfect Virgin, the Kind, Wondrous Mother of Our Savior, Our Lord Jesus Christ; [76]nevertheless his wish was not fulfilled. [77]The Bishop said that not only

on his [Juan Diego's] word would his petition be carried out, would what he requested happen, [78]but that some other sign was very necessary if he were to believe how the Queen of Heaven, personally, was sending him [Juan Diego] as Her messenger.

[79]As soon as Juan Diego heard that, he said to the Bishop: [80]"Señor Governor, think about what the sign you ask for will be, because then I will go ask for it of the Queen of Heaven who sent me." [81]And as the Bishop saw that he [Juan Diego] was in agreement, that he did not hesitate or doubt in the slightest, he dismissed him. [82]And as soon as he [Juan Diego] had left, the Bishop ordered some of his own household staff, in whom he had absolute trust, to go and follow him, to carefully observe where he went, whom he saw, and with whom he spoke. [83]And this they did. And Juan Diego went straight along, following the path. [84]But those who followed him, where the ravine opens, near Tepeyac, on the wooden bridge, came to lose him. And although they searched for him everywhere, they didn't see him anywhere.

[85]And so they turned back, not just because they had made terrible fools of themselves, but also because he had frustrated their attempt, he [Juan Diego] had made them angry. [86]So they went to tell the Reverend Bishop, they put into his head that he shouldn't believe him [Juan Diego], they told him how he was only telling him lies, that he was only making up what he came to tell him, or that he was only dreaming or imagining what he was telling him, what he was asking of him. [87]So they decided that if he came again, if he returned, they would grab him right there, and punish him severely, so that he would never again tell lies or get people all riled up.

[88]Meanwhile, Juan Diego was with the Most Holy Virgin, telling Her the response he brought from the Reverend Bishop: [89]and, when She heard it, She said to him: [90]"That's fine, my little son, you will come back here tomorrow so that you may take the Bishop the sign he has asked you for; [91]with that he will believe you, and he will no longer have any doubts about all this, nor will he be suspicious of you; [92]and know, my little son, that I will reward the care, the work and the fatigue that you have put into this for me; [93]so go now; I will be waiting for you here tomorrow."

[94]And on the following day, Monday, when Juan Diego was to take some sign in order to be believed, he did not return. [95]Because when he arrived at his house, the sickness had struck an uncle of his, named Juan

Bernardino, who had become very ill. [96]He [Juan Diego] went to get the doctor, who treated him, but it was too late; he was dying. [97]And when night fell, his uncle begged him that, when it was still the early hours of the morning, when it was still dark, he [Juan Diego] go to Tlatelolco to call one of the priests to come and hear his [Juan Bernardino's] confession, to get him ready, [98]because it was in his heart that it was truly now time, that now he would die, because he would no longer get up, he would no longer get well.

[99]And Tuesday, when it was still very dark, he left from there, from his house, to go to Tlatelolco to call a priest, [100]and when he reached the side of the little hill, at the foot of Tepeyácac, the end of the mountain range, where the road comes out, towards where the sun sets, where he had always gone before, he said: [101]"If I follow the road straight ahead, I don't want this Noble Lady to see me because, for sure, just like before, She'll stop me so I can take the sign to the Governing Priest for Her, as She ordered me to do. [102]First we must get rid of our first affliction; first I must quickly call the priest since my poor uncle anxiously awaits him." [103]He immediately went around the hill, climbed up the middle, crossing over it, and emerged towards where the sun rises; so he could quickly arrive in Mexico City, so that the Queen of Heaven would not stop him. [104]He thought that where he made the turn the one who sees everywhere perfectly would not see him.

[105]But he saw how She was coming down from up on the hill, and that from there she had been looking at him, from where she saw him before. [106]She came to meet him beside the hill, she came to block his way; she said to him: [107]"My youngest son, what's going on? Where are you going? Where are you headed?" [108]And he, perhaps he grieved a little, or perhaps he became ashamed? Or perhaps he became afraid of the situation, became fearful? [109]He prostrated himself before Her, he greeted Her, he said to Her: [110]"My little Maiden, my youngest Daughter, my Little Girl, I hope you are happy; how are you this morning? Does your beloved little body feel well, my Lady, my Girl?

[111]"Though it grieves me, I will cause your face and your heart anguish: I must tell you, my little Girl, that one of your servants, my uncle, is very ill. [112]A terrible sickness has taken hold of him; he will surely die from it soon. [113]And now I shall go quickly to your little house in Mexico , to call one of the ones beloved of Our Lord, one of our priests, so

that he will go to hear his [my uncle's] confession and prepare him. [114]Because in reality for this we were born, we who came to await the task of our death.

[115]"But, while I am going to do this, afterwards I will return here again to go carry your venerable breath, your venerable word, Lady, my Little Girl. [116]Forgive me, be patient with me a little longer, because I am not deceiving you with this, my youngest Daughter, my Little Girl, tomorrow without fail I will come in all haste."

[117]As soon as She heard Juan Diego's words, the Merciful Perfect Virgin answered him: [118]"Listen, put it into your heart, my youngest son, that what frightened you, what afflicted you is nothing; do not let it disturb your face, your heart; do not fear this sickness or any other sickness, nor any sharp or hurtful thing. [119]Am I not here, I who have the honor to be your mother? Are you not in my shadow and under my protection? Am I not the source of your joy? Are you not in the hollow of my mantle, in the crossing of my arms? Do you need anything more?

[120]"Let nothing else worry you, disturb you; don't grieve over your uncle's illness, because he will not die of it for now, you may be certain that he is already healed." [121](And at that very moment his uncle was healed, as he later found out). [122]And Juan Diego, when he heard the venerable breath, the venerable word, of the Queen of Heaven, he was greatly comforted by it, his heart became peaceful; [123]and he begged her to send him immediately as messenger to see the Governing Bishop, to take him Her sign, for proof, so that he [the Bishop] would believe.

[124]And the Queen of Heaven ordered him then to go to the top of the little hill, where he had seen her before. [125]She said to him: "Go up, my youngest son, to the top of the hill, to where you saw me and I told you what to do; [126]there you will see spread out several kinds of flowers: cut them, gather them, put them all together: then come right down; bring them here, into my presence." [127]And then Juan Diego climbed the little hill, [128]and when he reached the top, he marveled at how many flowers were spread out there, their blossoms were open, flowers of every kind, lovely and beautiful, like those of Castille, when it was not yet their season [129]because it was when the frost was worst. [130]The flowers were giving off an extremely soft fragrance, like precious pearls, as if filled with the night's dew. [131]Right away he began to cut them, gathered them all and put them in the hollow of his tilma. [132]The top of the little hill was

certainly not a place in which any flowers grew, because it was rocky, there were burs, thorny plants, prickly pear, and an abundance of mesquite bushes. [133]And though some small grasses might grow, it was then the month of December, in which the ice eats everything up and destroys it.

[134]And immediately he came back down, he came to bring the Heavenly Maiden the different kinds of flowers which he had gone up to cut. [135]And when She saw them, She took them with her venerable hands; [136]then She put them back in the hollow of Juan Diego's tilma and said to him: [137]"My youngest son, these different kinds of flowers are the proof, the sign that you will take to the Bishop; [138]you will tell him from me that in them he is to see my wish and that therefore he is to carry out my wish, my will; [139]and you, you who are my messenger, in you I place my absolute trust. [140]And I strictly order you that only alone, in the Bishop's presence, will you open your tilma and show him what you are carrying; [141]and you will tell him everything exactly, you will tell him that I ordered you to climb to the top of the little hill to cut the flowers, and everything you saw and admired; [142]so that you can convince the Governing Priest, so that he will then do what is entrusted to him, to build my little sacred house that I have asked for."

[143]And as soon as the Heavenly Queen gave him Her orders, he returned to the path, he went straight to Mexico, and now he went happily, [144]his heart was tranquil now, because it was going to come out fine, the flowers would see to that. [145]Along the way, he was very careful of what was in the hollow of his tilma, lest he lose something. [146]As he went, he enjoyed the fragrance of the different kinds of exquisite flowers.

[147]When he arrived at the Bishop's house, the doorkeeper and the Governing Priest's other servants went to meet him. [148]He begged them to tell him that he wanted to see him, but none of them was willing; they didn't want to listen to him, or perhaps because it was still very dark. [149]Or maybe because they knew him by now, and all he did was bother and inconvenience them. [150]And their companions [the other servants] had already told them about him, the ones who lost him when they were following him. [151]For a long, long time he [Juan Diego] waited for his request to be granted. [152]And when they [the servants] saw that he was simply standing there for a very long time, with his head down, doing nothing, in case he should be called, and how he was carrying something

in the hollow of his tilma; then they came close to him to see what it was he was bringing and thus to satisfy their curiosity.

[153]And when Juan Diego saw that there was no way he could hide from them what he was carrying, and that therefore they would harass him, push him, or perhaps beat him, he gave them a little peek and they saw that it was flowers. [154]And when they saw that they [the flowers] were all fine, different flowers, like those from Castille, and that it wasn't the season for them to be blooming, they admired them [the flowers] greatly, how fresh they were, with their buds open, how good they smelled, beautiful. [155]And they wanted to grab them and pull a few out. [156]They dared to try to take them three times, but there was no way they could do it, [157]because when they tried, they couldn't see them [the flowers] anymore, instead they looked painted or embroidered or sewn into the tilma.

[158]They [the servants] went immediately to tell the Governing Bishop what they had seen, [159]and how the lowly Indian who had come the other times wanted to see him, and that he had been waiting a very long time there for permission, because he wanted to see him [the Bishop]. [160]And the Governing Bishop, as soon as he heard this, already had it in his heart that that was the sign to convince him, so he would carry out the work that the humble man had asked of him. [161]He immediately ordered that they [the servants] let him in to see him. [162]And, having entered, he [Juan Diego] prostrated himself in his [the Bishop's] presence, as he had done before. [163]And again he [Juan Diego] told him about all he had seen, what he had admired, and his message. [164]He said to him: "My Lord, Governor, I have truly done it, I carried out your orders; [165]I went to tell the Lady, my Mistress, the Heavenly Maiden, Saint Mary, the Beloved Mother of God, that you asked for a sign in order to believe me, so that you would make her sacred little house, there where She asked that you build it; [166]and I also told Her I had given you my word to come and bring you some sign, some proof of Her venerable will, as you told me to do. [167]And She listened well to your venerable breath, your venerable word, and was pleased to receive your request for the sign, the proof, so that Her beloved will can be done, can be carried out. [168]And now, when it was still nighttime, She ordered me to come again to see you; [169]and I asked Her for Her sign so that I would be believed, as She said she would give to me, and immediately She kept her promise. [170]And She sent me to the top of the

little hill where I had seen Her before, to cut some different flowers there, like those from Castille. [171]And when I had cut them, I took them down to Her below; [172]and with Her venerable hands she took them. [173]Then, again, She put them in the hollow of my tilma, [174]so that I would come to bring them to you, so that I would deliver them to you personally. [175]Although I knew well that the top of the hill isn't a place where flowers grow, because it's just rocks, burs, thorny plants, wild prickly pear and mesquite bushes, I didn't doubt because of that; I didn't hesitate because of that. [176]When I reached the top of the little hill, I saw that it was now the Flowered Land [paradise]. [177]There had sprung forth various flowers, like Castillian roses, the finest that there are, full of dew, splendid; so I went to cut them. [178]And She told me that I should give them to you from Her, and that in this way I would prove it; so that you would see the sign you requested in order to carry out Her venerable will, [179]and so that it would be clear that my word, my message, is the truth. [180]Here they are; please receive them."

[181]And then he opened his white tilma, in the hollow of which were the flowers. [182]And all the different flowers, like those from Castille, fell to the floor. [183]Then and there his tilma became the sign, there suddenly appeared the Beloved Image of the Perfect Virgin Saint Mary, Mother of God, in the form and figure in which it is now, [184]where it is preserved in her beloved little house, in her sacred little house in Tepeyac, which is called Guadalupe. [185]And as soon as the Governing Bishop and all those who were there saw it, they knelt, they were full of awe, [186]they stood up to see it, they were moved, their hearts were troubled, their hearts as well as their minds were raised. [187]And the Governing Bishop, in tears, with sadness, begged Her, he asked Her forgiveness for not having carried out Her venerable will, Her venerable breath, Her venerable word.

[188]And the Bishop got up, and untied Juan Diego's garment, his tilma, from his neck where it was tied, [189]on which appeared the venerable sign of the Heavenly Queen. [190]And then he took it and placed it in his private chapel. [191]And Juan Diego still stayed for the day in the Bishop's house, who still kept him there. [192]And on the next day he [the Bishop] said to him: "Come, let's go so you can show me where it is that the venerable will of the Queen of Heaven wants Her chapel built." [193]Immediately the order was given to make it, to build it. [194]And Juan Diego, as soon as he showed where the Lady of Heaven had ordered that Her sacred little house

be built, asked for permission to leave. [195]He wanted to go home in order to see his uncle, Juan Bernardino, who was very ill when he left him, when he had gone to call on one of the priests in Tlatelolco to hear his confession and prepare him, the one whom the Queen of Heaven had said was already cured. [196]But they didn't let him go alone, instead people went with him to his house. [197]And when they arrived they saw that his venerable uncle was healthy, absolutely nothing pained him. [198]And he, for his part, greatly admired the way in which his nephew was so accompanied and honored. [199]He asked his nephew why this was happening, that they so honored him; [200]and he [Juan Diego] told him [Juan Bernardino] how, when he left to go call on a priest to hear his confession, to prepare him, there in Tepeyácac the Lady of Heaven appeared to him. [201]And She sent him to Mexico City to see the Governing Bishop, so that there he would build Her house in Tepeyácac.

[202]And She told him not to worry, because his uncle was already cured, and this very much consoled him. [203]His uncle told him it was true, that She healed him at that exact moment, [204]and he saw Her in exactly the same way She had appeared to his nephew. [205]And She told him that she was also sending him to Mexico City to see the Bishop; [206]and that also, when he went to see him, he should reveal absolutely everything to him, he should tell him what he had seen [207]and the wonderful way in which She had healed him, [208] and that he should properly name Her Beloved Image thus: THE PERFECT VIRGIN, SAINT MARY OF GUADALUPE.

[209]And right away they took Juan Bernardino into the presence of the Governing Bishop, so that he could come to speak to him, to give him his testimony. [210]And together with his nephew Juan Diego, the Bishop lodged them in his house for a few days, [211]while the sacred little house of the Heavenly Maiden was built there in Tepeyac, where She revealed Herself to Juan Diego. [212]And after some time, the Reverend Bishop moved the beloved Image of the Heavenly Maiden to the main church. [213]He [the Bishop] took it from his palace, from his chapel where it had been, so that everyone could see and admire Her precious Image. [214]And absolutely everyone, the entire city, without exception, trembled when they went to behold, to admire Her precious Image. [215]They came to acknowledge it as something divine. [216]They came to offer Her their prayers. [217]They marveled at the miraculous way it had appeared [218]since absolutely no one on Earth had painted Her beloved Image.

APPENDIX B
Chronology of Guadalupan Events

1474: An Indian named Cuauhtlatoatzin ("eagle that speaks") is born in Cuautitlán.

1476: Juan de Zumárraga is born in Spain.

1492: Christopher Columbus discovers the Americas, when he makes landfall on an island he calls San Salvador.

1517: Martin Luther writes his Ninety-Five Theses, commencing the Protestant Reformation.

1517: Francisco Hernández de Córdoba discovers Mexico.

1519-1521: Hernán Cortes lands in Mexico and conquers the capital city of the Aztecs.

1522: The first missionaries, including Pedro de Gante, arrive in Mexico.

1524: Official missionary activity begins with the arrival of twelve missionaries in Mexico City.

1525: The Indian Cuauhtlatoatzin is baptized and receives the Christian name of Juan Diego (John James).

1526: Dominican missionaries arrive in Mexico.

1528: Friar Juan de Zumárraga arrives in the New World.

1528: The first civil government, called the First Audience, arrives in New Spain, headed by President Nuño de Guzmán.

1529: Juan Diego's wife, María Lucía, dies.

1529, August 27: Problems arise between the First Audience officials and the evangelizing missionaries.

1530: There is a plot to assassinate bishop-elect Juan de Zumárraga, but he escapes harm.

1531: A series of natural events, including earthquakes, the appearance of Halley's comet, and a solar eclipse, leads the Indians to believe the world is about to end.

1531, December 9-12: During the winter solstice, Our Lady of Guadalupe appears to a Juan Diego Cuauhtlatoatzin, and asks him to be her messenger. The *tilma* is presented to bishop-elect Juan de Zumárraga.

1531: The first chapel to Our Lady of Guadalupe of Tepeyac is built, and on December 26, the tilma with Our Lady of Guadalupe's image is carried in procession to this first chapel.

1531: The *Pregón del Atabal* is composed, pairing pre-Conquest Aztec melodies with new words celebrating the procession of the *tilma* to the chapel on the Tepeyac.

1537, June 9: Pope Paul III issues the papal bull *Sublimis Deus*, which declares that Indians are able to receive the sacraments, encourages their catechesis, and defends their humanity.

1537: A *junta eclesiástica* is convened to consider modifications of the baptismal ceremony which had been proposed and practiced to accommodate the unusually large number of baptisms. These discussions would continue for a couple decades.

1541: The Franciscan friar Toribio de Benavente, an early historian of New Spain, writes that some nine million Indians had converted to Christianity.

1544, May 15: The uncle of Juan Diego, Juan Bernardino, dies.

1545: During a great drought and plague, a pilgrimage of young children goes to the Guadalupan shrine.

c1545-1548: The *Nican Mopohua*, an account of the apparitions of Our Lady of Guadalupe, is written down by a mestizo named Antonio Valeriano.

1548: Both Juan Diego and Bishop Juan de Zumárraga die in the same year.

Mid- to late sixteenth-century: Three of the most important extent manuscripts are written.

-The earliest extent manuscript of the *Nican Mopohua* is written; the manuscript now resides in the New York Public Library;

-The *Códice 1548* or *Codex Escalada* is composed on deerskin, depicting the two of the apparitions of Our Lady of Guadalupe at the Tepeyac and Juan

Diego wearing the tilma with the image on it; this manuscript also contains the date of Juan Diego's death, his name, a brief inscription in Náhuatl, and signatures of significant persons including Antonio Valeriano (author of the *Nican Mopohua*) and Sahagún;

-The *Codex Saville* is written, a pictorial calendar in which a depiction of Our Lady of Guadalupe is place in the position representing the year 1531.

1555: In the Provincial Council, archbishop of Mexico, Alonso de Montúfar, formulates canons that indirectly approve the apparitions.

1555-1556 - The Chapel of the Tepeyac is put on the "Uppsala map" (named for the city—Uppsala—where the map is presently located.

1556: Archbishop Montúfar orders an investigation into the Guadalupan devotion during which several testimonies are taken that ultimately affirm the devotion as true expression of Christian faith and practices.

1556 - Archbishop Montúfar begins the construction of the second church in honor of Our Lady of Guadalupe.

1556: A chapel is built next to Juan Diego's house in Cuauhtitlán and another is built in Tulpetlac

c.1559: The daughter of Juan Martín García gives a detailed testimony about Juan Diego and his wife, María Lucía, including such details as where they were married and where they lived.

1562: A census, now located in the Basilica Museum, is conducted by Martín de Aranguren and speaks of the Virgin of Guadalupe.

1564: An image of Our Lady of Guadalupe is carried on the first formal expedition to the Philippine Islands.

1567: The new church begun by Archbishop Montúfar is completed.

1568: Bernal Díaz del Castillo, in his work *Verdadera Historia del Conquista de la Nueva España*, twice mentions the Sanctuary of Our Lady of Guadalupe and notes that many miracles took place there.

1568: The pirate Miles Philips describes the great devotion of the Spaniards and Indians to Our Lady of Guadalupe.

1568: Friar Bernardino of Sahagún writes of the growing popularity of devotion to Our Lady Guadalupe on Tepeyac.

1570: Archbishop Montúfar sends King Philip II of Spain a copy of the image of Our Lady of Guadalupe done in oil paints.

1571: Admiral Giovanni Andrea Doria carries a copy of the image of Our Lady of Guadalupe aboard his ship during the battle of Lepanto and later credits the Virgin of Guadalupe with the victory over the Ottoman Empire forces.

1573: The historian Juan de Tovar, who transcribed the story of the apparitions from an earlier source, probably that written by Juan González, Zumárraga's translator, writes the "Primitive Relation."

1576: Pope Gregory XIII extends indulgences and blessings to the chapel at Tepeyac.

1582: Two important documents in the *File of Chimalhuacán Chalco*, an exvoto (a sign of gratitude for a favor) and a sonnet, describe the apparitions of Guadalupe.

1589: In his *Treatise on the History of the Indies*, Suárez de Peralta speaks of the apparition of Our Lady of Guadalupe.

1590: The *Nican Motecpana* is written, providing an account of the apparitions and the virtuous life of Juan Diego.

1590: A sixteenth-century drawing that captures the apparition of Our Lady of Guadalupe to Juan Diego is completed.

1606: The first copy of the *tilma*, dated and signed by Baltasar de Echave, is made.

1615: The artist Johannes Stradanus creates a copper engraving of the apparition of Our Lady of Guadalupe and the miracles attributed to her intercession.

1622: A publication from *Publicación de Diego Garrido* captures the image of Our Lady of Guadalupe.

1647: The image of Our Lady of Guadalupe on the *tilma* is covered with glass for the first time.

1648: For the 100th anniversary of Juan Diego's death, the priest Miguel Sánchez publishes *Imagen de la Virgen María, Madre de Dios de Guadalupe*, a work recounting in Spanish the apparition story.

1649: Luis Lasso de la Vega publishes *Huei–Tlamahuicoltica*, telling the story of the apparitions in Náhuatl and including earlier Náhuatl sources.

1650: The construction of the Indians' parish is completed, and the chapel is now used as a sacristy.

1666, February 18-March 22: A formal inquiry and investigation are conducted by the Church in order to inquire into the apparitions at Guadalupe and the miraculous tilma. The Vatican latter confirms the quality of investigation, designating them on the level of an Apostolic Visitation.

1666: The Chapel of the Cerrito is built at the highest point on the Tepeyac.

1667: Pope Clement IX institutes the feast of Our Lady of Guadalupe on December 12

1689: Carlos de Sigüenza y Góngora writes *Piedad Heroyca de don Fernando Cortés*, in which he speaks of the apparitions of Guadalupe.

1695: The first stone of the new sanctuary is laid, and the sanctuary is solemnly dedicated in 1709.

1723: Another formal investigation ordered by Archbishop Lanziego y Eguilaz is conducted.

1737: The Most Holy Mary of Guadalupe is chosen as the patroness of Mexico City.

1746: The patronage of Our Lady of Guadalupe is accepted for all of New Spain, which includes the regions from northern California to El Salvador.

1746: Pope Benedict XIV approves the building of the Our Lady of Guadalupe College.

1746: The knight Boturini Benaducci promotes the solemn and official coronation of the image.

1754: Pope Benedict XIV approves the Virgin's patronage of New Spain and grants a Mass and Office proper to the celebration of her feast on December 12.

1756: The famous painter Miguel Cabrera publishes his study of the *tilma* and image in the book *Maravilla Americana.*

1757: The Virgin of Guadalupe is named patroness of the city of Ponce in Puerto Rico.

1757: Pope Benedict XV allows King Ferdinand VII to use the offices and Masses of Our Lady of Guadalupe in the Spanish territories.

1767: When the Society of Jesus is expelled from the Spanish territory, the Jesuits carry the image with them around the world.

1787: Dr. Jose Ignacio Bartolache conducts an experiment on the tilma's miraculous preservation and commissions a group of artist to examine the Virgin's image.

1795: During a routine cleaning of the image's frame, acid is accidentally poured on the image of Our Lady of Guadalupe, yet miraculously the image is not damaged, except for a minor stain.

1810: Fr. Miguel Hidalgo y Costilla, leader of Mexico's movement for independence, takes the image of Guadalupe as his flag.

1821: Agustín de Iturbide puts the Mexican nation in the hands of Our Lady of Guadalupe and proclaims her Patroness and Empress of Mexico.

1895: Many of the bishops from throughout the Americas attend the pontifically authorized coronation of Our Lady of Guadalupe.

1899: The First Plenary Council of Latin America takes place in Rome and recognizes the special protection of Our Lady of Guadalupe.

1900: Pope Leo XII proclaims that the offices and Masses of Our Lady of Guadalupe are to be celebrated in perpetuity.

1904: Pope Pius X elevates the Church of Our Lady of Guadalupe to a minor basilica.

1910: Pope Pius X declares Our Lady of Guadalupe Patroness of Latin America.

1911: A church is built on the site of Juan Bernardino's home.

1921, November 14: A bomb placed beneath the image explodes, causing a great deal of damage within the basilica, but the *tilma* is unharmed.

1926-1929: The Cristeros, fighting against Mexico's anticlerical government, adopt the battle cry: "Viva Cristo Rey, viva la Virgen de Guadalupe!" ("Long live Christ the King and Our Lady of Guadalupe!"). The North American episcopate and the Knights of Columbus support the persecuted Catholic Church in Mexico.

1926: For the first time, the feast of Our Lady of Guadalupe is celebrated at the Basilica without any priests participating, due to government restrictions on religion.

1928: A copy of the image is crowned in Santa Fe, Argentina.

1929: Photographer Alfonso Marcue makes the first documented discovery of an apparent reflection of a man's head in the right eye of the Virgin.

1931: In celebration of the 400th anniversary of the apparitions, the infants baptized in the Archdiocese of Guadalajara this year are given the name Guadalupe or José Guadalupe.

1933: The day Our Lady of Guadalupe was first proclaimed Patroness of Latin America is commemorated in St. Peters Basilica in Rome.

1935: Pope Pius XI names Our Lady of Guadalupe Patroness of the Philippines.

1938: The president of the Holy Name Society in California declares Our Lady of Guadalupe to be the Queen of the New World, who should be honored by all Catholics in the United States and Canada.

1941: Delegates representing twenty countries gather at the Basilica of Our

Lady of Guadalupe to pray for peace. Among those attending is Archbishop John J. Cantwell of Los Angeles, who leads a delegation of American clergy to Mexico City and petitions that Our Lady of Guadalupe be named Patroness of the United States. The archbishop of Mexico City, Luis María Martínez, gives a small piece of the *tilma* to Archbishop Cantwell.

1945: Pope Pius XII declares that the Virgin of Guadalupe is the Queen of Mexico and Empress of the Americas and upholds the divine origins of her miraculous image.

1946: Pope Pius XII declares Our Lady of Guadalupe Patroness of the Americas.

1951: Carlos Salinas examines the image and finds the reflection of a man's head in the right eye of the image of Our Lady.

1956 - Dr. Javier Torroella Bueno, an ophthalmologist, examines the eyes of the Virgin on the *tilma* and confirms the existence of a reflection in her eyes.

1958: Dr. Rafael Torija-Lavoignet publishes his study of the Purkinje-Sanson effect as exhibited in the Guadalupan image.

1961: Pope John XXIII prays to Our Lady of Guadalupe as the Mother of the Americas and calls her the mother of and teacher of the faith to all people in the Americas.

1962: Studying a photograph of the image enlarged twenty-five times, Dr. Charles Wahlig, O.D., announces the discovery of two images reflected in the eyes of the Virgin.

1962: During a diplomatic visit to Mexico, President John F. Kennedy and the first lady Jacqueline Kennedy attend Mass at the Basilica of Our Lady of Guadalupe.

1966: Pope Paul VI sends a golden rose to the basilica of Our Lady of Guadalupe.

1975: The glass covering the image is removed so another ophthalmologist, Dr. Enrique Graue, can examine the image.

1976: The new basilica of Our Lady of Guadalupe, located four miles from central Mexico City, is dedicated.

1979: Pope John Paul II celebrates Mass in the sanctuary of Our Lady of Guadalupe during his first international pilgrimage.

1979: Dr. José Aste Tönsmann finds at least four human figures reflected in both eyes of the Virgin.

1981: The process of Juan Diego's canonization is officially opened.

1988: The liturgical celebration of Our Lady of Guadalupe on December 12 is raised to the status of a feast in all dioceses in the United States.

1990, May 3-6: Jose Barragan Silva fractures his skull and sustains life-threatening injuries in a fall from a balcony, but is healed through the intercession of Juan Diego. This miracle would become the miracle that would further Juan Diego's cause of canonization.

1990, May 6: Juan Diego is declared Blessed by Pope John Paul II at the Vatican. Later that year, Pope John Paul II returns to the Basilica in Mexico City to perform the beatification ceremony of Juan Diego.

1992: Pope John Paul II dedicates a chapel in honor of Our Lady of Guadalupe in St. Peter's Basilica.

1999: Pope John Paul II proclaims Our Lady of Guadalupe as Patroness of the whole American continent.

1999: The tilma is examined as part of the investigation process for Juan Diego's canonization.

2002, July 31: Juan Diego Cuauhtlatoatzin is canonized by Pope John Paul II at the Basilica of Our Lady of Gaudalupe in Mexico City.

2003: A relic of the *tilma* tours the United States. The pilgrimage is organized by the Apostolate for Holy Relics and is sponsored by the Knights of Columbus and Holy Cross Family Ministries. The relic is then enshrined in the Cathedral of Our Lady of the Angels in Los Angeles.

2003: After the Juan Diego's canonization, Archbishop Norberto Rivera Carrera founds the Guadalupan Studies Institute to bring together scholars to further study the Guadalupan event.

2007, May 13: On his first apostolic journey, while in Brazil, Pope Benedict XVI underscores the continuing significance of Our Lady of Guadalupe by addressing the Bishops of Latin America and the Caribbean with the words she once spoke to Juan Diego centuries before.

APPENDIX C

Prayers

PRAYER TO OUR LADY OF GUADALUPE

Given by John Paul II on his first apostolic visit to Mexico in 1979[1]

O Immaculate Virgin,
Mother of the true God and Mother of the Church!
You, who from this place reveal
your clemency and your compassion
to all who seek your protection,
hear the prayer that we address to you with filial trust,
and present it to your Son Jesus, our sole Redeemer.

Mother of Mercy, Teacher of hidden and silent sacrifice,
to you, who come to meet us sinners,
we dedicate on this day all our being and all our love.
We also dedicate to you our life, our work,
our joys, our infirmities and our sorrows.

Grant peace, justice and prosperity to our peoples;
for we entrust to your care all that we have and all that we are,
our Lady and Mother.

*We wish to be entirely yours and to walk with you
along the way of complete faithfulness to Jesus Christ in His Church:
hold us always with your loving hand.*

*Lady of Guadalupe, Mother of the Americas,
we pray to you for all the Bishops, that they may lead the faithful along
    paths
of intense Christian life, of love and humble service to God and souls.*

*Contemplate this immense harvest, and intercede with the Lord
that He may instill a hunger for holiness in all the People of God,
and grant abundant vocations to the priesthood and religious life,
and that they be strong in the faith and zealous dispensers of God's
    mysteries.*

*Grant to our homes
the grace of loving and respecting life since its beginnings,
with the same love with which you conceived in your womb
the life of the Son of God.
Blessed Virgin Mary, Mother of Precious Love, protect our families,
so that they may always remain united, and bless the upbringing of our
    children.*

*You, our hope, look upon us with compassion,
teach us to go continually to Jesus and, if we fall, help us to rise again,
to return to Him, by confessing our faults
and sins in the Sacrament of Penance,
which brings peace to the soul.
We beg you to grant us a great love for all the holy Sacraments,
which are, as they were, the signs that your Son left us on earth.*

*Thus, Most Holy Mother, with the peace of God in our conscience,
with our hearts free from evil and hatred,
we will be able to bring to all true joy and true peace,
which come to us from your Son, our Lord Jesus Christ,
who with God the Father and the Holy Spirit,
lives and reigns forever and ever. Amen.*

PRAYER TO ST. JUAN DIEGO

From John Paul II's homily at the canonization of St. Juan Diego at the Basilica of Our Lady of Guadalupe in 2002[2]

Blessed Juan Diego, a good, Christian Indian,
whom simple people have always considered a saint!
We ask you to accompany the Church...
so that she may be more evangelizing and more missionary each day.

Encourage the Bishops, support the priests,
inspire new and holy vocations,
help all those who give their lives
to the cause of Christ and the spread of his Kingdom.
Happy Juan Diego, true and faithful man!

We entrust to you our lay brothers and sisters
so that, feeling the call to holiness,
they may imbue every area of social life
with the spirit of the Gospel.
Bless families, strengthen spouses in their marriage,
sustain the efforts of parents
to give their children a Christian upbringing.

Look with favor upon the pain of those who are suffering
in body or in spirit, on those afflicted by poverty,
loneliness, marginalization or ignorance.
May all people, civic leaders and ordinary citizens,
always act in accordance with the demands of justice
and with respect for the dignity of each person,
so that in this way peace may be reinforced.

Beloved Juan Diego, "the talking eagle"!
Show us the way that leads to the "Dark Virgin" of Tepeyac,
that she may receive us in the depths of her heart,
for she is the loving, compassionate Mother
who guides us to the true God. Amen.

CONSECRATION OF THE FAMILY
TO OUR LADY OF GUADALUPE

Holy Mary, Mother of God
you fled into Egypt with your husband Joseph
to save your child from a death defended by unjust laws,
seeking protection in a foreign land.

Holy Mary, Mother to Juan Diego,
on the Tepeyac hill you came not as an exile
but as a mother offering protection and peace
to a new family in this new land, bringing with you such beauty
that could only compare with his dreams of the heavenly.

Come now to the Tepeyac of our family.
To you we consecrate not only ourselves as individuals,
but we consecrate our shared life — our unity of love as a family.

Our family has shared many joys,
and you have known them all.
Continue to watch over us and strengthen us
in our shared life and love.

When one of us faces difficulty,
help us all to be supportive.
When division seems inevitable,
help us all to be patient and to grow together.
When we are lost in ourselves and our own cares,
distracted by demands,
when anger rises and unkind words lash out,
help us all to forgive and to seek forgiveness,
and to see our good in the good of our family.

Holy Mary, come to the Tepeyac of our hearts,
make such a presence of Christ there
that we may no longer roam the empty places

where difficulties are unanswered,
but find instead in you a way to Christ,
and find in Christ the way of love,
transforming even hard times into opportunities for love.

Help our family to create a place of love
for the unborn children with us,
for the sick and the elderly among us,
for the persons dying before us.
And when comfort seems inexpressible
and help seems beyond our abilities,
let your words and your hands guide us.

To those who seem far from your healing presence,
let our family radiate your love of Christ.
To those whose families have been broken by hardship,
who can no longer see the obscured or severed bond of love,
let our family be a refuge, an extension of your mantle.
To those who cannot see the face of Christ in their lives,
let our family's life in Christ, our domestic church,
become a place for meeting God.

Holy Mary, Mother at Guadalupe,
We, your children, trust you with the safety of our family,
Save us from tolerating evil, encourage our defense of the good,
that our family may become a thing of beauty
in building a civilization truly worthy of God's family.

PRAYER FOR LIFE

From John Paul II 1995 encyclical "The Gospel of Life" (Evangelium Vitae)[3]

O Mary,
bright dawn of the new world,

Mother of the living,
to you do we entrust the cause of life.

Look down, O Mother,
upon the vast numbers
of babies not allowed to be born,
of the poor whose lives are made difficult,
of men and women
who are victims of brutal violence,
of the elderly and the sick killed
by indifference or out of misguided mercy.

Grant that all who believe in your Son
may proclaim the Gospel of life
with honesty and love
to the people of our time.

Obtain for them the grace
to accept that Gospel
as a gift ever new,
the joy of celebrating it with gratitude
throughout their lives
and the courage to bear witness to it
resolutely, in order to build,
together with all people of good will,
the civilization of truth and love,
to the praise and glory of God,
the Creator and lover of life.

PLEDGE TO OUR LADY OF GUADALUPE

Our Lady of Guadalupe,
by saying "yes" to God's gift of life,
you brought life to the world.

May I, like you, always be prepared
to accept the gift of new life.

You who told us that you would be our Mother,
always keep me close to your motherly heart.
May all the sons and daughters of this great land
yet to be born always be welcomed and protected.

O Virgin Mary, you who are
the Immaculate tabernacle of the Sacramental Jesus,
today I consecrate myself entirely to you,
and so I promise you that I will defend human life
from conception until the moment
when our Lord calls each person to His presence.

MAGNIFICAT

Also known as the Canticle of Mary, spoken by Mary at the Visitation in the Gospel[4]

My soul proclaims the greatness of the Lord;
my spirit rejoices in God my savior
for he has looked upon his lowly servant.

From this day all generations will call me blessed:
the Almighty has done great things for me,
and holy is his Name.

He has mercy on those who fear him
in every generation.

He has shown the strength of his arm,
he has scattered the proud in their conceit.

He has cast down the mighty from their thrones,
and has lifted up the lowly.

He has filled the hungry with good things,
and the rich he has sent away empty.

He has come to the help of his servant Israel
for he has remembered his promise of mercy,
the promise he made to our fathers,
to Abraham and his children for ever.

PRAYER FOR A CONTINENT OF HOPE AND LOVE

John Paul II's prayer from his homily given at the Basilica of Our Lady of Guadalupe in Mexico City in 1999[5]

O Mother! You know the paths followed
by the first evangelizers of the New World,
from Guanahani Island and Hispaniola
to the Amazon forests and the Andean peaks,
reaching to Tierra del Fuego in the south
and to the Great Lakes and mountains of the north.
Accompany the Church working in the nations of America,
so that she may always preach the Gospel
and renew her missionary spirit.
Encourage all who devote their lives
to the cause of Jesus and the spread of his kingdom.

O gentle Lady of Tepeyac, to you we present
this countless multitude of the faithful
praying to God in America.
You who have penetrated their hearts,
visit and comfort the homes, the parishes,
and the dioceses of the whole continent.
Grant that Christian families

may exemplarily raise their children
in the Church's faith and in love of the Gospel,
so that they will be the seed of apostolic vocations.
Turn your gaze today upon young people
and encourage them to walk with Jesus Christ.

O Lady and Mother of America!
Strengthen the faith of our lay brothers and sisters,
so that in all areas of social, professional, cultural and political life
they may act in accord with the truth and the new law
which Jesus brought to humanity.
Look with mercy on the distress of those suffering
from hunger, loneliness, rejection or ignorance.
Make us recognize them as your favorite children
and give us the fervent charity to help them in their needs.

Holy Virgin of Guadalupe, Queen of Peace!
Save the nations and peoples of this continent.
Teach everyone, political leaders and citizens,
to live in true freedom and to act
according to the requirements of justice
and respect for human rights,
so that peace may thus be established once and for all.
To you, O Lady of Guadalupe,
Mother of Jesus and our Mother,
belong all the love, honor, glory and endless praise
of your American sons and daughters!

NOTES

INTRODUCTION

1. Cardinale, "First Stop Puebla."
2. John Paul II, *Rise, Let Us Be on Our Way,* 55.
3. John Paul II, Homily at the Basilica of Our Lady of Guadalupe, January 27, 1979, §2.
4. León-Portilla addresses this authorship and dating in *Tonantzin Guadalupe.*
5. For example, *Información de 1556.*
6. Cf. Pardo, *The Origins of Mexican Catholicism*, especially Chapter I on conversion and baptism, 20–48.
7. For example, on March 7, 1530, Friar Zumárraga excommunicated several members of the governing body, the First Audience, for torturing and killing a Crown priest, Cristóbal de Angulo, and García de Llerena, a servant to Cortés. Cf. García Icazbalceta, *Fray Juan de Zumárraga,* 54–61.
8. John Paul II, General Audience, February 14, 1979, §6.
9. Benedict XVI, Address at the Inaugural Session of the Fifth General Conference of the Bishops of Latin America, §6.
10. John Paul II, *Ecclesia in America*, §11.
11. Ibid.
12. Ibid.
13. Ibid., §12.

14. Ibid., §33.
15. Benedict XVI, Address at the Inaugural Session of the Fifth General Conference of the Bishops of Latin America, §4.

CHAPTER 1

1. Luke 1:38.
2. "Actas e Informes Médicos y Técnicos sobre el Caso del Joven Juan José Barragán," in the Archive for the Cause of the Canonization of Saint Juan Diego, in the Congregation for the Causes of Saints, Holy See.
3. Cf. Sigüenza y Góngora, *Piedad Heróica de D. Fernando Cortés*, 31.
4. Specifically, the *macehuales* were "free commoners." See Owensby, *Empire of Law and Indian Justice in Colonial México*, 16. Some of the early works about Juan Diego include: Alva Ixtlilxóchitl, "Nican Motecpana"; Becerra Tanco, *Felicidad de México*; Sigüenza y Góngora, *Piedad Heróica de D. Fernando Cortés*; and Florencia, *Estrella del Norte de México*. Early testimonies about Juan Diego can be found in "Informaciones Guadalupanas de 1666 y 1723," in de la Torre Villar and Navarro de Anda, eds., *Testimonios Históricos Guadalupanos*. Finally, for some contemporary sources, see Chávez, *Juan Diego: La Santidad de un Indio Humilde* and Chávez, *Juan Diego: Una Vida de Santidad Que Marcó la Historia*.
5. *Informaciones Jurídicas de 1666*, f. 158r.
6. For an extended account of Cortés's conquest of the Aztec Empire, see Levy, *Conquistador*; also, for an excellent account specifically on Cortés's siege of Mexico City, see Hanson, *Carnage and Culture,* 170–93. For more on the practice of human sacrifice in the Aztec culture, see Carrasco, *City of Sacrifice*.
7. Throughout this chapter, the account of the apparition is based on Valeriano, *Nican Mopohua*. Full translation included in Appendix A.
8. Valeriano, *Nican Mopohua*, 9–10.
9. *Cantares Mexicanos*, fol. 16v.
10. In the Aztec civilization, corn was of such great importance that it took on profound religious significance; the Aztecs had several gods of corn to whom they made numerous offerings and for whom they performed human sacrifices. In *Patterns in Comparative Religion,* Mircea Eliade describes one rite when, just as the corn seed began to sprout, the Aztecs

would go out to the fields "to find the god of the maize," "a shoot which they brought back to the house and offered food, exactly as they would a god." He continues: "In the evening, [the sprout] was brought to the temple of Chicome-coatl, goddess of sustenance, where a group of young girls were gathered, each carrying a bundle of seven ears of maize saved from the last crop, wrapped in red paper and sprinkled with sap. The name given to the bundle, *chicomolotl* (the sevenfold ear), was also the name of the goddess of the maize. The girls were of three different ages, very young, adolescent, and grown up—symbolizing, no doubt, the stages in the life of the maize—and their arms and legs were covered in red feathers, red being the colour of the maize divinities. This ceremony, intended simply to honour the goddess and obtain her magic blessing upon the newly-germinating crop, did not involve any sacrifice. But three months later, when the crop was ripe, a girl representing the goddess of the new maize, Xilonen, was beheaded." See Eliade, *Patterns in Comparative Religion*, 343.

11. Valeriano, *Nican Mopohua*, 12.

12. Ibid., 17.

13. Ibid., 18–21.

14. Ibid., 24.

15. Ibid., 26.

16. Ibid., 26–31.

17. See, for instance, the analysis of the *Codex Mendoza* in Carrasco, *City of Sacrifice*, 25.

18. For more information on Friar Zumárraga, see García Icazbalceta, *Fray Juan de Zumárraga*.

19. Letter from June 12, 1531. Regarding the destruction of the codices, see Von Hagen, *The Aztec and Maya Papermakers*, 31–32.

20. Valeriano, *Nican Mopohua*, 54–56.

21. Quoted in Lockhart, *Nahuas and Spaniards*, 5–6; cf. Karttunen and Lockhart, *The Art of Náhuatl Speech.*

22. Valeriano, *Nican Mopohua*, 57–62.

23. Luke 1:52, the Magnificat.

24. Mendieta, *Historia Eclesiástica Indiana*, 514.

25. Sahagún, *Historia General*, 546.

26. Sahagún, *Florentine Codex*, VI, 35.

27. The plagues that ravaged Mexico throughout the sixteenth century were

catastrophic, beginning with the smallpox epidemic of 1519–20, when between five million and eight million people perished, and perhaps culminating—though by no means ending—with the epidemic of cocoliztli of 1545–48. This later epidemic, responsible for the death of Juan Diego's uncle in 1545, killed between five million and fifteen million people, or up to 80 percent of the native population of Mexico. As pointed out by Acuña-Soto in "Megadrought and Megadeath in 16th Century Mexico": "In absolute and relative terms the 1545 epidemic was one of the worst demographic catastrophes in human history, approaching even the Black Death of bubonic plague, which killed approximately 25 million in western Europe from 1347 to 1351 or about 50% of the regional population."

28. Valeriano, *Nican Mopohua*, 107.

29. Ibid., 114.

30. Ibid., 115–16.

31. Ibid., 118–19.

32. *Testimonios de la Antigua Palabra*, 161.

33. Lockhart, *Nahuas and Spaniards*, 6.

34. Valeriano, *Nican Mopohua*, 120.

35. Ibid., 137–39.

36. In order to come near the distinctiveness of the Nahuatl concepts, it is important to keep in mind the *difrasismos* (the "disguises"): in different texts written in Nahuatl in the sixteenth-century we find certain linguistic forms that have definitive discursive contexts. These forms have been given several names: metaphors, couplets, *difrasismos*, or paired phrases. The word difrasismo was coined by Father Angel Maria Garibay, one of the first scholars of Náhuatl language and culture in Mexico. See especially Garibay K., *History of Náhuatl Literature*, 926. The main characteristic is the juxtaposition of two or even three words that create a meaning that is not the sum of its parts, but rather produces a third meaning.

Later we shall see the difrasismo "face-heart," which the Indians used to refer to the human person or individual, as well as the difrasismo "*in alt, in tepetl*," meaning nation or civilization; equally present in Indian speech and writing is the difrasismo "*in xóchitl, in cuícatl*," meaning "flower and song." As León-Portilla notes in *Aztec Thought and Culture*, 75, beyond its literal meaning, "the phrase is a metaphor for poetry or a poem." And poetry—"flower and song"—was prized by the Indians as "the only truth on earth." Thus the above identification of flower and song with truth.

37. Anawalt, *Indian Clothing Before Cortés*, 27.

38. Valeriano, *Nican Mopohua*, 208.

39. Luke 18:42; Matthew 9:22.

40. To this day, countless historical anthropologists and specialists in the Náhuatl language have yet to reach a consensus regarding the origin of the Virgin's name. Around the time of the first official inquiry of 1666, Luis Becerra Tanco, one of the most influential commentators on the Guadalupan event, argued in his work *Felicidad de México* that Juan Bernardino, a native Náhuatl-speaker, would not have understood the Spanish "Guadalupe," because the sounds for "g" and "d" do not occur in the Náhuatl language, a language that was at the time still used by a vast majority of the Indians. Becerra Tanco then suggested two alternative Náhuatl names that sounded similar to the Spanish "Guadalupe": *Tequatlanopeuh*, "she whose origins were in the rocky summit," and *Tequantlaxopeuh*, "she who banishes those who devoured us." See Becerra Tanco, *Felicidad de México*, 21. Becerra Tanco's argument has over the years inspired countless scholars to propose alternative indigenous names that, as these scholars contend, were more likely to have been used by the Guadalupan Virgin and Juan Bernardino. Yet Becerra Tanco and others fail to take into account three important facts. First, at the time of the apparition, Juan Bernardino and Juan Diego would have been familiar with the "g" and "d" sounds, which were necessary in the pronunciation of their baptismal names received in 1525. Second, prior to the 1675 publication of Becerra Tanco's *Felicidad de México*, there is no historical evidence indicating that the Virgin was called by any of the names proposed by Becerra Tanco or later Náhuatl scholars, including the earliest account of the event written in Náhuatl. Third, there is a wealth of historical documents, written by the early Spaniards and the Franciscan friars, contending that the Virgin's title be changed to *Tepeaquilla* or *Tepeaca*, thus indicating that the original name was "Guadalupe" and not an Indian name, for had it been a Náhuatl name, there would have been no controversy. See, for instance, the 1556 testimony of the Franciscan Friar Alonso de Santiago in "Información de 1556 ordenada realizar por Alonso de Montúfar," in de la Torre Villar and Navarro de Anda, (eds.), *Testimonios Históricos Guadalupanos*, 61–62.

41. The name "Guadalupe" has been analyzed by a number of authors, most of whom agree that the first part of the name means "river", and as for the second part the name, some authors propose that it derives from a Latin word "lupus" meaning "wolf." However, it is little probable that a word would be partly derived from Arabic and partly from Latin, and agree with the analysis that it come from *lub*, meaning in Arabic "black lava," "black gravel," "black stones," or as "hidden" (that is, staying in the dark or darkness). This interpretation points to the very bottom of the river, that which is "hidden" or "in blackness" – that is, the riverbed which carries the water and moves it about. (Cf. Guerrero, *The Nican Mopohua*, T. I, 92).

42. Crémoux, *Pélerinages et Miracles*, 10–12.

43. An early chronicle on the Aztec migration and discovery of the eagle-sign recounts: "Seeing that everything / was filled with mystery, / [the Aztecs] went on, to seek / the omen of the eagle / and wandering from place to place / they saw the cactus and on it the eagle, / with its wings spread out to the rays of the sun, / enjoying its warmth and the cool of the morning, / and in its claws it held an elegant bird / with precious and resplendent feathers. / . . . [T]hey began to weep and give vent to their feelings, / and to make displays and grimace and tremble, as a sign of their joy and happiness, and as an expression of thanks, saying: 'How have we deserved such a blessing? Who made us worthy of such grace / and greatness and excellence? / Now we have seen what we have sought, / and we have found our city and place. / Let us give thanks to the Lord of creation / and to our god Huitzilopochtli.' / [T]hen, the next day, the priest / Cuauhtloquetzqui said to all of the tribe, / 'My children, we should be grateful to our god / and thank him for the blessing he has given us. / Let us all go and build at the place of the cactus / a small temple where our god may rest." See Durán, *Historia de las Indias de Nueva España*, cited in Matos Moctezuma, "Templo Mayor: History and Interpretation," in Broda, Carrasco, and Matos Moctezuma, eds., *The Great Temple of Tenochtitlan*, 29–30. Also, for the above-cited information on the eagle in Aztec culture and religion, as well as the etymological information on Tenochtitaln, see Miller and Taube, *An Illustrated Dictionary*, 83.

44. The name of this first chapel, commonly called in Spanish the "hermita", can be confusing. This is in part due to the fact that this building had a particular unique history and unique uses as a shrine to Our Lady, as a

chapel where Mass was celebrated, as a pilgrimage site, and as the place where Juan Diego lived. Throughout the book, we tend to refer to the "hermita" as the hermitage, following the tradition of several Guadalupan scholars.

45. Valeriano, *Nican Mopohua*, 214–18.
46. Alva Ixtlilxóchitl, "Nican Motecpana," 305.
47. John Paul II, Homily for the Canonization of St. Juan Diego, §5.
48. Ibid.

CHAPTER 2

1. Damascene, *On Holy Images,* 48.
2. Cf. González Fernández et al, *El Encuentro de la Virgen de Guadalupe.*
3. Andrade, "Testimonio de Manuel Ignacio Andrade," ff. 19v–20v.
4. Ibid.
5. Molina, *Química Aplicada al Manto de la Virgen de Guadalupe*, 3.
6. Cf. Bartolache y Posadas, "Manifiesto Satisfactorio" in de la Torre and Navarro de Anda, eds., *Testimonios Históricos Guadalupanos.* Bartolache's study consisted of two parts, one being the experiment described above. The other part was an examination of the tilma by several expert painters. After examining the image, the painters gave testimony as to their findings. When asked, "Taking into account the rules of your faculty, and without any personal passion or desire, do you consider this Holy Image as having been painted miraculously?" the artists responded: "Yes, inasmuch as what is considered substantial and [original], in our Holy Image, but not inasmuch as certain touch-ups and details which without a doubt, seem to have been done later by impudent hands" (ibid., 648).
7. Molina, *Química Aplicada al Manto de la Virgen de Guadalupe*, 3.
8. The team of artists included Juan Salguero, an art teacher for more than thirty years; Thomas Conrado, an art teacher for more than eight years; Sebastián López de Ávalos, a painter for more than thirty years; Nicolás de Fuenlabrada, a painter for over twenty years; Nicolás de Angulo, an art teacher and painter for more than twenty years; Juan Sánchez, an art teacher and painter for more than fifteen years; and Alonso de Zárate, an art teacher and painter for over fourteen years. See ibid.
9. *Informaciones Jurídicas de 1666*, ff. 138v–140r.

10. The chemists on the team included Dr. Lucas de Cárdenas Soto, Dr. Jerónimo Ortiz, and Dr. Juan Melgarejo. See Molina, *Química aplicada al manto de la Virgen de Guadalupe*, 3.

11. *Informaciones Jurídicas de 1666*, f. 185r–185v. As the *Informaciones Jurídicas de 1666* notes, the Hermitage was built on the ground bordering the south side of the lake which extended almost to the very edge of the Hermitage near the main entrance. Even at this time, the chemists saw evidence of the humidity of the sacristy and the church. Not only did the Hermitage suffer from the breezes constantly blowing from the lake, but during the rainy season, waters would rise up from the lake and reach the Hermitage, thus making the area around the Hermitage very wet and allowing the ground's humidity to seep through the foundation from underneath. See ibid. ff. 182v–183r.

12. Ibid., f. 187r.

13. Ibid.

14. Aste Tönsmann, *El Secreto de Sus Ojos*, 48.

15. Alva Ixtlilxóchitl, "Nican Motecpana," 307.

16. Second Council of Nicaea, "Decree of the Holy, Great, Ecumenical Synod, the Second of Nicaea."

17. Sahagún, *Florentine Codex*, XII, f. 25r.

18. See *Coloquios y Doctrina Cristiana con que los Doce Frailes de San Francisco Enviados por el Papa Adriano VI y por el Emperador Carlos V*, f.34r and f.35r, respectively.

19. For example, Hernández Illescas and Fernando Ojeda Llanes. See also Hernández Illescas, Rojas Sánchez, and Salazar, *La Virgen de Guadalupe y las Estrellas*.

20. The complete text and its judicial ratification are in the Sacred Congregation for the Causes of the Saints, Archive for the Cause of the Canonization of Juan Diego.

21. Cf. especially Carrasco, *City of Sacrifice: the Aztec Empire and the Role of Violence in Civilization*.

22. The difference between the day of the winter solstice in 1531 and now is due to the change from the Julian calendar to the Gregorian calendar (used today); while the Julian calendar was largely satisfactory, it failed to take into account the need for adding an extra day (leap day) every fourth year, causing a ten-day difference between the calendars.

23. González et al., *El Encuentro de la Virgen de Guadalupe y Juan Diego*, 213.

24. Mendieta, *Historia Eclesiástica Indiana*, 99.

25. Soustelle and O'Brian, *Daily Life of the Aztecs*, 46–47.

26. *Testimonios de la Antigua Palabra,* 77.

27. The complete text and its judicial ratification are in the Sacred Congregation for the Causes of the Saints, Archive for the Cause of the Canonization of Juan Diego.

28. This is also seen in the early catechetical artwork, depicting the crucifixion only symbolically, showing the instruments of the crucifixion—the nails, the crown of thorns, the spear – instead of showing the body of Christ himself.

29. Ochoterena, Análisis de Unas Fibras del Ayate de Juan Diego o Icono de Nuestra Señora de Guadalupe.

30. Benedict XVI, *On the Way to Jesus Christ*, 74.

31. López Trujillo, Address at the Opening of the International Theological Pastoral Congress Fourth World Meeting of Families; cf. *Documento Final de Santo Domingo* (IV Conferencia Episcopal Latinoamericano, 1992), 30.

32. John Paul II, Address at Vigyan Bhavan.

33. Paul VI, *Ecclesiam Suam*, §87.

CHAPTER 3

1. Fr. Mario Rojas developed the concept of the indigenous glyphs in a way that can easily be compared with those that the Virgin of Guadalupe had on her dress. Cf. Rojas Sánchez, *Guadalupe: Símbolo y Evangelización*.

2. Boone, *Stories in Red and Black*, 23.

3. For example, the island city of Tenochtitlan itself was designed according to it, divided into four quadrants by four roads, all connecting to the central temple, the Templo Mayor. For more on the symbolism of the Templo Mayor in relation to the Aztec religion and cosmology, see Matos Moctezuma, "Symbolism of the Templo Mayor."

4. During his reign, which ended with his death in 1472, Nezahualcóyotl, the great poet, philosopher, and king, erected a temple directly opposite the temple of Huitzilopochtli, which was previously built in recognition of Tenochtitlan's political supremacy. Unlike the temples of Tenochtitlan, this new temple was dedicated to Tloque Nahuaque, "lord of the close and near, invisible as the night and intangible as the wind,"

and held no images or idols. See León-Portilla, *Fifteen Poets of the Aztec World*, 76.

5. As suggested, the four-petal flower over the Virgin's womb is in the position of the *Nahui Ollin,* meaning constant movement. The *Nahui Ollin* is represented in several Indian codices, such as the *Codex Ríos* and the *Telleriano Remensis* manuscript, and in certain artistic and archeological works, including some found in the Templo Mayor as well as the so-called "Sun Stone," depicting the Aztec calendar. In Rojas Sánchez's *Guadalupe: Símbolo y evangelización* (p. 151-154 and Plates No. 55), the four-petal flower is related to Indian cosmology and solar symbols. In this, some of the important Indian cosmological concepts to keep in mind are: *Tonatih* (the Sun itself), *Nahui Ollin* (four movements), *Chalchiuhmichihuacan* (where the master of the jade fish lives; life), and *Omeyocan* (place of duality, of god). Significantly, each of these concepts is expressed through the four-petal flower. And thus, the flower on the Virgin's womb, representing Christ, draws on each of these concepts, thereby expressing to the Indians a God who is singular, omnipotent, eternal, and in constant movement. That is, a God who is the Lord of life, of the heavens, and of the earth.

To better understand the symbolic richness and synthesis of these concepts, see León-Portilla, *La Filosofía Náhuatl*, particularly chapters II and III. Here, León-Portilla considers the following passage from *Manuscript 1558*, in which the Indians identify the Sun with the Nahui Ollin and connect these with the preservation of life: "This Sun, named four movement, this is the Sun on which we live now." Analyzing this passage, León-Portilla writes: "Just as the text states, this can also be seen at the marvelous Sun stone, where the central figure represents the face of *Tonatiuh* (Sun), inside the sign of 4 movement (nahui ollin) from *Tonalámatl*. Given that this fifth Sun makes its entrance into the Nahuatl cosmological thought, the idea of movement becomes extremely important in the image of the world and its destiny" (*La Filosofía Náhuatl*, 8).

Notably, the idea of a single deity was not foreign to some of the Indians, specifically the Indian sages or *tlamatinime*. As León-Portilla notes: "In sharp contrast with the popular worship of the sun god *Huitzilopochtli*, the *tlamatinime* kept the ancient belief in a single god who exists beyond all heavenly levels." Called by many names, this god, while absolutely one, was at the same time seen as having two aspects or faces, one masculine and the other feminine, hence his popular title Ometéotl, meaning "the god of duality." See León-Portilla, *Visión de los vencidos*. See also López Austin, "The Mexicas and Their Cosmos," 26.

6. Valeriano, *Nican Mopohua*, 26.

7. Second Vatican Council, *Ad Gentes*, §11.

8. Acts 17:27–28.

9. For more information on Aztec cosmology and Ometéotl, see León-Portilla, *Aztec Thought and Culture*, 62–103.

10. For more information on the Aztec calendar system, see Aguilar-Moreno, *Handbook to Life in the Aztec World*, 290–98.

11. Cf. Hassig, *Time, History and Belief in Aztec and Colonial Mexico*, 7–17.

12. Luke 2; traditional "Christmas Proclamation" from the *Roman Martyrology*.

13. Valeriano, *Nican Mopohua*, 1.

14. As suggested, for the natives, the difrasismo "*in atl in tepetl*" or "water and mountain" means "village," "city," or "civilization." The mountain—the stone, the wood, the cavern, etc.—provided protection, while the water was associated with life. For the natives, the two realities together signified civilization. Cf. Luis Becerra Tanco, *Felicidad de México*, 1979 translation; León-Portilla, *Tonantzin Guadalupe*, 92-93; Guerrero, *El Nican Mopohua*, T. I, 109.

15. León-Portilla, *Fifteen Poets of the Aztec World*, 148.

16. Ibid., 147–48.

17. For more on the symbolism of the Templo Mayor in relation to Aztec cosmology, see Matos Moctezuma, "Symbolism of the Templo Mayor," 185–209.

18. Broda, "The Provenience of the Offerings: Tribute and Cosmovisión," 230–31.

19. Sahagún, quoted and discussed in ibid.

20. León-Portilla, *Aztec Thought and Culture*, 8.

21. The Náhuatl sage, as León-Portilla explains, "was called *te-ix-tlamach-tiani*, 'teacher of people's faces.'" Additionally, describing the task of the Aztec educator, one Aztec poet wrote: "He makes wise the countenances of others; / he contributes to their assuming a face; / he leads them to develop it. . . . / Thanks to him, people humanize their will." See León-Portilla, *Aztec Thought and Culture*, 115. Cf. Sahagún, *Códice Matritense de la Real Academia*, VIII, f. 118v.

22. León-Portilla, *Aztec Thought and Culture*, 142–43.

23. Ezekiel 11:19–20.

24. The complete text and its judicial ratification are in the Sacred Congregation for the Causes of the Saints, Archive for the Cause of the Canonization of Juan Diego.

25. *Testimonios de la Antigua Palabra*, 145.

CHAPTER 4

1. Benedict XVI, Address to the Local Population and the Young People.

2. Words from 1 John 4:8; quoted in Benedict XVI, *Deus Caritas Est,* §1.

3. Ibid., §6.

4. Carrasco, *City of Sacrifice*, 96. Carrasco writes: "[I]n this fearful night, women were closed up in granaries to avoid their transformation into fierce beasts who would eat men, pregnant women put on masks of maguey leaves, and children were punched and nudged awake to avoid being turned into mice while asleep." Also, as is relayed in the *Florentine Codex*, on that night, the people of Mexico "became filled with dread that the sun would be destroyed forever. All would be ended, there would be evermore be night. Nevermore would the sun come forth. Night would prevail forever, and the demons of darkness would descend, to eat men." See Sahagún, *Florentine Codex*, 7:27, quoted in Carrasco, *City of Sacrifice*, 97. Finally, León-Portilla cites ancient annals that provide mythological information on the previous four creations or "suns" and also gives more specific information about the anticipated apocalypse: "Under this sun [the fifth sun or present age] there will be earthquakes and hunger, and then our end shall come." See *Annals of Cuauhtitlán* and *Leyenda de los Soles*, cited in León-Portilla, *Aztec Thought and Culture*, 39.

5. John 3:16.

6. John Paul II, Address at the Puebla Conference, Mexico, 1979.

7. Benedict XVI (Joseph Cardinal Ratzinger), *God and the World*, 181.

8. Benedict XVI, *Deus Caritas Est*, §9.

9. Genesis 1:27.

10. John Paul II, *Christifideles Laici*, §17.

11. For more on John Paul II's Theology of the Body, see Anderson and Grenados, *Called to Love: Approaching John Paul II's Theology of the Body.*

12. Benedict XVI, *Deus Caritas Est*, §17.

13. John Paul II, *Letter to Families*, February 2, 1994, §19.

14. John Paul II, Address to Participants in the International Games for Disabled Persons, §7.

15. Benedict XVI, Homily for the Inauguration of his Pontificate.

16. Benedict XVI, General Audience, November 23, 2008.

17. Benedict XVI, Interview with Deutsche Welle.

18. Saraiva Martins, "The Face of Christ in the Face of the Church," §2.

19. Pope Benedict XVI, Message for the Celebration of the World Day of Peace, January 1, 2007.

20. Benedict XVI, *Sacramentum Caritatis*, §70.

21. John 19:34.

22. Chrysostom, "Catecheses", 3, 13–19.

23. Benedict XVI, Meeting with Catholic Educators.

CHAPTER 5

1. John Paul II, Message for the World Day of Peace 1981, §11.

2. John Paul II (Karol Wojtyla), Homily at Jasna Góra (Czestochowa), 1978. Quoted in Boniecki, *The Making of the Pope of the Millennium,* 739.

3. Mendieta, *Historia Eclesiástica Indiana*, 311–12. "And fearing that the friars would send notice of their tyrannies to the King and to his advisors, they placed the potential stagecoach under watch as well as interrupted all of the roads and trails so that word could not get through. And so they decreed that no one take a letter from religious men without the authorities reading it first. And subsequently they ordered inspections of the ships upsetting everything down to the ballast, looking for letters from the friars. And not content with this, for one or another reason, they wished to forestall, at the expense of the honor of the innocents, that if any letter arrived from them it should be discredited. To this effect, since they themselves were the witnesses and secretaries, they wrote their reports slandering the Holy Bishop and the friars with ugly and unimaginable comments."

4. For a fuller account, see García Icazbalceta, *Fray Juan de Zumárraga,* 36.

5. Zumárraga, *Letter from Friar Juan de Zumárraga to the King of Spain.*

6. Ibid., f. 314 v.

7. Mendieta, *Historia Eclesiástica Indiana,* 53.

8. Ibid., 49.

9. Sahagún, *Historia General,* 17.

10. This began scarcely one year after the twelve Franciscans arrived, beginning in Texcoco and later continuing in Mexico, Tlaxcala, and Huejotzingo. Motolinia provides us with interesting detailed news of this first "battle" against the idols by the Franciscans under the cover of night with the aid of some of their young catechism students: "Idolatry was as well established as before until, on the first day of the year 1525, which in that year fell on a Sunday, in *Texcoco,* the location of most and greatest of the *teocallis* or temples, and those most filled with idols and which were very well serviced by priests or ministers, on that very night three monks, from ten at night until dawn, scared and drove away all those who were in the houses and halls of the devils; and that day, after mass, they preached to them forbidding them to murder and ordering them, on behalf of God and the King, not to do that again otherwise they would be punished according to how God commanded such to be punished. This was the first battle against the devil, and then in Mexico and its surroundings, and in *Coauthiclan* [Cuautitlan]." Motolinia, *History of the Indians of New Spain,* 22.

11. John Paul II, *Letter to Men and Women Religious of Latin America.* Also quoted in John Paul II, *Message for the IV World Day of the Sick*, October 11, 1995, which was held at the Basilica of Our Lady of Guadalupe in Mexico.

12. Motolinia took great pains in calculating the number of baptisms, acquiring figures from missionaries and provinces. See his *History of the Indians of New Spain*, 131–33.

13. Macpherson, "St. Ethelbert." As the eighth-century English historian St. Bede the Venerable described the situation: "When he [King Ethelbert], among the rest, believed and was baptized, . . . greater numbers began daily to flock together to hear the Word, and, forsaking their heathen rites, to have fellowship, through faith, in the unity of Christ's Holy

Church. It is told that the king, while he rejoiced at their conversion and their faith, yet compelled none to embrace Christianity, but only showed more affection to the believers, as to his fellow citizens in the kingdom of Heaven. For he had learned from those who had instructed him and guided him to salvation, that the service of Christ ought to be voluntary, not by compulsion." Bede, *Historia Ecclesiastica Anglorum*, Book I, Chapter 26.

14. This especially became apparent in the Peace of Augsburg in 1555, based upon the principle of *cujus regio, ejus religio* (whose region, his religion), which declared that the religion of the ruling prince dictated the religion permitted in his realm, effectively forcing religious segregation.

15. Motolinia, *History of the Indians of New Spain*, Bk. 2, Ch. III, 131.

16. Ibid. Cf. Pardo, *The Origins of Mexican Catholicism*, 23–24, and 170–71 n. 10.

17. Hanson, *Carnage and Culture*, 175.

18. Sahagún, *Florentine Codex*, VI, 35.

19. Cf. León-Portilla, *Aztec Thought and Culture*.

20. *Coloquio y Doctrina Cristiana,* f. 36r. Also see León-Portilla, *El Reverso de la Conquista*, 25.

21. Cf. León-Portilla, *Visión de los Vencidos.* Also see León-Portilla, *El Reverso de la Conquista*.

22. Benedict XVI, *Spe Salvi*, §24.

23. Benedict XVI (Joseph Cardinal Ratzinger), *Principles of Catholic Theology*, 391.

24. González Fernandez, et al., *El Encuentro de la Virgen de Guadalupe y Juan Diego,* 204.

25. "Carta de Vasco de Quiroga al Consejo de Indias" in *Documentos Inéditos*, Torres de Mendoza, T. XIII, 421, in Cuevas, *Historia de la Iglesia en México*, T. I, 312.

26. Sahagún, "Sobre Supersticiones," in his *Historia General de las Cosas de Nueva España.* Available in de la Torre Villar and Navarro de Anda, eds., *Testimonios Históricos Guadalupanos,* 142–44.

27. Valeriano, *Nican Mopohua*, 26: "Sancta Maria in inantzin in huel nelli Teotl Dios" (Holy Mary, mother of the true God).

28. Mendieta, *Historia Eclesiástica Indiana*, 276.

29. Charny, *The Book of Chivalry of Geoffroi de Charny*, 177.

30. For more on the Spanish monarchy and its policies toward the Indians of the New World, see especially Owensby, *Empire of Law and Indian Justice in Colonial Mexico*.

31. Similarly, in 1503, Queen Isabel issued a decree ordering that the Indians be treated "as the free people they are, and not as serfs" (ibid., 134).

32. Another important figure in the debates regarding the humanity and rights of the Indians is the missionary Bartolomé de las Casas. Las Casas first came to the New World with his father in 1502, settling on Hispaniola, where he was given a *repartimiento*. However, in 1514, after a dramatic conversion, las Casas gave up his own *repartimiento* and became an adamant defender of the Indians. Later, he joined the Dominican Order, and dedicated much of his time to denouncing both in his preaching and scholarly writing the unjust treatment of the Indians, admitting, however, that "no account, no matter how lengthy, how long it took to write, nor how conscientiously it was compiled, could possibly do justice to the full horror of the atrocities committed." Bartolomé de las Casas, *A Short Account of the Destruction of the Indies*, 43. For more information on De las Casas and New World rights, see Vickery, *Bartolomé de las Casas: Great Prophet of the Americas*.

33. Mark 12:31.

34. Benedict XVI (Joseph Cardinal Ratzinger), *God and the World*, 300.

35. Benedict XVI (Joseph Cardinal Ratzinger), *Principles of Catholic Theology*, 391.

36. "His uncle told him it was true, . . . and he saw her in exactly the same way she had appeared to his nephew. And she told him that she was also sending him to Mexico City to see the Bishop." Valeriano, *Nican Mopohua*, 203–5.

37. Leies, *Mother for a New World*, 231–35.

38. Benedict XVI, *Deus Caritas Est*, §28b.

39. John Paul II, *Message for the World Day of Peace*, January 1, 2003, §9.

40. Congregation for the Doctrine of the Faith and Joseph Cardinal Ratzinger, *Instruction on Christian Freedom and Liberation*, §63.

41. Benedict XVI (Joseph Cardinal Ratzinger), *The Ratzinger Report*, 173.

42. Ibid., 176.

43. Ibid.

44. De la Vega, *El Gran Acontecimiento*. Regarding the study of Tepeyac hill, see Letter from Guillermo Gándara (director of the Mexico City

Herbario) to Fr. Jesús García Gutiérrez (secretary of the Academia de la Historia Guadalupana), February 19, 1924. The study by Ign. Carlos F. de Landero was conducted September 15, 1923; quoted in Benítez, *El Misterio de la Virgen de Guadalupe*, 204.

45. According to the *New York Times,* June 2, 1921, even prior to the successful bombing, another bombing attempt was made: "Three persons disguised as beggars, one of them said to be carrying a dynamite bomb, were arrested last night at the village of Guadalupe, near here, charged with attempting to break up religious services being held in the cathedral there under the auspices of the Knights of Columbus. They were later released upon orders from Celestino Gasca, Governor of the Federal District, who declared there was no evidence against them." Incidentally, Celestino Gasca was also a leader of the CROM. "Vera Cruz Radicals in 24-Hour Strike."

46. In fact, all churches in Mexico were asked to hold prayer services. See *Brownsville Herald,* "Catholics Make Solemn Atonement for Desecration," November 19, 1921. Regarding Obregon's visit, see "Two Goddesses," *New York Times*, November 20, 1921.

47. Meyer, *La Cristiada: El conflicto entre la iglesia y el estado*, 148–51.

48. Ibid., 148.

49. "A group of Separatists, known as the Knights of Guadalupe, has requested the Mexican Government to give the Basilica of Guadalupe to the National or Separatist Church as the seat of the Mexican Catholic religion. The knights say their intention is to make Guadalupe the Vatican of Mexico." "One Dead, Three Hurt in Mexico City Riot," *New York Times*, February 24, 1925.

50. Ibid.; "Calles Closes Church." *New York Times*, March 15, 1925.

51. Álvaro Obregón, quoted in "Papal Notes," *Time*, September 1, 1924.

52. Alva Ixtlilxóchitl, "Nican Motecpana," 307.

53. Leies, *Mother for a New World*, 266.

54. Suzanne Silvercruys, "Eusebio F. Kino."

CHAPTER 6

1. Benedict XVI (Joseph Cardinal Ratzinger) and Seewald, *God and the World,* 296.

2. Regarding the *Información*, quoted in Johnson, *The Virgin of Guadalupe*, 47.

3. Onis, "Mexican Pilgrims Flock to the Shrine of Our Lady of Guadalupe."

4. Cf. *Información de 1556* and the *Letter of the Hieronymite Brother Diego de Santa María*.

5. John Paul II, General Audience, December 16, 1987, §1.

6. John Paul II, General Audience, December 9, 1987, §3.

7. Ibid., §1.

8. John Paul II, General Audience, December 16, 1987, §1.

9. John Paul II, General Audience, December 16, 1987, §1.

10. Luke 16:19-31.

11. Benedict XVI, "Thoughts on the Place of Marian Doctrine and Piety in Faith and Theology as a Whole," in Benedict XVI (Joseph Cardinal Ratzinger) and Von Balthasar, *Mary: the Church at the Source*, 36.

12. Ibid.

13. Betancourt, Interview on Vatican Radio. Quoted in "Betancourt Trusting Our Lady for End to Conflict."

14. Ibid.

15. Mendieta, *Historia Eclesiástica Indiana*, 277.

16. Valeriano, *Nican Mopohua*, 55.

17. John Paul II, *Crossing the Threshold of Hope*, 212-13.

18. Synod of Bishops, *Encounter with the Living Jesus Christ:The Way to Conversion, Communion and Solidarity in America*, §14.

19. John 2:1-11. Quotation from John 2:5. New American Bible translation.

20. Benedict XVI, General Audience, February 21, 2007.

21. Benedict XVI, Homily at the Lower Basilica of St. Francis.

22. Benedict XVI, General Audience, February 21, 2007.

23. Churchill, Radio Broadcast, London, October 1, 1939. In Churchill, *Never Give In*, 199.

24. Groeschel, *Spiritual Passages*, 54-55.

25. Philippians 2:8.

26. Nietzsche, *Antichrist*, §2.

27. John Paul I, Address to the Roman Clergy.

28. John Paul II, *Homily for the Inauguration of his Pontificate,* §5.

29. Benedict XVI, *Homily for the Inauguration of his Pontificate.*

30. Valeriano, *Nican Mopohua*, 55.

31. Ibid., 58-59.

32. Mark 15:34; see also Psalm 22, verse 1.

33. Luke 23:46.

34. Benedict XVI, General Audience, November 26, 2008.

35. John Paul II, *Rise, Let Us Be On Our Way*, 56.

36. Benedict XVI, *Co-Workers of the Truth*, 390-91.

37. Mother Teresa and González-Balado, *Mother Teresa*, 35.

38. Thornton and Varenne, *The Essential Pope Benedict XVI*, 335.

39. Benedict XVI, *God and the World*, 299.

CHAPTER 7

1. John Paul II, Address at Czestochowa.

2. Valeriano, *Nican Mopohua*, 32.

3. Leies, *Mother for a New World*, 188–93.

4. Matthew 28:20.

5. Matthew 28:16–20.

6. Valeriano, *Nican Mopohua*, 26–28.

7. Most authors translate verses 27 and 28 of the *Nican Mopohua* as: "in order to show all my love, compassion, aid, and defense in [the temple]." However, in Nahuatl, different words—and thus different concepts—can be created by joining them or bringing them together in single words, enabling Náhuatl to express rich, multilayered concepts with few words. Breaking down the Nahuatl version of the Virgin's words, these layers are made visible: "Notlazotlaliz" means "my love." "Noicnoitaliz" means "my compassion" and can also be literally translated as "my compassionate glance." However, the Nahuatl text in the *Nican Mopohua* says: "Notetlazotlaliz," "noteicnoitaliz": this -*te*- does not refer to "something," which means that it does not refer to the action that she is carrying out, but to "someone," a person. Thus, she is not talking about herself but of someone else. Therefore, the literal translation of this is "Notetlazotlaliz," "my love-person"; "Noteicnoitaliz," "my compassionate glance-person"; "Notepale-huiliz," "my aid-person"; "Note- manahuiliz," "my salvation-person." This would be hard to pronounce in many languages, including English and Spanish, but from a theological point of view, it has a very

profound meaning, given that it is obvious that Saint Mary of Guadalupe is talking with her Son. That is why the most faithful translation, taking into account all the richness and implications, is: "He who is my love"; "He who is my compassionate glance"; "He who is my aid"; "He who is my salvation." It is also interesting to note that the translators of Nican Mopohua had not paid attention to the syllable -te-, which we can clearly observe in the original text, because in their own philological notes about the usage of the syllable -te- they mention that it makes reference to "someone." It seems, though, that they might have done this in order make the reading of the text in Spanish easier, given the difficulty translating these concepts literally. The result is that these content-rich words that join the syllable -te- end up being translated more simply and clearly in Spanish as "my love" or "my compassionate glance," which, even if not completely incorrect, do not express the richness of this expression. José Luis Guerrero was a pioneer in capturing the deep theological significance of taking into account the syllable -te-, which attaches itself to the word. Even though this makes the translation more literal and thus more difficult to articulate in common Spanish, it helps one capture the depth and richness of the words of Saint Mary of Guadalupe, given that she is making reference to "someone," who evidently is her Son Jesus Christ. Cf. Guerrero, *El Nican Mopohua: Un Intento de Exégesis,* 171–77.

8. John Paul II, General Audience, April 13, 1997, §5.

9. Ibid.

10. Valeriano, *Nican Mopohua,* 24.

11. Ibid.

12. Benedict XVI, *The God of Jesus Christ,* 69–84.

13. Ibid., 78.

14. Von Balthasar, quoted in Benedict XVI, *The God of Jesus Christ,* 75.

15. Benedict XVI, *The God of Jesus Christ,* 77.

16. For more information about the uses and interpretations of the ending -tzin as an expression of courtesy and reverence toward another person, see Ortiz de Montellano, *Nican Mopohua,* 275. Also cf. Guerrero, *El Nican Mopohua: Un Intento de Exégesis,* 136, 142–43. For more information about -tzin as acknowledging honor in one's own situation, see Guerrero, *El Nican Mopohua: Un Intento de Exégesis,* 321. Cf. also Chávez, *La Verdad de Guadalupe,* 318.

17. John 19:26–27.

18. John Paul II, *Redemptoris Mater*, §45.

19. Quoted by John Paul II, Homily at Mass, Accra, Ghana, §2: "You have shown your faith in action, worked for love and persevered through hope, in your Lord Jesus Christ."

20. Benedict XVI, in Benedict XVI (Joseph Cardinal Ratzinger) and Von Balthasar, *Mary: The Church at the Source*, 31.

21. Cf. John Paul II, *Mulieris Dignitatem*, §2-5, as well as John Paul II, *Letter to Women*, §10.

22. John Paul II, Homily at Mass, Suva.

23. John Paul II, *Mulieris Dignitatem*, §22.

24. Benedict XVI, in Benedict XVI and Von Balthasar, *Mary: The Church at the Source*, 25.

25. Ibid., 25.

26. Quoted in González Fernandez, *Guadalupe: Pulso y Corazón de un Pueblo*, 187–88.

27. Mendieta, *Historia Eclesiástica Indiana*, 278.

28. Wainwright and Tucker, eds., *The Oxford History of Christian Worship*, 631–48.

29. Benavente, *History of the Indians of New Spain*, 22.

30. Torquemada, *Monarquía Indiana*, III:140.

31. Mendieta, *Historia Eclesiástica Indiana*, 282–83.

32. Sahagún, *Historia General*, 38.

33. Cameron, Homily.

CHAPTER 8

1. Paul VI, *Apostolicam Actuositatem*, §2.

2. Mendieta, *Historia Eclesiástica Indiana*, 429.

3. For example, one such artistic representation, dated to the sixteenth century, was presented in 1983 by the commission for the beatification of Juan Diego. Done on wood by an unknown Indian artist, this portrait depicts Juan Diego crowned with a halo and wearing the Franciscan habit. Also presented as evidence for Juan Diego's beatification was a sculpture of Juan Diego, again done by an anonymous Indian artist, portraying Juan Diego as a Franciscan, with a missionary staff.

4. Toribio de Benavente discussed this in *Memoriales* and in *History of the Indians of New Spain*. See Pardo, *Origins of Mexican Catholicism*, 49.

5. Pardo, *The Origins of Mexican Catholicism*, 52.

6. Paul VI, *Apostolicam Actuositatem*, §2.

7. Benedict XVI, General Audience, August 20, 2008.

8. John Paul II (Karol Wojtyla), Vatican Radio, November 25, 1963. Quoted in Boniecki, *The Making of the Pope of the Millennium*, 221.

9. Benedict XVI, Address to the Bishops of Switzerland, November 9, 2006.

10. John Paul II, Messaggio per la Giornata Mondiale del Migrante 1992, §6.

11. Benedict XVI, *Deus Caritas Est*, §14.

12. John Paul II (Karol Wojtyla), quoted in Boniecki, *The Making of the Pope of the Millennium*, 196.

13. "Testimonio de Marcos Pacheco," in *Informaciones Jurídicas de 1666*, f. 15r–15v, facsimile and translation available in Chávez, *La Virgen de Guadalupe y Juan Diego*.

14. John Paul II, Address for the Arrival Ceremony in Mexico, July 30, 2002, §3.

15. "Eucharistic Prayer I," in *The Sacramentary*, 546.

16. Benedict XVI, General Audience, August 20, 2008.

17. Of course, all Catholics are in some measure "witnesses" to the faith, participating in the evangelization through their actions if not their words as well; likewise, the margin of Indians who did convert became witnesses in this same capacity. However, Juan Diego still stood out in recognition by others, in that he was hailed as a good Christian, an exemplary witness of the life of faith.

18. Benedict XVI (Joseph Cardinal Ratzinger), "The New Evangelization: Building the Civilization of Love."

19. John Paul II, Address to a Spanish-Speaking Parish, in *The Pope Speaks to the American Church*, 222, §3.

20. Benedict XVI (Joseph Cardinal Ratzinger) and Peter Seewald, *Salt of the Earth*, 265.

21. John Paul II, Homily at the Basilica of Our Lady of Guadalupe, January 23, 1999, §8.

22. John Paul II, Ad Limina Address to the Bishops of Indianapolis, Chicago and Milwaukee; John Paul II, *Ecclesia in Oceania*, §19.

23. John Paul II, Address at the Puebla Conference. Quoted in John Paul II, *Ecclesia in America*, §66.

CHAPTER 9

1. John Paul II, Homily at the Basilica of Our Lady of Guadalupe, January 23, 1999, §8.
2. Acuña-Soto, et al., "Megadrought and Megadeath in 16th Century Mexico."
3. López Luján, *The Offerings of the Templo Mayor of Tenochtitlan*, 151. See also Juan Alberton Román Berrelleza, "Offering 48 of the Templo Mayor: A Case of Child Sacrifice," in Boone, ed., *The Aztec Templo Mayor.*
4. This pilgrimage is recounted in the *Nican Motecpana* and in Miguel Sánchez's *Imagen de la Virgen* (1648). Both available in de la Vega, ed., *The Story of Guadalupe*, 94–97 and 142–43, respectively.
5. Luke 1:39–56; quotation from Luke 1:42. *New American Bible translation.*
6. Luke 1:43. *New American Bible translation.*
7. Benedict XVI (Joseph Cardinal Ratzinger) and Von Balthasar, *Mary: The Church at the Source,* 102–3.
8. Benedict XVI (Joseph Cardinal Ratzinger), "Truth and Freedom."
9. Ibid.
10. Ibid.
11. Merton, *No Man Is an Island*, 3.
12. Genesis 1:31.
13. John Paul II, General Audience, April 9, 1986, §4.
14. Valeriano, *Nican Mopohua*, 114.
15. Ibid., 119.
16. Weil, *Waiting for God*, 65.
17. Benedict XVI, Homily for the Inauguration of his Pontificate.
18. For more information on the role of sacrifice in Aztec cosmology, see León-Portilla, *Aztec Thought and Culture*, especially 25–61.
19. Durán, *Historia de las Indias*, I, 242. Quoted also in León-Portilla, *Aztec Thought and Culture*, 163–64.
20. Sahagún, *Historia General*, 384–85. Quoted in Chávez, *Our Lady of Guadalupe and Saint Juan Diego*, 55–56.

21. Benedict XVI, *Spe Salvi*, §34.

22. Valeriano, *Nican Mopohua*, 26–32.

23. Benedict XVI, Address at the Conclusion of the Meeting with the Bishops of Switzerland.

24. Benedict XVI, *Spe Salvi*, §34.

25. Ibid., §35.

26. Paul VI, *Evangelica Testificatio*, §39.

27. Benedict XVI, Address to an International Congress, "Oil on the Wounds."

28. Valeriano, *Nican Mopohua*, 107.

29. Benedict XVI, Homily at the Basilica of Notre-Dame du Rosaire.

30. Psalm 27.

CHAPTER 10

1. John Paul II, *Ecclesia in America*, §11.

2. Benedict XVI, Address at the Inaugural Session of the Fifth General Conference of the Bishops of Latin America, §3.

3. Synod of Bishops, Message of the Special Assembly for America, §4.

4. John Paul II, *Ecclesia in America*, §44, quoting from *Propositio* 54.

5. Benedict XVI, "Die Ecclesiologie des Zweiten Vatikanums."

6. John Paul II, *Ecclesia in America*, §11.

7. Leies, *Mother for a New World*, 323–29.

8. Benedict XVI, Address at the Inaugural Session of the Fifth General Conference of the Bishops of Latin America, §4.

9. Benedict XVI, *Deus Caritas Est*, §16.

10. David Rieff, "Nuevo Catholics."

11. John Paul II, Letter to World Movement of Christian Workers.

12. Quoted in Boniecki, *The Making of the Pope of the Millennium*, 720.

13. Von Balthasar, *Unless You Become Like This Child*, 73.

14. Paul VI, Homily for Beatification, November 1, 1975 .

15. Benedict XVI, Address to the Fathers of the General Congregation of the Society of Jesus.

16. Benedict XVI, Address at the Inaugural Session of the Fifth General Conference of the Bishops of Latin America, §4.

APPENDIX A

1. Burrus, *The Oldest Copy of the Nican Mopohua*, 3–4. Observations on the Spanish and Náhuatl textual similarities first made by Fr. Mario Rojas Sánchez.
2. Ibid.
3. León-Portilla, *Tonantzin Guadalupe*, 87.
4. Translation provided by the Instituto Superior de Estudios Guadalupanos.

APPENDIX C

1. John Paul II, Prayer.
2. John Paul II, Homily for the Canonization of St. Juan Diego Cuauhtlatoatzin, §5.
3. John Paul II, *Evangelium Vitae*, §105.
4. Luke 1:46–55.
5. John Paul II, Homily at the Basilica of Our Lady of Guadalupe, January 23, 1999, §9.

BIBLIOGRAPHY

"Actas e Informes Medicos y Técnicos sobre el Caso del Joven Juan José Barragán." Archive for the Cause of the Canonization of Saint Juan Diego, in the Congregation for the Causes of Saints, Holy See.

Acuña-Soto, Rodolfo, et al. "Megadrought and Megadeath in 16th Century Mexico." *Emerging Infectious Diseases* 8, 4 (2002).

Aguilar-Moreno, Manuel. *Handbook to Life in the Aztec World.* New York: Facts on File, 2006.

Álbum Conmemorativo del 450 Aniversario de las Apariciones de Nuestra Señora de Guadalupe. Mexico City: Buena Nueva, 1981.

Álbum de la Coronación de la Sma. Virgen de Guadalupe. 2 vols. Mexico City: El Tiempo, 1895.

Alcalá Alvarado, Alfonso. "El Milagro del Tepeyac: Objeciones y Respuestas Desde la Historia." *Libro Anual 1981–1982.* Mexico City: Instituto Superior de Estudios Eclesiásticos, 1984.

Alva Ixtlilxóchitl, Fernando de. "Nican Motecpana." In Ernesto de la Torre Villar and Ramiro Navarro de Anda, *Testimonios Históricos Guadalupanos.* Mexico: Ed. FCE, 1982.

Anawalt, Patricia Rieff. *Indian Clothing Before Cortés: Mesoamerican Costumes from the Codices.* Norman: University of Oklahoma Press, 1981.

Anderson, Carl. *A Civilization of Love: What Every Catholic Can Do to Transform the World.* New York: HarperOne, 2008.

Anderson, Carl, and José Grenados. *Called to Love: Approaching John Paul II's Theology of the Body.* New York: Doubleday, 2009.

Andrade, Manuel Ignacio. "Testimonio de Manuel Ignacio Andrade." In *Instrumento Jurídico sobre el agua fuerte que se derramó, casualmente, hace muchos años, sobre el Sagrado lienzo de la portentosa Imagen de N. Sra. De Guadalupe,* 1820. Historical Archives of the Basilica of Guadalupe, Correspondence with the Supreme Government. Box 3, File 54., ff. 19v-20v.

Anticoli, Esteban. *Historia de la aparición de la Santísima Virgen María de Guadalupe en México desde el año MDCCCI al de MDCCCXCV.* 2 vols. Mexico City: La Europea, 1897.

Ascensio, Luis Medina. *The Apparitions of Guadalupe as Historical Events.* Washington, D.C.: Center for Applied Research in the Apostolate, 1979.

Aste Tönsmann, José. *El Secreto de Sus Ojos.* Mexico: El Arca Editores, 2004.

Augustine, Saint. *Confessions.* Transated by Henry Chadwick. New York: Oxford University Press, 1998.

Bartolache, Jose Ignacio and Díaz de Posadas. "Manifiesto Satisfactorio." In Ernest de la Torre Villar and Ramiro Navarro de Anda, *Testimonios Históricos Guadalupanos.* Mexico City: FCE, 1982.

Becerra Tanco, Luis. *Felicidad de México.* Mexico City: Jus, 1979.

Bede, Venerable. *Ecclesiastical History of the English People.* Translated and Edited by David Farmer and Leo Sherley-Price. Harmondsworth Eng.: Penguin, 1990.

Benavente, Toribio de [Motolinia]. *Historia de los Indios de la Nueva España.* Mexico: Porrúa Eds. 1973.

———. *History of the Indians of New Spain.* Trans. Elizabeth Andros Foster. Berkeley, CA: Cortés Society, 1950.

———. *Memoriales o Libro de las Cosas de la Nueva España.* Mexico City: UNAM, Historic Research Institute, 1971.

Benedict XVI. Address at the Conclusion of the Meeting with the Bishops of Switzerland. November 9, 2006. Vatican City: Libreria Editrice Vaticana, 2006. http://www.vatican.va/holy_father/benedict_xvi/speeches/2006/november/documents/hf_ben-xvi_spe_20061109_concl-swiss-bishops_en.html

———. Address at the Inaugural Session of the Fifth General Conference of the Bishops of Latin America. Shrine of Aparecida, May 13, 2007. Vatican City: Libreria Editrice Vaticana, 2007. http://www.vatican.va/holy_father/benedict_xvi/speeches/2007/may/documents/hf_ben-xvi_spe_20070513_conference-aparecida_en.html.

———. Address to Participants in an International Congress, "Oil on the Wounds." April 5, 2008. Vatican City: Libreria Editrice Vaticana, 2008. http://www.vatican.va/holy_father/benedict_xvi/speeches/2008/april/documents/hf_ben-xvi_spe_20080405_istituto-gpii_en.html

———. Address to the Fathers of the General Congregation of the Society of Jesus. February 21, 2008. Vatican City: Libreria Editrice Vaticana, 2008. http://www.vatican.va/holy_father/benedict_xvi/speeches/2008/february/documents/hf_ben-xvi_spe_20080221_gesuiti_en.html

———. Address to the Local Population and the Young People. Pastoral Visit to Santa Maria di Leuca and Brindisi. Brindisi, Italy. June 14, 2008. Vatican City: Libreria Editrice Vaticana, 2008. http://www.vatican.va/holy_father/benedict_xvi/speeches/2008/june/documents/hf_ben-xvi_spe_20080614_lenio-flacco_en.html

———. Angelus Address. Prairie, Lourdes. September 14, 2008. Vatican City: Libreria Editrice Vaticana, 2008. http://www.vatican.va/holy_father/benedict_xvi/angelus/2008/documents/hf_ben-xvi_ang_20080914_lourdes_en.html

———. Angelus Address. St. Peter's Square. February 19, 2006. Vatican City: Libreria Editrice Vaticana, 2006. http://www.vatican.va/holy_father/benedict_xvi/angelus/2006/documents/hf_ben-xvi_ang_20060219_en.html

———. *Deus Caritas Est.* Vatican City: Libreria Editrice Vaticana, 2005. http://www.vatican.va/holy_father/benedict_xvi/encyclicals/documents/hf_ben-xvi_enc_20051225_deus-caritas-est_en.html

———. General Audience. February 21, 2007. Libreria Editrice Vaticana, 2007. http://www.vatican.va/holy_father/benedict_xvi/audiences/2007/documents/hf_ben-xvi_aud_20070221_en.html

———. General Audience. November 26, 2008. Vatican City: Libreria Editrice Vaticana, 2008. http://www.vatican.va/holy_father/benedict_xvi/audiences/2008/documents/hf_ben-xvi_aud_20081126_en.html.

———. General Audience. August 20, 2008. Summer Papal Residence, Castel Gandolfo. Vatican City: Libreria Editrice Vaticana, 2008. http://www.vatican.va/holy_father/benedict_xvi/audiences/2008/documents/hf_ben-xvi_aud_20080820_en.html

———. Homily at the Basilica of Notre-Dame du Rosaire. Apostolic Visit to Lourdes, France. September 15, 2008. Vatican City: Libreria Editrice Vaticana, 2008. http://www.vatican.va/holy_father/benedict_xvi/homilies/2008/documents/hf_ben-xvi_hom_20080915_lourdes-malati_en.html

———. Homily at the Lower Basilica of St Francis. Pastoral Visit to Assisi, Italy. June 17, 2007. Vatican City: Libreria Editrice Vaticana, 2007. http://www.vatican.va/holy_father/benedict_xvi/homilies/2007/documents/hf_ben-xvi_hom_20070617_assisi_en.html

———. Homily at St. Peter's Square. Mass for the Imposition of the Pallium and Conferral of the Fisherman's Ring for the Beginning of the Petrine Ministry of the Bishop of Rome. April 24, 2005. Vatican City: Libreria Editrice Vaticana, 2005. http://www.vatican.va/holy_father/benedict_xvi/homilies/2005/documents/hf_ben-xvi_hom_20050424_inizio-pontificato_en.html

———. Homily for the Inauguration of his Pontificate. Saint Peter's Basilica, April 24, 2005.

Libreria Editrice Vaticana, 2005. http://www.vatican.va/holy_father/benedict_xvi/homilies/documents/hf_ben-xvi_hom_20050424_inizio-pontificato_en.html

———. Inaugural Session of the Fifth General Conference of the Bishops of Latin America and the Caribbean. May 13, 2007. Vatican City: Libreria Editrice Vaticana, 2007. http://www.vatican.va/holy_father/benedict_xvi/speeches/2007/may/documents/hf_ben-xvi_spe_20070513_conference-aparecida_en.html

———. Interview with Deutsche Welle. August 13, 2006. Available from AD2000. http://www.ad2000.com.au/articles/2006/oct2006p8_2359.html.

———. Meeting with Catholic Educators. April 17, 2008. Libreria Editrice Vaticana, 2008. http://www.vatican.va/holy_father/benedict_xvi/speeches/2008/april/documents/hf_ben-xvi_spe_20080417_cath-univ-washington_en.html.

———. Message for the World Day of Peace, January 1, 2007. Libreria Editrice Vaticana, 2007. http://www.vatican.va/holy_father/benedict_xvi/messages/peace/documents/hf_ben-xvi_mes_20061208_xl-world-day-peace_en.html

———. On the Way to Jesus Christ. San Francisco: Ignatius Press, 2005.

———. Sacramentum Caritatis. February 22, 2007. Vatican City: Libreria Editrice Vaticana, 2007. http://www.vatican.va/holy_father/benedict_xvi/apost_exhortations/documents/hf_ben-xvi_exh_20070222_sacramentum-caritatis_en.html

———. Spe Salvi. Vatican City: Libreria Editrice Vaticana, 2007. http://www.vatican.va/holy_father/benedict_xvi/encyclicals/documents/hf_ben-xvi_enc_20071130_spe-salvi_en.html

——— (Joseph Cardinal Ratzinger). Co-Workers of the Truth. San Francisco: Ignatius Press, 1992.

———. "Die Ecclesiologie des Zweiten Vatikanums." L'Osservatore Romano. December 16, 1985.

———. The God of Jesus Christ. Chicago: Franciscan Herald Press, 1978.

———. "The New Evangelization: Building the Civilization of Love." http://www.ewtn.com/new_evangelization/Ratzinger.htm

———. Principles of Catholic Theology. San Francisco: Ignatius Press, 1987.

———. The Ratzinger Report. Trans. Salvator Attanasio and Graham Harrison. San Francisco: Ignatius, 1985.

———. "Truth and Freedom." Communio: International Catholic Review. Spring, 1996. Full text available on the EWTN website: http://www.ewtn.com/library/THEOLOGY/TRUE-FREE.HTM

———. What It Means to Be a Christian. San Francisco: San Francisco: Ignatius Press, 2006.

Benedict XVI (Joseph Cardinal Ratzinger), and Hans Urs Von Balthasar. Mary: The Church at the Source. San Francisco: Ignatius Press, 2005.

Benedict XVI (Joseph Cardinal Ratzinger) and Peter Seewald. God and the World: A Conversation with Peter Seewald. San Francisco, CA: Ignatius Press, 2002.

———. Salt of the Earth. San Francisco: Ignatius Press, 1997.

"Betancourt Trusting Our Lady for End to Conflict," Zenit. September 4, 2008. http://www.zenit.org/article-23549?l=english.

Boniecki, Adam. The Making of the Pope of the Millennium. Stockbridge, MA: Marian Press, 2000.

Boone, Elizabeth. Stories in Red and Black: Pictorial Histories of the Aztecs and Mixtecs. Austin: University of Texas Press, 2000.

———, ed. The Aztec Templo Mayor. Washington, D.C.: Dumbarton Oaks, 1987.

Broda, Johanna. "The Provenience of the Offerings: Tribute and Cosmovisión." In Boone, The Aztec Templo Mayor.

Broda, Johanna, David Carrasco, and Eduardo Matos Moctezuma. The Great Temple of Tenochtitlan. Berkeley: University of California Press, 1989.

Burland, C. A. Montezuma: Lord of the Aztecs. New York: G. P. Putnam's Sons, 1973.

Burrus, Ernest J. The Basic Bibliography of the Guadalupan Apparitions (1531–1723). Washington, D.C.: Center for Applied Research in the Apostolate, 1983.

———. The Oldest Copy of the Nican Mopohua. Washington, D.C.: Center for Applied Research in the Apostolate, 1981.

Butler, Matthew. *Faith and Impiety in Revolutionary Mexico.* Basingstoke: Palgrave Macmillan, 2007.

Cabrera, Miguel. *Maravilla Americana y conjunto de raras maravillas observadas con la dirección de las reglas del Arte de la pintura en la Prodigiosa Imagen de Nuestra Señora de Guadalupe de México.* Mexico City: Imprenta del Real y más antiguo Colegio de San Ildefonso, 1756.

Calderón, Luis. *Virtudes y Méritos de Juan Diego.* Mexico City: Tradición, 1989.

Callahan, Philip. *My Search for Traces of God.* Metairie, LA: Acres Publishing, 1997.

Cameron, Fr. Peter John. Homily on the Feast of Our Lady of Guadalupe. New Haven, CT. December 12, 2008.

Cantares Mexicanos. Facsimile reproduction in *Colección de Cantares Mexicanos.* Edited by Antonio Peñafiel. Mexico, 1904.

Cantos y Crónicas del México Antiguo. Ed. Miguel León-Portilla. Madrid: Dastin, 2003.

Cardinale, Gianni. "First Stop Puebla" (interview with Alfonso Cardinal López Trujillo). *30 Days,* January 2004.

Carrasco, David. *City of Sacrifice.* Boston: Beacon Press, 1999.

———. *Religions of Mesoamerica.* Prospect Heights, IL: Waveland Press, 1998.

———. "The Virgin of Guadalupe and Two Types of Religious Experience: The Personal Illumination and the Ceremonial Landscape." In *Religionen— die religiöse Erfahrung/Religions—The Religious Experience,* ed. Matthias Riedel and Tilo Schabert. Würzburg: Königshausen and Neumann, 2008.

Carrasco, David, and Scott Sessions. *Daily Life of the Aztecs: People of the Sun and Earth.* Indianapolis: Hackett, 1998.

Charny, Geoffroi de. *The Book of Chivalry of Geoffroi de Charny.* Ed. Richard W. Kaeuper and Elspeth Kennedy. Philadelphia: University of Pennsylvania Press, 1996.

Chauvet, Fidel. *El Culto Guadalupano del Tepeyac. Sus Orígenes y sus Críticos del siglo XVI.* Mexico City: Centro de Estudios Fray Bernardino de Sahagún, 1978.

Chavero, Alfredo. *Los Azteca o Mexica Fundación de México Tenochtitlan.* Mexico City: Porrúa, 1983.

Chávez, Eduardo. *Juan Diego: El Mensajero de Santa María de Guadalupe.* Mexico City: Instituto Mexicano de Doctrina Social Cristiana, 2001.

———. *Juan Diego: La Santidad de un Indio Humilde.* Mexico City: Basilica de Guadalupe, 2001.

———. *Juan Diego: Una Vida de Santidad que Marcó la Historia.* Mexico City: Porrúa, 2002.

———. *Our Lady of Guadalupe and Juan Diego: The Historical Evidence.* Trans. Carmen Treviño and Verónica Montaño. Lanham, MA: Rowman & Littlefield, 2006.

———. *La Verdad de Guadalupe.* Mexico City: Empresad Ruz, 2008.

———. *La Virgen de Guadalupe y Juan Diego en las Informaciones Jurídicas de 1666.* Mexico City: Ángel Servin Impresores, 2002.

Chorba, Carrie. *Mexico, from Mestizo to Multicultural.* Nashville: Vanderbilt University Press, 2007.

Chrysostom, Saint John. "Catecheses." *Baptismal Instructions.* Trans. Paul W. Harkins. Westminster, MD: Newman Press, 1963.

Churchill, Winston. *Never Give In: The Best of Winston Churchill's Speeches.* Ed. Winston S. Churchill. New York: Hyperion, 2003.

Coloquios y Doctrina Cristiana con que los doce frailes de san Francisco enviados por el Papa Adriano sexto y por el Emperador Carlos quinto convirtieron a los indios de la Nueva España en lengua Mexicana y Española. Vatican Secret Archive, Misc. Arm-I-91.

Cook, S.F. and L. B. Simpson. "The Population of Central Mexico in the Sixteenth Century." In *Ibero Americana,* 31. Berkeley: University of California Press, 1948.

Cook, Noble David. *Born to Die: Disease and New World Conquest, 1492–1650.* Cambridge: Cambridge University Press, 1998.

Congregation for the Doctrine of the Faith and Joseph Cardinal Ratziner. *Instruction on Christian Freedom and Liberation.* Vatican City: Libreria Editrice Vaticana, 1986.

Crémoux, Françoise. *Pélerinages et Miracles.* Madrid: Casa de Velázquez, 2001.

Cuevas, José de Jesús. *La Santísima Virgen de Guadalupe.* Mexico City: Círculo Católico, 1887.

Cuevas, Mariano. *Álbum Histórico Guadalupano del IV Centenario.* Mexico City: Tip. Salesiana, 1930.

――――. *Historia de la Iglesia en México.* 5 vols. El Paso, TX: Revista Católica, 1928.

Damascene, John. *On Holy Images.* Transated by Mary H. Allies. London: Thomas Baker, 1898.

De la Torre Villar, Ernesto, and Ramiro Navarro de Anda, eds. *Testimonios Históricos Guadalupanos.* Mexico City: FCE, 1982.

Díaz, Juan, A. de Tapia, B. Vázquez, and F. de Aguilar. *La Conquista de Tenochtitlan.* Ed. Germán Vázquez Chamorro. Madrid: Dasti, 2003.

Dolan, Jay, and Gilberto Hinojosa. *Mexican Americans and the Catholic Church, 1900–1965.* Notre Dame, IN: University of Notre Dame Press, 1994.

Dunnington, Jacqueline. *Guadalupe: Our Lady of New Mexico.* Santa Fe: Museum of New Mexico Press, 1999.

Durán, Diego de. *Historia de las Indias de Nueva España y Islas de Tierra Firme.* Mexico: Porrúa, 1967.

Eliade, Mircea. *Patterns in Comparative Religion.* Lincoln: University of Nebraska Press, 1996.

Florencia, Francisco de. *Estrella del Norte de México.* Barcelona: Antonio Velázquez, 1741.

Gallegos Rocafull, José María. "La Filosofía en México en los Siglos XVI y XVII." In *Estudios de Historia de la Filosofía en México.* Ed. Miguel León- Portilla. Mexico City: UNAM, 1963.

García Icazbalceta, Joaquín. *Don Fray Juan de Zumarraga: Primer Obispo y Arzobispo de Mexico.* Ed. Rafael Aguayo Spencer and Antonio Castro Leal. Mexico City: Porrúa, 1947.

García, Jaime. *La Conquista de Mexico-Tenochtitlan.* Mexico City: Porrúa, 2001.

González Fernández, Fidel. *Guadalupe: Pulso y Corazón de un Pueblo.* Madrid: Encuentro, 2004.

González Fernández, Fidel, Eduardo Chávez Sánchez, and José Luis Guerrero Rosado. *El Encuentro de la Virgen de Guadalupe y Juan Diego.* Mexico City: Porrúa, 1999.

Groeschel, Benedict. *Spiritual Passages: The Psychology of Spiritual Development.* New York: Crossroad, 2000.

Guerrero Rosado, José Luis. *Los dos mundos de un indio santo. Cuestionario preliminar*

――――. *Los Dos Mundos de un Indio Santo: Cuestionario Preliminar De La Beatificación De Juan Diego.* Mexico City: Cimiento, 1992.

――――. *Flor y canto del nacimiento de México.* Ed. F. Fernández. Mexico City: Librería Parroquial de laveria, 1990.

――――. *El manto de Juan Diego.* Mexico City: Limusa, 1990.

――――. *El Nican Mopohua: Un Intento de Exégesis.* 2 vols. Mexico City: Universidad Pontificia de México, 1996.

Hanke, Lewis. *The Spanish Struggle for Justice in the Conquest of America.* Philadelphia: University of Pennsylvania Press, 1949.

Hanson, Victor. *Carnage and Culture.* Garden City, NY: Doubleday, 2001.

Hassig, Ross. *Time, History, and Belief in Aztec and Colonial Mexico.* Austin: University of Texas Press, 2001.

Hernández Illescas, Juan Homero. "Estudio de la Imagen de la Virgen de Guadalupe." Breves Comentarios. *Histórica.* 1, 3: 2-21.

――――. "La Imagen de la Virgen de Guadalupe, un Códice Náhuatl." In *Histórica.* 1, 2: 7-20.

Hernández Illescas, Juan Homero, Mario Rojas Sánchez, and Enrique R. Salazar S. *La Virgen de Guadalupe y Las Estrellas.* Mexico: Centro de Estudios Guadalupanos, 1995.

"Información de 1556, ordenada realizar por Alonso de Montufar, arzobispo de Mexico." In Ernesto de la Torre Villar and Ramiro Navarro de Anda, *Testimonios Historicos Guadalupanos.* Mexico: Ed. FCE, 1982.

Informaciones Jurídicas de 1666. Copy of April 14, 1666. History of the Basilica of Guadalupe Archives, Ramo Histórico, Mexico. In *La Virgen de Guadalupe y Juan Diego en las Informaciones Jurídicas de 1666,* translated by Eduardo Chávez Sánchez. Mexico: Instituto de Estudios Teológicos e Históricos Guadalupanos, 2002.

John Paul I. Address to the Roman Clergy. September 7, 1978. Vatican City: Libreria Editrice Vaticana, 1978. http://www.vatican.va/holy_father/john_paul_i/speeches/documents/hf_jp-i_spe_07091978_roman-clergy_en.html.

John Paul II. Ad Limina Address to the Bishops of Indianapolis, Chicago and Milwaukee. May 28, 2004. Vatican City: Libreria Editrice Vaticana, 2004. http://www.vatican.va/holy_father/

john_paul_ii/speeches/2004/may/documents/hf_jp-ii_spe_20040528_ad-limina-usa-reg-vii_en.html.

———. Address at Czestochowa, Jasna Góra. June 4, 1997. Vatican City: Libreria Editrice Vaticana, 1997. http://www.vatican.va/holy_father/john_paul_ii/travels/documents/hf_jp-ii_spe_04061997_prayer_en.html.

———. Address at the Arrival Ceremony in Mexico. International Airport of Mexico City. July 30, 2002. Vatican City: Libreria Editrice Vaticana, 2002. http://www.vatican.va/holy_father/john_paul_ii/speeches/2002/july/documents/hf_jp-ii_spe_20020730_arrival-mexi-co_en.html.

———. Address at the Puebla Conference. January 28, 1979. Vatican City: Libreria Editrice Vaticana, 1979. http://www.vatican.va/holy_father/john_paul_ii/speeches/1979/january/documents/hf_jp-ii_spe_19790128_messico-puebla-episc-latam_en.html.

———. Address at Vigyan Bhavan. November 7, 1999. Vatican City: Libreria Editrice Vaticana, 1999. http://www.vatican.va/holy_father/john_paul_ii/travels/documents/hf_jp-ii_spe_07111999_new-delhi_meeting%20other%20religions_en.html.

———. Address to Participants in the International Games for Disabled Persons. April 3, 1981. Vatican City: Libreria Editrice Vaticana, 1981. http://www.vatican.va/holy_father/john_paul_ii/speeches/1981/april/documents/hf_jp-ii_spe_19810403_mondiali-handicappati_en.html.

———. *Crossing the Threshold of Hope.* Trans. Jenny McPhee and Martha McPhee. New York: Alfred A. Knopf, 1994.

———. *Ecclesia in America.* Vatican City: Libreria Editrice Vaticana, 1999. http://www.vatican.va/holy_father/john_paul_ii/apost_exhortations/documents/hf_jp-ii_exh_22011999_ecclesia-in-america_en.html.

———. *Ecclesia in Oceania.* Vatican City: Libreria Editrice Vaticana, 2001. http://www.vatican.va/holy_father/john_paul_ii/apost_exhortations/documents/hf_jp-ii_exh_20011122_ecclesia-in-oceania_en.html.

———. General Audience. February 14, 1979. Libreria Editrice Vaticana, 1979. http://www.vatican.va/holy_father/john_paul_ii/audiences/1979/documents/hf_jp-ii_aud_19790214_en.html.

———. General Audience. April 9, 1986. Libreria Editrice Vaticana, 1986. http://www.vatican.va/holy_father/john_paul_ii/audiences/alpha/data/aud19860409en.html.

———. General Audience. December 9, 1987. Vatican City: Libreria Editrice Vaticana, 1987. http://www.vatican.va/holy_father/john_paul_ii/audiences/alpha/data/aud19871209en.html.

———. General Audience. December 16, 1987. Vatican City: Libreria Editrice Vaticana, 1987. http://www.vatican.va/holy_father/john_paul_ii/audiences/alpha/data/aud19871216en.html.

———. General Audience. April 13, 1997. Vatican City: Libreria Editrice Vaticana, 1997. http://www.vatican.va/holy_father/john_paul_ii/audiences/1997/documents/hf_jp-ii_aud_13081997_en.html.

———. Homily at a Spanish-Speaking Community, "Our Lady of Guadalupe Plaza." *The Pope Speaks to the American Church.* New York: HarperCollins, 1992.

———. Homily at Mass, Suva (Fiji). November, 21, 1986. Vatican City: Libreria Editrice Vaticana, 1986. http://www.vatican.va/holy_father/john_paul_ii/homilies/1986/documents/hf_jp-ii_hom_19861121_suva-fiji_en.html.

———. Homily at Mass, Accra, Ghana. May 8, 1980. Vatican City: Libreria Editrice Vaticana, 1980. http://www.vatican.va/holy_father/john_paul_ii/homilies/1980/documents/hf_jp-ii_hom_19800508_accra-africa_en.html.

———. Homily for the Canonization of St. Juan Diego. Basilica of Our Lady of Guadalupe, Mexico City. July 31, 2002. Vatican City: Libreria Editrice Vaticana, 2002. http://www.vatican.va/holy_father/john_paul_ii/homilies/2002/documents/hf_jp-ii_hom_20020731_canonization-mexico_en.html

———. Homily for the Inauguration of his Pontificate. Saint Peter's Basilica, October 22, 1978. Vatican City: Libreria Editrice Vaticana, 1978. http://www.vatican.va/holy_father/john_paul_ii/speeches/1978/documents/hf_jp-ii_spe_19781022_inizio-pontificato_en.html

———. Homily at the Basilica of Our Lady of Guadalupe, January 23, 1999. Vatican City:

Libreria Editrice Vaticana, 1999. http://www.vatican.va/holy_father/john_paul_ii/homilies/1999/documents/hf_jp-ii_hom_19990123_mexico-guadalupe_en.html.

———. Homily at the Basilica of Our Lady of Guadalupe, January 27, 1979. Vatican City: Libreria Editrice Vaticana, 1979. http://www.vatican.va/holy_father/john_paul_ii/homilies/1979/documents/hf_jp-ii_hom_19790127_messico-guadalupe_en.html.

———. *Letter to Families.* Vatican City: Libreria Editrice Vaticana, 1994. http://www.vatican.va/holy_father/john_paul_ii/letters/documents/hf_jp-ii_let_02021994_families_en.html.

———. *Letter to Women.* Vatican City: Libreria Editrice Vaticana, 1995. http://www.vatican.va/holy_father/john_paul_ii/letters/documents/hf_jp-ii_let_29061995_women_en.html.

———. *Letter to World Movement of Christian Workers.* May 7, 2000. Vatican City: Libreria Editrice Vaticana, 2000. http://www.vatican.va/holy_father/john_paul_ii/letters/2000/documents/hf_jp-ii_let_20000512_katame_en.html

———. *Letter to Men and Women Religious of Latin America on the Fifth Centenary of the Evangelization of the New World.* June 29, 1990. In *Acta Apostolicae Sedis* 83 (1991): 26–27.

———. Message for the IV World Day of the Sick. October 11, 1995. Vatican City: Libreria Editrice Vaticana, 1995. http://www.vatican.va/holy_father/john_paul_ii/messages/sick/documents/hf_jp-ii_mes_11101995_world-day-of-the-sick-1996_en.html

———. Message for the World Day of Peace, January 1, 1981. Libreria Editrice Vaticana, 1981. http://www.vatican.va/holy_father/john_paul_ii/messages/peace/documents/hf_jp-ii_mes_19801208_xiv-world-day-for-peace_en.html.

———. Message for the World Day of Peace, January 1, 2003. Libreria Editrice Vaticana, 2003. http://www.vatican.va/holy_father/john_paul_ii/messages/peace/documents/hf_jp-ii_mes_20021217_xxxvi-world-day-for-peace_en.html.

———. Messaggio per la Giornata Mondiale del Migrante 1992. February 2, 1992. Vatican City: Libreria Editrice Vaticana, 1992. http://www.vatican.va/holy_father/john_paul_ii/messages/migration/documents/hf_jp-ii_mes_19920731_world-migration-day-1992_it.html.

———. *Mulieris Dignitatem.* Vatican City: Libreria Editrice Vaticana, 1988. http://www.vatican.va/holy_father/john_paul_ii/apost_letters/documents/hf_jp-ii_apl_15081988_mulieris-dignitatem_en.html.

———. *The Pope Speaks to the American Church.* New York: HarperCollins, 1992.

———. Prayer to the Virgin of Guadalupe. Apostolic Visit to Mexico, Mexico City, January 25, 1979. Vatican City: Libreria Editrice Vaticana, 1979. http://www.vatican.va/holy_father/john_paul_ii/speeches/1979/january/documents/hf_jp-ii_spe_19790125_preghiera-guadalupe_sp.html

———. *Rise, Let Us Be on Our Way.* New York: Warner Books, 2004.

———. *Redemptoris Mater.* Vatican City: Libreria Editrice Vaticana, 1987. http://www.vatican.va/holy_father/john_paul_ii/encyclicals/documents/hf_jp-ii_enc_25031987_redemptoris-mater_en.html.

Johnson, Maxwell E. *The Virgin of Guadalupe.* Lanham, MD: Rowman and Littlefield, 2002.

Karttunen, Frances, and James Lockhart. *The Art of Náhuatl Speech.* Los Angeles: UCLA Latin American Center Publications, University of California, 1987.

Langford, Joseph. *Mother Teresa: In the Shadow of Our Lady.* Huntington, IN: Our Sunday Visitor, 2007.

Las Casas, Bartolomé de. *A Short Account of the Destruction of the Indies.* New York: Penguin, 1992.

Laso de la Vega, Luis. *El Gran Acontecimiento {Huei tlamahuicoltica}.* Translated and Edited by Jesús García Gutiérrez and Feliciano Velázquez. Mexico: Carreño, 1926.

———. *The Story of Guadalupe.* Trans. and ed. Lisa Sousa, Stafford Poole, and James Lockhart. Stanford: Stanford University Press, 1998.

Leies, Herbert F. *Mother for a New World: Our Lady of Guadalupe.* Westminster, MD: Newman Press, 1964.

León-Portilla, Miguel. *Los Antiguos Mexicanos a Través de sus Crónicas y Cantares.* Mexico City: FCE, 1983.

———. *Aztec Thought and Culture: A Study of the Ancient Nahuatl Mind.* Norman, OK: University of Oklahoma Press, 1990.

_____. *Bernardino De Sahagun, First Anthropologist.* Norman: University of Oklahoma Press, 2002.

_____. *The Broken Spears.* Boston: Beacon Press, 2007.

_____. *Fifteen Poets of the Aztec World.* Norman: University of Oklahoma Press, 2000.

_____. *La Filosofía Náhuatl Estudiada en sus Fuentes.* Mexico City: UNAM, 1974.

_____. *El Reverso de la Conquista.* Mexico: Joaquín Mortiz, 2007.

_____. *Toltecáyotl. Aspectos de la Cultura Náhuatl.* Mexico City: FCE, 1980.

_____. *Tonantzin Guadalupe.* Mexico: El Colegio Nacional Fondo de Cultura Económica, 2002.

_____. *Visión de los Vencidos.* Mexico City: UNAM, 1969.

León-Portilla, Miguel, et al. *Historia Documental de México.* 2 vols. Mexico City: UNAM, Instituto de Investigaciones Históricas, 1974.

Levy, Buddy. *Conquistador.* London: Bantam, 2008.

Lockhart, James. *Nahuas and Spaniards: Postconquest Central Mexican History and Philology.* Stanford: Stanford University Press, 1991.

López Luján, Leonardo. *The Offerings of the Templo Mayor of Tenochtitlan.* Trans. Bernard R. Ortiz de Montellano and Thelma Ortiz de Montellano. Albuquerque: University of New Mexico Press, 2005.

López Austin, Alfredo. "Los mexicas y su cosmos." In Aa. Vv., *Dioses del México Antiguo.* Mexico: DGE Ediciones, 1995.

López Trujillo, Alfonso Cardinal. Address at the Opening of the International Theological Pastoral Congress Fourth World Meeting of Families. Manila, January 22, 2003. http://www.vatican.va/roman_curia/pontifical_councils/family/documents/rc_pc_family_doc_20030122_iv-meeting-families-manila-trujillo_en.html

Maccagnan, Valerio. *Guadalupe: Evangelio y Cultura.* Guadalajara: Centro Mariano, 2001.

MacPherson, E. "St. Ethelbert." In *Catholic Encyclopedia.* New York: Appleton, 1909.

Matos Moctezuma, Eduardo. "Symbolism of the Templo Mayor." In *The Aztec Templo Mayor,* ed. Elizabeth Boone. Washington, D.C.: Dumbarton Oaks, 1987.

Matovina, Timothy. *Guadalupe and Her Faithful.* Baltimore: Johns Hopkins University Press, 2005.

Mendieta, Gerónimo de. *Historia Eclesiástica Indiana.* Mexico City: Porrúa, 1980.

Mendoza, Victor Campa. *La Literatura Náhuatl Guadalupana.* Mexico City: Instituto Tecnológico de Durango, 2006.

Merton, Thomas. *No Man Is an Island.* Boston: Shambhala, 2005.

Meyer, Jean. *La Cristiada: El Conflicto entre la Iglesia y el Estado.* Mexico: Siglo XXI, 2002.

Miller, Mary, and Karl Taube. *An Illustrated Dictionary of the Gods and Symbols of Ancient Mexico and the Maya.* London: Thames and Hudson, 1997.

Molina, Alejandro Javier. "Química Aplicada al Manto de la Virgen de Guadalupe." In the Archive for the Cause of the Canonization of Saint Juan Diego, in the CCS, Holy See.

Montes de Oca, Luis T. *Las Tres Primeras Ermitas Guadalupanas del Tepeyac.* Mexico City: n.p., 1934.

Nietzsche, Friedrich. *The Antichrist.* N.p.: Wilder Publications, 2008.

Noguez, Xavier. "El Culto Prehispánico en el Tepeyac." *Arqueología Mexicana* 4 (1996): 50–55.

_____. *Documentos Guadalupanos. Un Estudio sobre las Fuentes de Información Tempranas en Torno a las Mariofanías en el Tepeyac.* Mexico City: El Colegio Mexiquense y FCE, 1993.

Ochoterena, Isaac. Análisis de unas fibras del ayate de Juan Diego o Icono de Nuestra Señora de Guadalupe, realizado por el Instituto de Biología de la UNAM, Mexico, June 7, 1946. Instituto de Biología, UNAM, oficio 242, file 812.2/-2. Available in the Archive for the Cause of the Canonization of Juan Diego, in the Congregation for the Causes of Saints, Holy See.

Oliva de Coll, Josefina. *La Resistencia Indígena ante la Conquista.* Mexico City: Siglo XXI, 1974.

Onis, Juan de. "Mexican Pilgrims Flock to the Shrine of Our Lady of Guadalupe." *New York Times,* December 14, 1969. http://select.nytimes.com/gst/abstract.html?res=F60B14FD345F 127A93C6A81789D95F4D8685F9&scp=2&sq=guadalupe&st=p

Ortiz de Montellano, Guillermo. *Nican Mopohua.* Mexico: Universidad Iberoamericana, Departamento de Ciencias Religiosas, Departamento de Historia, 1990.

Owensby, Brian. *Empire of Law and Indian Justice in Colonial America*. Stanford: Stanford University Press, 2008.

Pardo, Osvaldo. *The Origins of Mexican Catholicism*. Ann Arbor: University of Michigan Press, 2004.

Parsons, Wilfrid. *Mexican Martyrdom*. Rockford: Tan Books, 1987.

Paul III. *Sublimus Dei*. Promulgated May 29, 1537. http://www.ewtn.com/library/PAPALDOC/P3SUBLI.HTM

Paul VI. *Apostolicam Actuositatem*. Vatican City: Libreria Editrice Vaticana, 1965. http://www.vatican.va/archive/hist_councils/ii_vatican_council/documents/vat-ii_decree_19651118_apostolicam-actuositatem_en.html.

———. *Ecclesiam Suam*. Vatican City: Libreria Editrice Vaticana, 1964. http://www.vatican.va/holy_father/paul_vi/encyclicals/documents/hf_p-vi_enc_06081964_ecclesiam_en.html.

———. *Evangelica Testificatio*. Vatican City: Libreria Editrice Vaticana, 1971. http://www.vatican.va/holy_father/paul_vi/apost_exhortations/documents/hf_p-vi_exh_19710629_evangelica-testificatio_en.html.

———. Homily for Beatification, November 1, 1975. Vatican City: Libreria Editrice Vaticana, 1975: http://www.vatican.va/holy_father/paul_vi/homilies/1975/documents/hf_p-vi_hom_19751101_it.html.

Perea, Francisco J. *450 Años a la Sombra del Tepeyac*. Mexico City: Universo, 1981.

———. *El Mundo de Juan Diego*. Mexico City: Diana, 1988.

Pomar, Juan Bautista, and Alonso de Zorita. *Relación de Texcoco y de la Nueva España*. Mexico: Chávez Hayhoe, 1941.

Pompa y Pompa, Antonio. *El Gran Acontecimiento Guadalupano*. Mexico City: Jus, 1967.

Poole, Stafford. *Our Lady of Guadalupe: The Origins and Sources of a Mexican National Symbol, 1531–1797*. Tucson: University of Arizona Press, 1995.

Puente de Guzmán, Alicia. *Promoción y Dignidad de la Mujer a la Luz del Evento Guadalupano*. Mexico City: Instituto Superior de Estudios Eclesiásticos, 1984.

Rieff, David. "Nuevo Catholics," *New York Times Magazine*, December 24, 2006.

Rojas Sánchez, Mario. *Guadalupe: Símbolo y Evangelización*. Mexico : M. Rojas Sanchez, 2001.

———. *Nican Mopohua*. Introduction by Manuel Robledo Gutiérrez. Buenos Aires: La Peregrinación, 1998.

Romero Salinas, Joel. *Juan Diego, su Peregrinar a los Altares*. Mexico City: Paulinas, 1992.

Sahagún, Bernardino de. *Codice Matritense de la Real Academia de la Historia*. Ed. by Francisco del Paso y Troncoso. Madrid: Hauser y Menet, 1907.

———. *Florentine Codex*. Santa Fe, NM: Monographs of the School of American Research, 1950–69.

———. *Historia General de las Cosas de la Nueva España*. Mexico City: Porrúa, 1982.

———. *A History of Ancient Mexico*. Translated by Fanny R. Bandelier. Nashville, TN: Fisk University Press, 1932.

Salinas, Carlos. *Juan Diego en los Ojos de la Santísima Virgen de Guadalupe*. Mexico City: Tradición, 1974.

Salinas, Carlos, and Manuel de la Mora. *Descubrimiento de un Busto Humano en los Ojos de la Virgen de Guadalupe*. Mexico City: Tradición, 1976.

Saraiva Martins, José Cardinal. "The Face of Christ in the Face of the Church." Vatican City: Libreria Editrice Vaticana, 2002. http://www.vatican.va/roman_curia/congregations/csaints/documents/rc_con_csaints_doc_20021210_martins-rosto-de-cristo_en.html.

Schroeder, Susan, and Stafford Poole. *Religion in New Spain*. Albuquerque: University of New Mexico Press, 2007.

Schwartz, Stuart. *Victors and Vanquished*. Boston: Bedford/St. Martin's, 2000.

Second Council of Nicaea. "Decree of the Holy, Great, Ecumenical Synod, the Second Council Of Nicea." *The Seven Ecumenical Councils of the Undivided Church*. Trans. by H. R. Percival. Grand Rapids, MI: Wm. B. Eerdmans, 1955.

Second Vatican Council. *Ad Gentes*. Vatican City: Libreria Editrice Vaticana. http://www.

vatican.va/archive/hist_councils/ii_vatican_council/documents/vat-ii_decree_19651207_ad-gentes_en.html

Shein, Max, and Jorge Flores. *The Precolumbian Child.* Lancaster: Labyrinthos, 1992.

Sigüenza y Góngora, Carlos de. *Piedad Heróica de D. Fernando Cortés.* Mexico: Talleres de la Librería Religiosa, 1898.

Siller Acuña, Clodomiro L. *Para Comprender el Mensaje de María de Guadalupe.* Buenos Aires: Guadalupe, 1989.

Simpson, Lesley Byrd. *The Laws of Burgos of 1512–1513.* Santa Barbara, CA: Greenwood Press, 1979.

Smith, Jody. *The Image of Guadalupe.* Macon, GA: Mercer University Press, 1994.

Smith, Michael. *The Aztecs.* Cambridge: Blackwell, 1996.

Soustelle, Jacques. *La Pensée Cosmologique des Anciens Mexicains.* Paris: Hermann, 1940.

Soustelle, Jacques, and Patrick O'Brian. *Daily Life of the Aztecs on the Eve of the Spanish Conquest.* London: Phoenix, 2002.

Stevenson, Mark. "Brutality of Aztecs, Mayas Corroborated." *Los Angeles Times,* January 23, 2005 in print edition A-4.

Synod of Bishops. *Encounter with the Living Jesus Christ:The Way to Conversion, Communion and Solidarity in America.* Lineamenta. Special Assembly for America. August 1, 1996. http://www.vatican.va/roman_curia/synod/documents/rc_synod_doc_01081996_usa-lin-eam_en.html

———. "Message of the Special Assembly for America." *Jubileum.* No. 6, December 1, 1997. http://www.vatican.va/jubilee_2000/magazine/documents/ju_mag_01121997_p-32_en.html

Teresa of Calcutta (Agnes Gonxha Bojaxhiu) and José González-Balado. *Mother Teresa: In My Own Words.* Compiled by José González-Balado. New York: Gramercy Book, 1997.

Testimonios de la Antigua Palabra. Ed. Miguel León-Portilla. Mexico City: Comisión Nacional Conmemorativa del V Centenario del Encuentro de Dos Mundos, 1988.

Thornton, John, and Susan Varenne. *The Essential Pope Benedict XVI.* New York: HarperOne, 2008.

Todorov, Tzvetan, and Richard Howard. *The Conquest of America.* Norman: University of Oklahoma Press, 1999.

Torquemada, Juan de. *Monarquía Indiana.* Introduction by Miguel León-Portilla. Mexico City: Ed. Porrúa, 1986.

Vázquez Santa Ana, Higinio. *Epigrafía, Iconografía y Literatura Popular de Juan Diego.* Mexico City: Museo Juan Diego, 1940.

"Vera Cruz Radicals in 24-Hour Strike." *New York Times.* June 2, 1921, Page 19. http://query.nytimes.com/gst/abstract.html?res=9805EED61F3FEE3ABC4A53DFB066838 A639EDE

Vera Fortino, Hipólito. *Informaciones sobre la Milagrosa Aparición de la Santísima Virgen de Guadalupe, Recibidas en 1666 y 1723.* Amecameca, Mexico: Colegio Católico, 1889.

Vickery, Paul S. *Bartolomé de las Casas: Great Prophet of the Americas.* New York, NY: Paulist Press, 2006

Von Hagen, Victor W. *The Aztec and Maya Papermakers.* New York: J. J. Augustin, 1944.

Von Balthasar, Hans Urs. *Unless You Become Like This Child.* Translated by Erasmo Leiva-Merikakis. San Francisco: Ignatius Press,1991.

Wainwright, Geoffrey, and Karen Westerfield Tucker, eds. *The Oxford History of Christian Worship.* New York: Oxford University Press, 2006.

Weil, Simone. *Waiting for God.* Trans. Emma Craufurd. New York, NY: HarperCollins Publishers, 2001.

Wood, Michael. *Conquistadors.* Berkeley: University of California Press, 2000.

Zavala, Silvio. *La Filosofía Política en la Conquista de América.* Mexico City: FCE, 1947.

———. *Repaso Histórico de la Bula Sublimis Deus de Paulo III, en Defensa de los Indios.* Mexico City: Universidad Iberoamericana, Departamento de Historia, 1991.

———. *El Servicio Personal de los Indios en la Nueva España.* Mexico City: Colegio Nacional, 1984–95.

Zumárraga, Juan de. Letter from Friar Juan de Zumarraga to the King of Spain. August 27, 1529. In Archivo de Simancas, Bibl. Miss., II, 229, carta 13. Muñoz collection, T. 78.